JOURNALISM BEYOND ORWELL

Journalism Beyond Orwell adapts and updates pioneering work by Richard Lance Keeble to explore George Orwell's legacy as a journalist in original, critical – and often controversial – ways.

Though best known as the author of *Animal Farm* and *Nineteen Eighty-Four*, Orwell was, throughout his career, a journalist. The essays in this collection explore Orwell's important legacy: as a practising activist journalist critical of the dominant media; as a polemicist, essayist and novelist constantly concerned with issues relating to war and peace; as a literary journalist determined to make 'political writing an art'; and as a writer who warned of the growing powers of the secret state. Through this highly individualistic essay collection that connects Orwellian themes to modern journalism, Richard Lance Keeble explores key topics, including:

- Orwell the 'proto-blogger'
- How Orwell put his political economy critique of the corporate press into practice
- Information warfare in an age of hyper-militarism
- The manufacture of the myth of heroic warfare in the reporting of the Afghan conflict
- The debates over the theory and practice of peace journalism
- The ethical challenges for journalists reporting on conflict
- The crucial role of the alternative media
- The pleasures and pitfalls of the celebrity profile.

This collection will be of particular interest to students and researchers in journalism studies, English literature, media, intelligence studies and international relations.

Richard Lance Keeble is Professor of Journalism at the University of Lincoln and Honorary Professor at Liverpool Hope University. Chair of the Orwell Society, he has written and edited 40 books. In addition, he has written more than 50 book chapters and over 30 academic journal articles.

JOURNALISM BEYOND ORWELL

A Collection of Essays

Richard Lance Keeble

LONDON AND NEW YORK

First published 2020
by Routledge
2 Park Square, Milton Park, Abingdon, Oxon OX14 4RN

and by Routledge
52 Vanderbilt Avenue, New York, NY 10017

Routledge is an imprint of the Taylor & Francis Group, an informa business

British Library Cataloguing-in-Publication Data
A catalogue record for this book is available from the British Library

Library of Congress Cataloging-in-Publication Data
A catalog record has been requested for this book

ISBN: 978-0-367-33356-0 (hbk)
ISBN: 978-0-367-33355-3 (pbk)
ISBN: 978-0-429-31936-5 (ebk)

Typeset in Bembo
by Taylor & Francis Books

MIX
Paper from
responsible sources
FSC
www.fsc.org   FSC® C013985

Printed in the United Kingdom
by Henry Ling Limited

CONTENTS

INTRODUCTION

Why journalism and Orwell matter

On the importance of journalism

As a lad, growing up in Nottingham during the early 1960s, my parents took the *Daily Mail* and *Daily Telegraph* and it was through reading their sports pages (I was mad on cricket and football) that my interest in the press began. From the age of around 13, I was determined on a career as a journalist. So I have been very lucky to realise that ambition – beginning on the *Guardian Journal*, in Nottingham, immediately after university in 1970. Following stints on the *Cambridge Evening News* and the *Teacher* (the weekly newspaper of the National Union of Teachers) I entered academia (while continuing as a freelance writer) in 1984 – running the International Journalism MA at City, University of London, along with Bob Jones.

My interest in the press may have been sparked by sports but since then it's fair to say that all my writings and teaching have been informed by an awareness of the enormous importance of journalism: culturally, ideologically, politically – and as an industry: both nationally and globally. In my research, I have tried to identify the ways in which journalism (and the prime focus throughout my career has been on print and more recently also online) has both covered and influenced British culture, politics and foreign policy – mainly since 1945. After all, it is through the news and journalism in general that we learn about the world beyond the narrow confines of our own experience. The corporate media influence enormously the dominant discourse – both nationally and internationally. The alternative media equally play significant roles in the alternative public sphere – both nationally and internationally. Indeed, it is because of journalism's social, political and cultural importance that it is so worthy of detailed, critical analysis – and of study as a creative, literary genre – by students as an academic subject.

Assessing Orwell's legacy

Orwell's novels *Animal Farm* (1945) and *Nineteen Eighty-Four* (1949) are deeply embedded in the culture and in education. I remember seeing a few years back a wonderful school production of *1984* in Louth, Lincolnshire, near where I live – the horror of the final torture scenes brilliantly captured by the students. Ask most people about Orwell and they will say they have read one or both of these novels at school – that's about it. But Orwell offers a treasure trove of other riches beyond these two iconic works. I have certainly used Orwell extensively in my teaching: on media ethics, literary journalism, investigative reporting, war correspondence, on the links between Fleet Street and the secret state and so on. As a progressive journalist committed to the alternative media Orwell has been a particular inspiration for me.

Paradoxically, while Orwell never went to university his whole life might be considered an educational project. His constant curiosity, questioning and desire to understand drove him – and through his writings he generously encouraged his readers to join him in his journey. And that is the essential Orwellian legacy I want to explore here. Orwell's writings covered a vast range of genres – letters, diaries, poetry, political analysis, polemic, novels (but interestingly no short stories), investigative reporting, columns, war correspondence, radio plays and commentaries, book, film and drama reviews, media analysis, essays and light sketches. Journalism, then, was for Orwell, a distinct field (after all it provided him with some money). But it is best seen as an integral element of his life as a politically engaged writer – in which his subject matter and styles of writing (for instance, documentary and memoir, poetry and political analysis, fiction and social commentary) are forever overlapping.

George Orwell: The activist journalist

Orwell, then, provides the stem around which this essay collection (drawn from just two publishers for copyright reasons) develops. Most importantly, his journalism reflects an overall *political activist* approach. The activist is very different from the *campaigning* journalist. Many corporate media (both national and local) run campaigns: to save a post office from closing, to ban hospital car parking charges, to change the law on stalking – and so on. Campaigning is, then, consistent with notions of 'professional autonomy'. The activist journalist, however, sees all journalism as essentially political – given the political economy of the media and its closeness to dominant economic, cultural and ideological forces – and links their political engagement with their journalism.

The first chapter looks at Orwell as activist journalist of the left and press critic. A number of features stand out. Firstly, Orwell's views on many topics shifted over time (see Dwan 2019). Yet his 'political economy' approach to the press remained remarkably consistent throughout his writing career. Significantly, he maintained the same approach when commenting on the BBC (where he worked as a talks producer for the Eastern Service from 1941–1943) (Keeble 2017). In many respects his political economy approach anticipates the work of theorists such as Noam Chomsky, Peter Golding, Edward S. Herman, Graham Murdock, Jeffery Klaehn and Florian Zollmann. Moreover, in this era of digital communications the approach remains highly relevant. Eli Noam's study of 30 countries suggests that the concentration of media ownership continues to escalate with the internet amplifying this process across national borders (Noam 2016; see also Christians 2019).

Closely linked to Orwell's *political attitude* is, then, his *practice* as an activist journalist with most of his journalism deliberately targeted at journals of the left. To a certain extent his working for the *Observer*, owned by the family of his friend, David Astor, contradicts this approach. Yet in this instance another principle is applied – that friendship takes priority.

Secondly, Orwell was remarkably imaginative in the ways he critiqued the press. In one instance, he used a letter from a Mrs Ada Dodd to *Tribune* (the leftist journal where he was literary editor from 1943–1947) in one of his 'As I Please' columns to mock the standards at a journalism training institution – and its reluctance to encourage students to promote any form of socialism. In another column he presents a list of the leading newspapers and then inverts it: one shows major newspapers in order of intelligence; the other in order of popularity. He comments (Orwell 1998 [1946a]: 500): 'It will be seen that the second list is very nearly – not quite, for life is never so neat as that – the first turned upside down.'

Thirdly, Orwell's detailed analyses of press content (as, for instance, an issue of the *Daily Mail*, a set of women's newspapers and even the American women's fashion magazine *Vogue*) are highly original. Orwell is known for founding, in some respects, the discipline of Cultural Studies with his essays on boys' weeklies, cups of tea, the common toad, sexy seaside postcards, junk shops and so on. The ways in which his press critiques anticipate approaches taken later by Media, Journalism and Communications academics are less well known.

The next two chapters examine Orwell's 80 'As I Please' columns for *Tribune* and his reporting from the continent for the *Observer* and *Manchester Evening News* during the dying days of the Second World War. Orwell's legacy is not without its problematics: a number of critics, for instance, rightly accuse him of misogyny (Beddoe 1984; Campbell 1984; Patai 1984; Newsinger 2019: 154). And yet, at the same time, Orwell can display distinctly un-misogynistic attitudes: in his memoir 'Such, Such Were the Joys' (Orwell 1970 [1952]: 4) he presents an account (how true, how fictional?) of his own sex life and of the sexual development of youths in general. Orwell was never much impressed by psychoanalysis, as biographer Gordon Bowker stresses (Bowker 2003: 48). Yet, if openness about feelings and sexuality (making the personal political) is another mark of today's New Man, then Orwell was ahead of his times (Keeble 2018a: 85).

Linked to his 1945 war reporting assignment, his possible involvement with British intelligence (using journalism as a cover) has to be considered (see also Keeble 2012). On his deathbed Orwell handed over a 'little list' of crypto-communists to the Information Research Department (IRD), the government's recently set up propaganda unit (Lashmar and Oliver 1998). James Smith (2013) is right when he argues that Orwell's flirtation with the secret state was 'a gross miscalculation … and should be condemned' (145). But given his earlier involvement with intelligence, it is tempting to see his work with the IRD as not an aberration (as generally thought). Rather, it is an action consistent with his attitudes and behaviour as they developed during the 1940s – particularly through his friendship with David Astor (Keeble 2019).

Orwell and the radical tradition of the press (in brief)

Orwell is best considered within a long tradition of radical, progressive, critical journalism too often marginalised in the conventional histories. Indeed, historically, the alternative media have helped provide the basis on which an alternative, global public sphere (and an alternative political culture) has been built. During the French Revolution of the 1790s, journalists such as Robespierre, Marat, Danton and Hébert played central roles (see Hartley 1996; Chapman 2008). Again, in the first half of the 19th century in the UK, a massively popular, radical, anti-royalist, anti-clerical, revolutionary, unstamped (and hence illegal) press played a crucial role in the campaigns for trade union rights and social and political reforms (Black 2001; Chalaby 1998; Conboy 2004; Curran and Seaton 2004; Keeble 2010).

Hopkin (1978: 298) calculates that several hundred thousands of workers' (often short-lived) newspapers were launched between 1890 and 1910 in the UK. In America, the long tradition of the dissident, pro-labour, anti-racist and feminist press is charted by Rodger Streitmatter (2001): from the founding of the *Mechanic's Free Press* in Philadelphia, in 1827, through to Julius Augustus Wayland's *Appeal to Reason* which published between 1895 and 1922. In 1905, it began the serialisation of Upton Sinclair's *The Jungle* which exposed the appalling conditions faced by immigrants in Chicago meat packing plants (ibid: 109–110). During the suffragette campaigns many women were both journalists (on newspapers such as the *Women's Suffrage Journal*) and activists (e.g. Sylvia Pankhurst: see Davis 1999). In the US, between 1911 and 1917, *The Masses* was 'a fully-fledged magazine of social protest in which editorial content and art joined in radical assault upon the social and political structure' – publishing the work of leading radicals such as Dorothy Day, Max Eastman and John Reed.[1]

The Mapping American Social Movements Project at the University of Washington describes the period 1880–1940 as 'the golden age' of labour journalism while, later, 'radical journalism enjoyed an extraordinary renaissance with the underground press movement of the 1960s and 1970s'.[2] In the UK, Orwell directed most of his journalism during the 1930s and 1940s to dozens of human rights, leftist, anarchist, pacifist, trade union journals (such as *The Adelphi, Commentary, Controversy, For Anarchism, Forward, Fortnightly Review, Gangrel, The Highway, Left News, Left Forum, Left Review, New English Weekly,* New York's

New Leader, New Republic, the pacifist *New Road, New Statesman and Nation, New Saxon Pamphlets, Polemic, Politics and Letters, Tribune*). During the Vietnam War, *I. F. Stone's Weekly* was one of the few journals to maintain a consistent opposition[3] while Jonathan Neale identifies around 300 anti-war newspapers in the US armed forces during the course of the conflict (Neale 2001: 122–130; see also Painter and Ferrucci 2019). The tradition continues today with sites (all to be read with the same critical attention as given the corporate media, of course) based in Australia, France, India, the US and UK – as highlighted in the last chapter of this book.

Moreover, particularly in his books *Down and Out in Paris and London* (1933), the part fictional/part memoir of his times with the beggars and hop pickers and working as a *plongeur* in a posh Parisian hotel, and *The Road to Wigan Pier* (1937), his investigation into poverty in the north of England, Orwell is maintaining the radical tradition of investigative journalism set by Elizabeth Banks, Nelly Bly, Stephen Crane, James Greenwood and Jack London (see Koven 2004). And it has continued since with the brave reporting by Felicity Arbuthnot, Wilfred Burchett, Duncan Campbell, Nick Davies, Paul Foot, Robert Fisk, Martha Gellhorn, Seymour Hersh, David Kay Johnston, Phillip Knightley, Paul Lashmar, John Pilger, Anna Politkovskaya, Nick Turse, and Gunter Wallraff – and many others (see Pilger 2004; Mair and Keeble 2011; for my profile of the Australian investigative reporter Antony Loewenstein see Keeble 2018b).

Making journalism an art: Literary journalism today

In 'Why I write', the essay he contributed to the short-lived alternative journal, *Gangrel*, Orwell stresses: 'What I have most wanted to do throughout the past ten years is to make political writing an art' (Orwell 1970 [1946b]: 28). In this, he was clearly drawing on the tradition of literary journalism set by Defoe, Hazlitt, Dickens, Steele and Stevenson. This part picks up the literary journalism (LJ) theme and offers three contrasting case studies. LJ effectively emerged as an academic discipline following the publication of Tom Wolfe's *The New Journalism* (Wolfe and Johnson 1973) which brought together the work of (largely white, male and American) journalists such as Truman Capote, Joan Didion, Barbara Goldsmith, Michael Herr, Norman Mailer, George Plimpton, Gay Talese and Hunter S. Thompson. Here was a practising journo (how amazing!) reflecting on his practice, identifying various elements of the unique style he was promoting (the New Journalism, no less) – and being, at the same time, highly combative and confident. Its effect was rather like that of a small earthquake in the fertile ground of Western culture: the after-effects are still being felt (Keeble 2018c). But Wolfe's legacy is not without its problematics for his concentration on journalistic *techniques* (which has proved so influential in the development of LJ in higher education internationally) crucially marginalises consideration of such elements as ideology and political economy – and ultimately promotes a form of cultural elitism (Keeble 2018d).

Challenging that dominant approach, these essays attempt to go beyond a study of technique and focus on deeper economic, cultural and political factors. Interestingly, Orwell describes Mark Twain as a 'licensed jester' given his constant retreating behind the 'amiable mask of the "public figure"' and his reluctance to 'attack established beliefs in a way that is likely to get him into trouble' (Orwell 1970 [1943]: 372). Indeed, I argue that it's useful to see Lynn Barber (the subject of this part's first essay) as a 'court jester'. Elites know they will be mocked and attacked. The court jester system originally served to contain that mockery. Today, a version of the court jester system still operates, in both the political and cultural spheres, and while there is no formal licensing, a subtler – and hence more powerful – unwritten licensing system helps define the limits of acceptable debate. As I argue, Barber, as a prominent Fleet Street journalist, is clearly a member of the 'court' of the cultural elite and, as a result, 'her witty put-downs can be seen not only as providing pleasure and entertainment but necessary features of the contemporary celebrity circus'.

Orwell constantly defies genre conventions in his writings – and Lara Pawson (the subject of Chapter 5) certainly does this in her memoir in which she explores with remarkable candour her role as a BBC foreign correspondent based in Africa. Finally in this part, I carry the tribute to my friend and University of Lincoln colleague, John Tulloch. In my writings on Orwell (too often associated with the doom and gloom of the dystopian world of *Nineteen Eighty-Four*) I have tried to celebrate him as one of England's greatest humourists (Keeble 2015). John was a polymath (just talking to him was an education in itself) and his writings on journalism are bristling with eclectic referencing (reflecting his Orwellian-like, voracious reading), theoretical depth, original ideas – and wit.

War, peace and the press: Yesterday and today

Orwell's attitudes to war and peace and violence were, not surprisingly, extremely complex. Issues surrounding violence (both individual and institutional) were a constant preoccupation during his lifetime. Indeed, the critique of the military/industrial complex and its need for constant warfare against manufactured enemies lies at the heart of his dystopian masterpiece *Nineteen Eighty-Four*.

As a policeman in Burma and as a Republican militiaman in the Spanish civil war he was prepared to take up a gun when he felt it was necessary. But in many respects his account of his time in the Spanish trenches, *Homage to Catalonia* (1937), is cleverly anti-war as he is always determined to expose the horror and absurdity of conflict – and any claims for heroism. They are fighting more the cold and boredom than the fascists, he writes. Certainly from 1936 to just about the outbreak of the Second World War he is distinctly anti-war. Any war would, he maintains, do nothing more than extend imperialist possessions and interests.

In 1938, while on holiday in Marrakech he adds his name to a *New Leader* manifesto 'If War Comes We Shall Resist'. It blames the imperialist treaties signed at the conclusion of the First World War and calls for 'world supplies' to be made equally available to all people 'on a basis of co-operation and social justice' (see Marks 2011: 71). While Orwell's support for the war effort 1939 to 1945 and his set-to with the pacifist Alex Comfort are well known he still uses his film reviewing for *Time and Tide* (1940–1941) to condemn the gratuitous violence of so many Hollywood movies (Tulloch 2012). And his essay 'Raffles and Miss Bland-ish', published in *Horizon*, in October 1944, amounts to a profound critique of pornography and violence.

Many of his colleagues and closest friends, such a Sir Richard Rees, editor of *Adelphi* – which published some of Orwell's earliest and most celebrated essays – and the anarchist photographer Vernon Richards were pacifists. Indeed, his won-derful and much-anthologised essay 'Why I write' appeared in the short-lived journal *Gangrel*, edited by John Pick, another celebrated pacifist, Quaker and conscientious objector during the Second World War. His ambivalence towards pacifism emerges particularly in his essay 'Reflections on Gandhi' published in the American journal *Partisan Review* in January 1949. While very critical of Gandhi he ends carefully on a positive note:

> One may feel, as I do, a sort of aesthetic distaste for Gandhi, one may reject the claims of sainthood made on his behalf (he never made such claims him-self, by the way), one may reject sainthood as an ideal and therefore feel that Gandhi's basic aims were anti-human and reactionary; but regarded simply as a politician, and compared with other leading political figures of our time, how clean a smell he has managed to leave behind (Orwell 1970 [1949]: 531).

Most significantly, when Orwell stayed at the Cranham Sanatorium in the Cots-wolds towards the end of his life, he was happy to leave his son, Richard, at the nearby anarchist/pacifist/Tolstoyan community of Whiteway. This was largely the result of Orwell's friendship with the anarchist/pacifist and Whiteway resident Lilian Wolfe (Taylor 2016).

Part III of *Journalism Beyond Orwell*, then, continues the theme of war and peace. The coverage of the 1991 Gulf conflict by the press in the US and UK was the subject of my PhD in 1996 (and published by John Libbey as *Secret State, Silent Press: New Militarism, the Gulf and the Modern Image of Warfare*, in 1997). And the research from that study (driven by my long-standing pacifism and particularly inspired by the work of Noam Chomsky, Phillip Knightley and John Pilger) has formed the basis for all my subsequent writings on war and peace: for instance, on the 2003 Iraq invasion (Chapter 7) and the now forgotten but, at the time, heavily-hyped Operation Moshtarak of 2010 during Britain's disastrous intervention in Afghanistan (Chapter 8). Underlying both essays is the argument (also embodied in the dissident 'The Theory and Practice of Oligarchic Collectivism' in *Nineteen Eighty-Four*) that the military/industrial complex requires both constant warfare –

to provide markets for armaments and keep the populace timidly conformist – and the constant manufacture of 'enemies'. This part's final chapter examines the contested terrain of peace journalism. Given the corporate media's historic function to promote overall the dominant political, military, economic, ideological and cultural interests in society, the chapter highlights the crucial role of the alternative media in confronting secret states – globally.

Scoops and spooks: Journalism in an age of surveillance capitalism

My interest in secrecy (secret warfare, secret diplomacy, secret coups and assassinations) developed during my research into the 1991 conflict coverage. The more I studied the period the more I realised most of the important information and sources were missing from the media. Indeed, it strikes me that one of the crucial functions of the corporate media, given its propaganda role for dominant economic/military/political interests, is to *silence* oppositional voices and perspectives. Fleet Street's ties to the constantly competing factions within the intelligence services reinforce this process.

Returning to Orwell, there were clearly many influences on him in the making of *Nineteen Eighty-Four*. Yet, given Orwell's introduction to the world of spooks by his friend and *Observer* editor David Astor, is it not surprising that his last great novel should describe a world of Big Brother, of child spies and tele-screens – and where the state's surveillance intrudes into the individual's inner-most private life? Orwell's ambivalent attitude to just about everything was reflected in his responses to the secret state. On the one hand, he supports it and becomes friends with some of its operators. But he also sees the secret state's growing powers and is horrified. So he dedicates all his energy (in what proves to be his final years) in his remote house on the Scottish island of Jura to composing the crucial warning.

The earlier essay on Orwell's 1945 war reporting assignment for Astor high-lights Orwell's possible links with intelligence. The first chapter in Part IV of *Journalism Beyond Orwell* provides a critical historical overview – suggesting that Orwell is not alone amongst Fleet Street journos in developing close ties to the secret state.

Chapter 11, looking at the press coverage of Col. Gaddafi, draws on a wide range of alternative sources to focus on the many secret attempts by Western powers to assassinate the President of Libya. This then is effectively a study of non-coverage: within the 24/7 bombardment of information through the digital media, the absent often remains the most important. The final chapter echoes Orwell's constant critique of journalists' professionalism, places the activities of Chelsea Manning at WikiLeaks and the NSA's Edward Snowden in the context of previous brave whistleblowing (taking a particularly critical view on the Watergate saga). It ends highlighting the role of international alternative websites which exploit the contradictions of surveillance capitalism (as examined by Shoshana Zuboff (2019)) to confront the myths, crimes and lies of the secret state.

Notes

1 See http://graphicwitness.org/historic/young1.htm
2 See http://depts.washington.edu/moves/
3 http://www.ifstone.org/index.php

Acknowledgements

The number of people who have helped me over the years (in the UK, Ireland, North and South America, Australia, New Zealand, throughout continental Europe and India) are too many to mention individually. Many thanks to you all! Thanks also to Richard and Pete Franklin at Abramis and colleagues at Routledge for giving me permission to use work they have published in this text – and to the anonymous reviewers. Special thanks to my partner, Maryline Gagnère, and our son, Gabriel, for their love and support. This book is dedicated to the memory of friend and colleague John Tulloch – and to John Mair, with thanks for all the fun we've had over the years editing so many books together.

References

Beddoe, Deirdre (1984) Hindrances and help-meets: Women in the writings of George Orwell, Norris, Christopher (ed.) *Inside the Myth: Orwell: Views from the Left*, London: Lawrence & Wishart pp 139–154

Black, Jeremy (2001) *The English Press 1621–1861*, Stroud, Gloucestershire: Sutton Publishing

Bowker, Gordon (2003) *George Orwell*, London: Little, Brown

Campbell, Beatrix (1984) Orwell: Paterfamilias or Big Brother?, Norris, Christopher (ed.) *Inside the Myth: Orwell: Views from the Left*, London: Lawrence & Wishart pp 128–136

Chalaby, Jean (1998) *The Invention of Journalism*, Basingstoke: Macmillan Press

Chapman, Jane (2008) Republican citizenship, ethics and the French revolutionary press, Keeble, Richard (ed.) *Communication Ethics Now*, Leicester: Troubador pp 131–141

Christians, Clifford (2019) *Media Ethics and Global Justice in the Digital Age*, Cambridge: Cambridge University Press

Conboy, Martin (2004) *Journalism: A Critical History*, London: Sage

Curran, James and Seaton, Jean (2004) *Power Without Responsibility: The Press, Broadcasting and New Media in Britain*, London: Routledge, seventh edition

Davis, Mary (1999) *Sylvia Pankhurst: A Life in Radical Politics*, London: Pluto

Dwan, David (2019) *Liberty, Equality and Humbug: Orwell's Political Ideals*, Oxford: Oxford University Press

Hartley, John (1996) *Popular Reality: Journalism, Modernity, Popular Culture*, London and New York: Arnold

Hopkin, Deian (1978) The socialist press in Britain, 1890–1910, Boyce, George, Curran, James and Wingate, Pauline (eds) *Newspaper History from the Seventeenth Century to the Present Day*, London: Constable pp 294–306

Keeble, Richard Lance (2010) Peace journalism as political practice: A new, radical look at the theory, Keeble, Richard Lance, Tulloch, John and Zollmann, Florian (eds) *Peace Journalism, War and Conflict Resolution*, New York: Peter Lang pp 49–68

Keeble, Richard Lance (2012) Orwell, *Nineteen Eighty-Four* and the spooks, Keeble, Richard Lance (ed.) *Orwell Today*, Bury St Edmunds: Abramis pp 151–163

Keeble, Richard Lance (2015) 'There is always room for one more custard pie': Orwell's humour, Keeble, Richard Lance and Swick, David (eds) *Pleasures of the Prose: Journalism and Humour*, Bury St Edmunds: Abramis pp 10–25

Keeble, Richard Lance (2017) Beyond Room 101, Orwell Society *Journal*, autumn pp 8–10

Keeble, Richard Lance (2018a) 'The art of Donald McGill': Orwell and the pleasures of sex, *George Orwell Studies*, Vol 3, No. 1 pp 21–36

Keeble, Richard Lance (2018b) Putting the politics into investigative reporting, Mair, John and Keeble, Richard Lance (eds) *Investigative Journalism Today: Speaking Truth to Power*, London: Bite-Sized Books pp 67–78

Keeble, Richard Lance (2018c) Literary journalism as a discipline and genre: The politics and the paradox, *Literary Journalism Studies*, Vol 10, No. 2 pp 83–98

Keeble, Richard Lance (2018d) Literary journalism as a discipline: Tom Wolfe and beyond, *Brazilian Journalism Review* Vol. 14, No. 3 pp 862–881

Keeble, Richard Lance (2019) Orwell, David Astor and the making of *Nineteen Eighty-Four*, *orwellsocietyblog*, 3 June. Available online at https://orwellsocietyblog.wordpress.com/2019/06/03/orwell-astor-1984/

Koven, Seth (2004) *Slumming: Sexual and Social Politics in Victorian London*, Princeton, NJ and Oxford: Princeton University Press

Lashmar, Paul and Oliver, James (1998) *Britain's Secret Propaganda War 1948–1977*, Stroud: Sutton

Mair, John and Keeble, Richard Lance (eds) (2011) *Investigative Journalism: Dead or Alive?* Bury St Edmunds: Abramis

Marks, Peter (2011) *George Orwell the Essayist: Literature, Politics and the Periodical Culture*, London: Continuum

Neale, Jonathan (2001) *The American War: Vietnam 1960–75*, London: Bookmarks

Newsinger, John (2019) *Hope Lies in the Proles: George Orwell and the Left*, London: Pluto Press

Noam, Eli M. (2016) *Who Owns the World's Media? Media Concentration and Ownership Around the World*, New York: Oxford University Press

Orwell, George (1970 [1943]) Mark Twain: Licensed jester, Orwell, Sonia and Angus, Ian (eds) *The Collected Essays, Journalism and Letters*, Vol. 2: *My Country Right or Left 1940–1943*, Harmondsworth, Middlesex: Penguin pp 369–374; *Tribune*, 26 November

Orwell, George (1998 [1946a]) As I Please, Davison, Peter (ed.) *Complete Works of George Orwell*, Vol. 17: *Smothered Under Journalism, 1946*, London: Secker & Warburg pp 497–500; *Tribune*, 22 November

Orwell, George (1970 [1946b]) Why I write, Orwell, Sonia and Angus, Ian (eds) *The Collected Essays, Journalism and Letters*, Vol. 1, Harmondsworth, Middlesex: Penguin pp 23–30; first published *Gangrel*, No. 4

Orwell, George (1970 [1949]) Reflections on Gandhi, Orwell, Sonia and Angus, Ian (eds) *The Collected Essays, Journalism and Letters*, Vol. 4: *In Front of Your Nose*, Harmondsworth, Middlesex: Penguin pp 523–531; *Partisan Review*, January

Orwell, George (1970 [1952]) Such, such were the joys, Orwell, Sonia and Angus, Ian (eds) *The Collected Essays, Journalism and Letters*, Vol. 4: *In Front of Your Nose*, Harmondsworth, Middlesex: Penguin pp 379–422; *Partisan Review*, September/October

Painter, Chad and Ferrucci, Patrick (2019) 'Ask what you can do to the Army': A textual analysis of the underground GI press during the Vietnam War, *Media, War and Conflict*, Vol 12, No. 3 pp 354–367

Patai, Daphne (1984) *The Orwell Mystique: A Study in Male Ideology*, Amherst: University of Massachusetts Press

Pilger, John (2004) *Tell Me No Lies: Investigative Journalism and Its Triumphs*, London: Jonathan Cape

Smith, James (2013) *British Writers and MI5 Surveillance 1930–1960*, Cambridge: Cambridge University Press

Streitmatter, Rodger (2001) *Voices of Revolution: The Dissident Press in America*, New York: Columbia University Press

Taylor, Antony (2016) The Whiteway anarchists in the twentieth century: A transnational community in the Cotswolds, *History*, Vol. 101, No. 344 pp 62–83

Tulloch, John (2012) Sceptic in the palace of dreams: Orwell as a film reviewer, Keeble, Richard Lance (ed.) *Orwell Today*, Bury St Edmunds: Abramis pp 79–101

Wolfe, T. and Johnson, E. W. (1973) *The New Journalism*, New York: Harper & Row

Zuboff, Shoshana (2019) *The Age of Surveillance Capitalism*, London: Profile Books

PART I

George Orwell: The activist journalist

1

THE MYTH OF FREEDOM

Orwell and the press

This chapter examines Orwell's involvement in the press – both as an activist journalist and as a media critic. While most well-known for his novels *Animal Farm* (1945) and *Nineteen Eighty Four* (1949), Orwell was throughout his writing career a journalist. Yet, until recently his journalism was largely ignored by the academy. The chapter will aim to explain that marginalisation, highlighting the 'low' status of journalism in the broader culture: significantly, Orwell also had a low opinion of his journalism describing it as 'mere pamphleteering'. Throughout all his writings on the press Orwell maintained a consistent 'political economy' approach, questioning the notion of press freedom, stressing the impact of advertisers and proprietorial control on content – and highlighting the close integration of mainstream newspapers with dominant financial, political and military interests and their essential propaganda role for the wealthy. Orwell also adopted many other original ways of examining the press: for instance, deconstructing an issue of the *Daily Mirror* and cheap women's newspapers – to highlight the manufacture of the 'sunshine mentality' – and even damning journalism training at the time.

Closely linked to Orwell's *political attitude* was his *practice* as an activist journalist – not without its contradictions – with most of his journalism deliberately targeted at journals of the left. Moreover, considering Orwell's biography, writing and political activism as inseparable, the chapter will highlight Lynnette Hunter's (1984) stress on the *writing process* adopted by Orwell and how he practised journalism as an integral part of his *life as a writer*.

Journalism as 'mere pamphleteering'

Despite the publication of *The Collected Essays, Journalism and Letters*, edited by Sonia Orwell and Ian Angus in 1968 (and two years later in paperback), the focus on Orwell remained for many years away from his journalism. His novels, particularly *Animal Farm* (1945) and *Nineteen Eighty-Four* (1949), tended to be the main focus – and to a slightly lesser extent the essays such as 'A Hanging' (1931), 'Shooting an Elephant' (1936) and 'Politics and the English Language' (1946). Reportage such as *The Road to Wigan Pier* (1937) and *Homage to Catalonia* (1938) was also covered. But until quite recently he was still considered primarily a novelist and so his forays into journalism – such as his 'As I Please' columns for the leftist journal, *Tribune*, between 1943 and 1947, and his war reporting for the *Observer* and *Manchester Evening News*, in 1945 – had been given no serious academic attention. Similarly, Charles Dickens was considered almost exclusively as a novelist: hardly ever as a journalist though he was an eminent editor and proprietor of magazines such as *Household Words* and *All the Year Round*. The same was true for the journalism of Willa Cather, Angela Carter. Daniel Defoe, Martha Gellhorn, Graham Greene, George Sand and Virginia Woolf (Keeble 2007).

Why was journalism, then, not considered Literature with a capital L – like Jane Austen, George Eliot, James Joyce? The reasons are complex and lie in the historic roots of journalism. The news media in the early 17th century tended to be associated with scandal, gossip and 'low' culture since they focused on sex, bawdiness, violence, monstrous births, murders and so on. By the early 18th century, in the UK, the derogatory term 'Grub Street' came to be associated with struggling, low-level publishing – often in the East End of London: hack (as in Hackney) being basically anything hired out or common (ibid: 3).

On a basic level journalism has provided writers with an income. Yet this very fact has reinforced journalism's position as a sub-literary genre. For while literature is often seen as the fruit of scholarship – hence pure and disinterested and above market considerations – journalistic writing is viewed as distorted by the constraints of the market, tight deadlines and word limits. All this has influenced writers' perceptions of their own journalism – many of them looking down on their journalism as a 'lower' form of writing. Orwell for instance, in 'Why I write' (Orwell 1970 [1946a]), says he dreamed of being a writer of enormous naturalistic novels with unhappy endings, full of purple passages. But when he became politically aware he had been forced into becoming 'a sort of pamphleteer' (ibid: 26).

Studies by Paul Anderson (2006), Peter Davison (2014) and Alex Woloch (2016) have focused critical attention on Orwell's journalism – yet he still remains in the public imagination primarily a novelist.

Orwell: Journalist from the beginning – and followed by the spooks

Journalism persisted as an activity for Orwell from the start of his writing career until ill-health forced him to stop in 1949 – while newspapers, censorship, freedom of speech, propaganda and language were subjects for constant study and critique. Resigning after five years as an Imperial Policeman in Burma in 1927, Eric Blair (as he then was) returns to England and (much to the horror of his family) determines to make his way as a journalist and writer. So he decides to spend months on end with the tramps in London's East End, with the hop pickers of Kent and as a *plongeur* in an up-market hotel in Paris. All this is part of his efforts (as he points out in the autobiographical, second section of *The Road to Wigan Pier*, of 1937) to exorcise his guilt for having been part of an illegitimate system of imperial oppression – but at the same time he is fully aware that his experiences could form the basis for journalistic copy.

While in Paris, he exploits the contacts his radical feminist Aunt Nellie and her partner Eugène Adam have with Henri Barbusse, the communist editor of the journal *Monde*, to contribute an article 'La censure en Angleterre'. He suggests the censorship of James Joyce's *Ulysses* and Radclyffe Hall's *The Well of Loneliness* is a result of 'that strange English puritanism which has no objection to dirt, but which fears sexuality and detests beauty' (see Marks 2016: 19). But as a result of his writing for Barbusse, Blair comes to the attention of British intelligence – who follow him closely throughout his career until his death (Keeble 2012; Smith 2013).

Monde also carries a short piece on the novelist John Galsworthy while his articles on an eclectic range of topics – unemployment in Britain, a day in the life of a tramp, beggars in London, and the British Empire in Burma – are published by another French journal *Le Progrès Civique*. Significantly, his first published piece in the UK, 'A farthing newspaper' (for Chesterton's review *G. K's Weekly*) adopts a political economy approach that he is to maintain throughout his writing career (Orwell 1970 [1928]: 34–37). *Ami du Peuple*, costing just ten centimes, has recently been launched in Paris with a manifesto claiming it is 'uncontaminated by any base thoughts of gain' (ibid: 34). Blair adds, ironically:

> The proprietors, who hide their blushes in anonymity, are emptying their pockets for the mere pleasure of doing good by stealth. Their objects, we learn, are to make war on the great trusts, to fight for a lower cost of living and above all combat the powerful newspapers which are strangling free speech in France (ibid: 34–35).

He proceeds to deconstruct, with polemical vigour, the paper's pretensions – noting that its proprietor is M. Coty 'a great industrial capitalist and also proprietor of the *Figaro* and the *Gaulois*'. In other words, it is merely putting across 'the sort of propaganda wanted by M. Coty and his associates' (see Dulley 2015: 16–17). According to D. J. Taylor, Blair's early essay lacks a conspicuous personal voice, being more what a modern commissioning editor would call a 'think piece' (Taylor 2003: 95). Yet, as Peter Davison (2014: 2) observes, Blair's first seven published articles 'encapsulate what would be his prime topics of interest – social justice, literary criticism, the evils of imperialism, censorship, and a format that he virtually created: popular culture'. And based on his experiences, his first book, *Down and Out in Paris and London* (1933) – part memoir, part fiction – is published. So George Orwell (the pen name Blair adopts) is born.

Spain and the lies of journalism

In December 1936, just a few weeks after marrying Eileen O'Shaughnessy, Orwell travels to Spain to report on the civil war which has erupted between Republicans and General Franco's fascist forces (Crick 1980: 315). But once in Barcelona he is overwhelmed by the revolutionary spirit he witnesses and immediately joins the Trotskyist POUM militia. In *Homage to Catalonia* (1938), he provides vivid accounts of his time on the front-line, witnessing the 'working class in the saddle' and then the attempts of the communists to crush the Trotskyists and anarchists. At one point he is even shot – and only narrowly escapes death.

At the heart of *Homage* (and his growing socialist commitment) is Orwell's anger at the coverage of the conflict by both mainstream and alternative/left newspapers – and his desire to put the record straight. As he writes: 'One of the dreariest effects of this war has been to teach me that the Left-wing press is every bit as spurious and dishonest as that of the Right' (though he excludes the *Manchester Guardian* from this criticism) (Orwell 1962 [1938]: 64). With typical wry humour, he tells of the 'fat Russian agent' at the Hotel Continental, in Barcelona: 'I watched him with some interest, for it was the first time that I had seen a person whose profession was telling lies – unless one counts journalists' (ibid: 135).

He later adds:

> In the English press, in particular, you would have to search for a long time before finding any favourable reference, at any period of the war, to the Spanish Anarchists. They have been systematically denigrated and, as I know by my own experience, it is almost impossible to get anyone to print anything in their defence (ibid: 153).

He spends the following nineteen pages (ibid. 153–172) in a meticulous content analysis – denouncing the lies in the communist and pro-communist press (the *Daily Worker, Imprecor, Daily Herald* and the Spanish *Verdad* and *Frente Rojo*) that the Trotskyists and anarchists are conspiring with the fascists to bring down the revolution. Significantly, in his long, reflective essay, 'Looking back on the Spanish War' (composed in 1942 and published the following year), he concludes:

> Early in life I had noticed that no event is ever correctly reported in a newspaper, but in Spain, for the first time, I saw newspaper reports which did not bear any relation to the facts, not even the relationship which is implied in an ordinary lie. I saw great battles reported where there had been no fighting, and complete silence where hundreds of men had been killed. I saw troops who had fought bravely denounced as cowards and traitors, and others who had never seen a shot fired hailed as the heroes of imaginary victories, and I saw newspapers in London retailing these lies and eager intellectuals building emotional superstructures over events that had never happened. I saw, in fact,

history being written not in terms of what happened but of what ought to have happened according to various 'party lines' (Orwell 1970 [1943a]: 294).

Orwell and the political economy of the press

Underlying Orwell's comments on the press throughout his career (from that early essay on *Ami du Peuple*, of 1928, onwards) is a desire to highlight the economic factors impacting on its operations and political bias. Thus, he is concerned over the ways proprietorial ownership and the pressures from advertisers seriously constrain the press. For instance, in *The Lion and the Unicorn* (Orwell 1970 [1941a]), written during some of the bleakest days of the Second World War when Britain seriously feared invasion by the Nazis, he writes bluntly: 'Is the English press honest or dishonest? At normal times it is deeply dishonest. All the papers that matter live off their advertisements and the advertisers exercise an indirect censorship over news' (ibid: 88).

Deconstructing the Daily Mirror

In 1943, Orwell leaves the BBC, where he has been a talks producer in the Indian Section of the Eastern Service since 1941, and takes up the position of literary editor of the leftist journal, *Tribune*. There he writes 80 'As I Please' columns (see Chapter 2), many of them focusing on the press. For instance, on 7 April 1944 – in a completely original way – he devotes his entire column to deconstructing the *Daily Mirror* issue of 21 January 1936 (Orwell 1998 [1944a]). First he provides a meticulously detailed quantitative analysis, highlighting the unreality of the world as manufactured by the press and, equally significantly, important events and perspectives missed by the media. He then moves on to make more general qualitative comments, comparing press output with that of the radio. He opens by providing background to the column (establishing the wry, critical tone which is to persist throughout):

> Sometimes, on top of a cupboard or at the bottom of a drawer, you come on a pre-war newspaper, and when you have got over your astonishment at its enormous size, you find yourself marvelling at its almost unbelievable stupidity (ibid: 145).

He admits it may be dangerous to draw too many inferences from this one edition since the *Daily Mirror* is the 'second silliest paper' after the *Sketch* and it contains the announcement of the death of George V. But, he argues (addressing his readers directly as 'you'), it is still worth analysing: 'If you want to know why your house has been bombed, why your son is in Italy, why the income tax is ten shillings in the pound and the butter ration is only just visible without a microscope, here is part of the reason' (ibid).

Most of the 28 pages, he calculates, are devoted to the Royal Family (those capital letters are in the original article): the first 17 being entirely focused on the dead king and the other royals. 'There is a history of the King's life, articles on his activities as a statesman, family man, soldier, sailor, big and small game shot, motorist, broadcaster and what-not, with, of course, photographs innumerable.' Pages 18–23 feature 'amusement guides, comic articles and so forth'. On page 24, 'some news begins to creep in': a highway robbery, a skating contest, the forthcoming funeral of Rudyard Kipling and details about a snake at the Zoo which is refusing food.

Then, on page 26 comes 'the sole reference to the real world' with the headline: 'Bombing pledge by Duce: No more attacks on Red Cross.' The article under-neath says il Duce 'deplores' the attacks on the Red Cross and adds that the League of Nations has just turned down Abyssinia's requests for assistance and refused to investigate the charges of Italian atrocities. Orwell continues ironically: 'Turning to more congenial topics the *Daily Mirror* then follows up with a selection of murders, accidental deaths and the secret wedding of Earl Russell' (ibid). The last page is headed 'LONG LIVE KING EDWARD VIII' and contains 'a short biography and a highly idealised photograph of the man whom the Conservative Party were to sack like a butler a year later' (ibid: 145–146). Orwell goes on to highlight important omissions: the two or three million unemployed, Hitler, the progress of the Abyssinian war, the political situations in France and Spain. He adds:

> And though this is an extreme instance, nearly all newspapers of those days were more or less like that. No real information about current affairs was allowed into them if it could possibly be kept out. The world – so the readers of the gutter Press were taught – was a cosy place dominated by royalty, crime, beauty-culture, sport, pornography and animals (ibid: 146).

On the power of advertisers and the manufacture of a 'sunshine mentality'

Orwell now returns to his long-standing, political economy critique, highlighting the impact of advertising and proprietorial monopolies on press content:

> The unbearable silliness of English newspapers from about 1900 onwards has two main causes. One is that nearly the whole of the press is in the hands of a few big capitalists who are interested in the continuance of capitalism and therefore in preventing the public from learning to think: the other is that in peacetime newspapers live off advertisements for consumption goods, building societies, cosmetics and the like and are therefore interested in maintaining a 'sunshine mentality' which will induce people to spend money. ... Therefore, don't let people know the facts about the political and economic situation; divert their attention to giant pandas, channel swimmers, royal weddings and other soothing topics (ibid).

In one of the 'London Letters' he contributes to the American leftist journal, *Partisan Review*, in 1941, he says he has detected a change in tone of the popular newspapers which have become 'politically serious while preserving their "stunt" make-up with screaming headlines etc' (Orwell 1970 [1941b]: 137–138). Now, in his 'As I Please' column, he returns to that same theme, suggesting that, during the war, the 'advertiser has temporarily lost his grip' and so newspapers 'are far more intelligent than they were five years ago' (Orwell 1998 [1944a]: 146). 'At the same time there has been an increase in censorship and official interference, but this is not nearly so crippling and not nearly so conducive to sheer silliness. It is better to be controlled by bureaucrats than by common swindlers' (ibid). His unrelenting critique continues:

> Most newspapers remain completely reckless about details of fact. The belief that what is 'in the papers' must be true has been gradually evaporating ever since Northcliffe set out to vulgarise journalism, and the war has not yet arrested the process. Many people frankly say that they take in such and such a paper because it is lively but that they don't believe a word of what it says (ibid).

In comparison, the BBC has gained in prestige since 1940 for its news, he says. 'Throughout most of the world the BBC is looked on as more reliable than that of other belligerent nations' (ibid: 147). How far is this justified?, Orwell asks.

> So far as my own experience goes, the BBC is much more truthful, in a negative way, than the majority of newspapers and has a much more responsible and dignified attitude towards the news. It tells less direct lies, makes more effort to avoid mistakes and – the thing the public probably values – keeps news in better proportion. But none of this alters the fact that the decline in the prestige of the newspapers as against radio is a disaster (ibid).

Orwell next appears to draw on his experience working at the BBC from 1941 to 1943. Then, everything broadcast had to be censored twice – once for security and once for policy. Even what appeared to be spontaneous talk had first to be checked (West 1985: 21). Radio, Orwell argues, is 'inherently totalitarian' since it can only be operated by the government. Moreover, while the BBC does not tell deliberate lies, 'it simply avoids every awkward question' (Orwell 1998 [1944a]: 147). 'In even the most stupid or reactionary newspaper every subject can at least be raised, if only in the form of a letter.' He concludes with these damning words:

> The Press is of its nature a more liberal, more democratic thing, and the Press lords who have dirtied its reputation, and the journalists who have more or less knowingly lent themselves to the process, have a lot to answer for (ibid).

Orwell's contempt for the *Daily Mirror* is to persist. Significantly, at the end of *Animal Farm*, the pigs take out subscriptions to *John Bull, Tit-Bits* and the *Mirror* – symbolically marking their ultimate betrayal of the revolution (Orwell 1976 [1945]: 63).

Orwell: Proto-blogger and the power of proprietors (again)

Typically, the issue does not end there. Orwell operates often in his 'As I Please' columns as a sort of proto-blogger encouraging dialogue with his readers (see Chapter 2). Here, after a letter from a reader, Frank Preston (identified by Peter Davison as possibly the assistant editor of *Practical Wireless*: see ibid), is carried in *Tribune* of 21 April 1944, criticising Orwell's suggestion that the BBC is a better source of news than the dailies, he responds in his column in the same issue:

> … in my experience the BBC *is* relatively truthful and, above all, has a responsible attitude towards the news and does not disseminate lies simply because they are 'newsy'. … the BBC sins much more by simply avoiding anything controversial than by direct propaganda (Orwell 1998 [1944b]: 164; italics in the original).

The correspondent asserts that the public and journalists rather than the proprietors are to blame 'for the silliness of English newspapers'. Orwell accepts that journalists share the blame – and adds wittily: 'In allowing their profession to be degraded they have largely acted with their eyes open, whereas, I suppose, to blame some-body like Northcliffe for making money in the quickest way is like blaming a skunk for stinking' (ibid).

In another 'As I Please' column later in 1944, Orwell highlights (with almost venomous fury) the ways in which the proprietorial and advertiser control of the press impacts even on the content of literary reviews and what he describes as 'the book racket' (Orwell 1998 [1944c]: 251–253):

> The literary papers of several well-known papers were practically owned by a handful of publishers who had their quislings planted in all the important jobs. These wretches churned forth their praise – 'masterpiece', 'brilliant', 'unforgettable' and so forth – like so many mechanical pianos. A book coming from the right publishers could be absolutely certain not only of favourable reviews, but of being placed on the 'recommended' list which industrious book-borrowers would cut out and take to the library the next day (ibid: 251–252).

On the power of advertisers, he writes: 'A book coming from a big publisher, who habitually spent large sums on advertisement, might get fifty or seventy-five reviews: a book from a small publisher might get only twenty' (ibid: 252).

In his lengthy essay, *The English People* (also written in 1944 but only published in 1947), Orwell's critique again focuses on the press:

> It is a fact that the much-boasted freedom of the British press is theoretical rather than actual. To begin with the centralised ownership of the press means in practice that unpopular opinions can only be printed in books or in newspapers with small circulations. Moreover, the English people as a whole are not sufficiently interested in the printed word to be very vigilant about this aspect of their liberties and during the last twenty years there has been much tampering with the freedom of the press, with no real popular protest. ... On the other hand, freedom of speech is a reality and respect for it almost general (Orwell 1998 [1947]: 208).

Orwell and the silencing role of the dominant consensus

Orwell constantly reads the press. Davison notes that in his diary between 2 July 1939 and 3 September 1939, Orwell quotes from 41 sources for the 297 entries. Of these, 138 (46.5 per cent) are from the *Daily Telegraph* (which he clearly considers a respectable 'journal of record'); others include *The Times, News Chronicle* and papers of the left such as *Socialist Correspondence* and *Revolutionary Proletarian* (Davison 2010: 156). And Orwell regularly uses press coverage as launch pads for his own journalism. For instance, in his 'As I Please' column on 7 July 1944, he responds to a letter from Lord Winterton in the *Evening Standard* on the 'remarkable reticence' of both parliament and press on matters endangering national security (Orwell 1998 [1944d]: 276):

> It is not only in war time that the British Press observes this voluntary reticence. One of the most extraordinary things about England is that there is almost no official censorship, and yet nothing that is acutely offensive to the governing class gets into print, at least in any place where large numbers of people are likely to read it.

To support his argument, he quotes the stanza (which he wrongly attributes to Hilaire Belloc, it's actually by Humbert Wolfe): 'You cannot hope to bribe or twist/ Thank God! The English journalist:/ But seeing what the man will do/ Unbribed, there is no reason to.' As an example of media silence, he cites the scandal surrounding Mrs Simpson: not even the communist *Daily Worker* mentions it 'although the American and European papers were having the time of their lives with the story' (ibid). The same kind of 'veiled censorship' applies to books. He concludes with a typical colourful flourish:

> Circus dogs jump when the trainer cracks his whip, but the really well-trained dog is the one that turns his somersault when there is no whip. And that is the state we have reached in this country thanks to three hundred years of living together without a civil war (ibid: 277).

The missing Animal Farm *Introduction*

Orwell's most sustained critique of press censorship lay unknown for many years. In 1944, the manuscript of *Animal Farm* is rejected by four publishers concerned over its implicit attack on the Soviet Union, then a crucial ally in the war against Hitler's Nazis. The Ministry of Information turns down Jonathan Cape's request – but the chief censor there is Peter Smollett, later revealed to be a Soviet spy (Bowker 2003: 312). At Faber, T. S. Eliot (who in 1931 rejected *Down and Out in London and Paris*, see ibid: 131) objects, somewhat obtusely, to the representation of the animals: 'What was needed was not more communism but more public-spirited pigs' (ibid: 313). After rejection letters arrive from publishers William Collins and André Deutsch, Orwell turns to his friend Paul Potts who runs the Whitman Press, a small anarchist imprint. For this edition, Orwell pens an eight-page 'Introduction' but when Secker & Warburg suddenly agrees to publish in March 1945 he ditches it. The manuscript is only discovered in 1971 among some of the books of Roger Senhouse, former business partner of Fredric Warburg (Crick 1972) – and published in full in the *Times Literary Supplement* on 15 September 1972. Orwell begins the polemic repeating the arguments developed over a number of 'As I Please' columns – hitting out at the monopoly control of the press (Orwell 1972: 1037):

> The British press is extremely centralized and most of it is owned by wealthy men who have every motive to be dishonest on certain important topics. But at the same kind of veiled censorship also operates in books and periodicals as well as in plays, films and radio.

Next he highlights the silencing function of the dominant consensus: 'Anyone who challenges the prevailing orthodoxy finds himself silenced with surprising effectiveness. A genuinely unfashionable opinion is almost never given a fair hearing, either in the popular press or in the highbrow periodicals' (ibid). He directs his venom, in particular, at 'the greater part of the English intelligentsia which have swallowed and repeated Russian propaganda from 1941 onwards'. As an example he cites the BBC celebrating the twenty-fifth anniversary of the Red Army without mentioning Trotsky: 'This was about as accurate as commemorating the battle of Trafalgar without mentioning Nelson but it evoked no protest from the English intelligentsia' (ibid: 1038).

He discounts the notion of absolute liberty, claiming there will always be 'some degree of censorship so long as organized societies endure'. However, he quotes approvingly Voltaire's 'famous words': 'I detest what you say: I will defend to the death your right to say it' and adds:

> If the intellectual liberty which without doubt has been one of the distinguishing marks of western civilization means anything at all, it means that everyone shall have the right to say and print what he believes to be the truth,

provided only that it does not harm the rest of the community in some quite unmistakeable way (ibid).

He is even prepared to defend the publication of the communist *Daily Worker* (accused by some of doubtful loyalty during war time) even though it has 'gone out of its way to libel me more than once' (ibid).

Confounding expectations: Orwell on women's papers

Feminist critics unite in condemning Orwell as a misogynist. According to Beatrix Campbell (1984: 131): 'Part of the problem is that Orwell's eye never comes to rest on the culture of women, their concerns, their history, their movements. He only holds women to the filter of his own desire – or distaste.' According to Deirdre Beddoe (1984: 140): 'Orwell was not only anti-feminist but he was totally blind to the role women were and are forced to play in the order of things.' And for Daphne Patai (1984), author of *The Orwell Mystique: A Study in Male Ideology*, Orwell cultivated 'a traditional notion of masculinity, complemented by a generalized misogyny' (ibid: 15). He 'polarizes human beings according to sex roles and gender identity and legitimizes male displays of dominance and aggression' (ibid: 17). John Newsinger is also critical of Orwell's attitudes to women. He writes: 'He regularly dismissed both "feminists" and "feminism". He was unfortunately one of those male socialists who were opposed to every oppression, except that of women' (Newsinger 2018: 154). Even Christopher Hitchens (2002), hardly noted as a feminist, argues (105): 'Every one of the female characters [in his novels] is practically devoid of the least trace of intellectual or reflective capacity.'

Yet, Orwell was a complex man with many sides to his personality – and one was distinctly un-misogynistic. Many of the women he was to be associated with (Jacintha Buddicom, Stevie Smith, Inez Holden, Mabel Fierz, Celia Kirwan – not to mention his two wives, Eileen O'Shaughnessy and Sonia Brownell) were forceful characters who would hardly have tolerated a misogynist. As a father to Richard Horatio, whom he and Eileen adopted in June 1944, Orwell certainly confounded the expectations of his day, displaying considerable affection for the child, taking him for walks in the pram – and even changing his nappies (though with a cigarette in his mouth) (Crick 1980: 483).

In one 'As I Please' column, responding again to a reader's letter, he uses a serious critique of women's papers – such as *Lucky Star*, the *Golden Star* and *Peg's Paper* – to explore the ways in which press proprietors and the ruling class in general promote the notion of the moral superiority of the poor as 'the deadliest form of escapism' (Orwell 1998 [1944e]: 305). He argues that it is all 'a sublimation of the class struggle' and adds, with typical dry irony: 'The vast majority of the people who will see a film are poor and so it is politic to make the poor man a hero. Film magnates, Press lords and the like amass quite a lot of their wealth by pointing out that wealth is wicked' (ibid).

Yet, he argues, reality enters these papers through the correspondence columns where you can read harrowing tales of 'bad legs' and haemorrhoids 'written by middle-aged women who give themselves such pseudonyms as "A Sufferer", "Mother of Nine" and "Always Constipated"': 'To compare these letters with the love stories that lie cheek by jowl with them is to see how vast a part mere day dreaming plays in modern life' (ibid).

And in another 'As I Please' column, on 8 November 1946, he begins: 'Someone has just sent me a copy of an American fashion magazine which shall be nameless' (Orwell 1998 [1946c]: 471). In fact, it was *Vogue*, which had been posted to his London address because, amongst its many photographs of glamorous women, was a profile of Orwell. So he proceeds to deconstruct the magazine, noting: 'One striking thing when one looks at these pictures is the overbred, exhausted, even decadent style of beauty that now seems to be striven after. Nearly all of these women are immensely elongated.' On the prose style of the advertisements, he says it's 'an extraordinary mixture of sheer lushness with clipped and sometimes very expressive technical jargon'. And, typically, Orwell focuses on what's missing:

> A fairly diligent search through the magazine reveals two discreet allusions to grey hair, but if there is anywhere a direct mention of fatness or middle age I have not found it. Birth and death are not mentioned either: nor is work, except that a few recipes for breakfast dishes are given (ibid).

Other idiosyncratic, imaginative ways of critiquing the press

Orwell is forever inventing new ways of examining the press. In a proto-blogger style, he devotes the first item in his 'As I Please' column of 6 October 1946 to responding to a letter from a reader who has been advised by a well-known school of journalism to 'avoid writing propaganda for Socialist newspapers' (Orwell 1998 [1994f]: 423). (Peter Davison identifies the correspondent as Mrs Ada Dodd, of Bridgend, Glamorgan, and the training institute as the London School of Journalism, ibid: 426.) Orwell responds with venom:

> What is significant is the assumption that nothing ever changes, that the public always will be and always must be the same mob of nitwits wanting only to be duped and that no sane person would sit down behind a typewriter with any other object than to produce saleable drivel (ibid: 424).

Orwell returns to the issue in his 17 November 1944 column. The proprietors have sent him the current issue of the *Writer* which he had wrongly stated earlier as being defunct. He is happy to correct himself, but goes on to examine the advertisements of people selling their journalism training services. One, for instance, reads: 'Plotting without tears. Learn my way. The simplest method ever. Money returned if dissatisfied. 5 shillings post free' (Orwell 1998 [1944g]: 464). Orwell comments with merciless wit: isn't it curious that the trainers are rarely well-known writers? 'If Bernard Shaw or J. B. Priestley offered to teach you how to make money out of writing, you might feel that there was something in it. But who would buy a bottle of hair restorer from a bald man?' (ibid).

Another intriguing way of critiquing the press appears in the 'As I Please' column on 22 November 1946. Here Orwell simply presents two lists and subjects them to 'ironic reversal', as Alex Woloch points out (2016: 246): one shows major newspapers in order of intelligence (*Manchester Guardian, Times, News Chronicle, Telegraph, Herald, Mail, Mirror, Express, Graphic*); the other in order of popularity (*Express, Herald, Mirror, News Chronicle, Mail, Graphic, Telegraph, Times, Manchester Guardian*). He comments (Orwell 1998 [1946b]: 500): 'It will be seen that the second list is very nearly – not quite, for life is never so neat as that – the first turned upside down.' For Orwell, the solution lies in the alternative press:

> In these circumstances it is difficult to foresee a radical change, even if the special kind of pressure exerted by owners and advertisers is removed. What matters is that in England we do possess juridical liberty of the Press, which makes it possible to utter one's true opinions fearlessly in papers of comparatively small circulation (ibid).

Again, the column provokes a couple of readers' letters to which Orwell responds in *Tribune*, 13 December 1946 (ibid: 501). He admits to a mistake in his list of circulations and tweaks it to read *Express, Mirror, Herald, Mail, News Chronicle*. On the issue of not including the communist *Daily Worker*, he says its circulation is too small for inclusion. 'But if it is to be included, it rather bears out my contention. I should put it fairly high in the list for intelligence, say about the level of the *Telegraph*, whereas it comes bottom in popularity' (ibid).

Putting principles into practice

Orwell not only lambasts the corporate press but puts his principles into practice by devoting most of his journalistic energies to the small circulation/alternative/left press. As Peter Marks (2011) writes: 'Some of these journals were almost unknown except to their subscribers, while most had circulations lower than 5,000' (4). In particular, his writings for dozens of human rights, leftist, anarchist, pacifist, trade union journals (such as the *Adelphi, Commentary, Controversy, For Anarchism, Forward, Fortnightly Review, Gangrel, Left News, Left Forum, Left Review, New English Weekly*, New York's *New Leader, New Republic*, the *Highway, New Road, New Statesman and Nation, New Saxon Pamphlets, Polemic, Politics and Letters, Tribune*) play a crucial role in the intellectual and political debates within the alternative public sphere of the 1930s and 1940s.

From January 1940 until the summer of 1946, Orwell clearly wants to demonstrate his commitment to the US. So he contributes a regular 'London Letter' not to the prestigious *New York Times* but to the left-wing, anti-communist, small circulation *Partisan Review* (see Newsinger 1999). According to Gordon Bowker (2003: 272), these pieces include 'some of his best wartime writing – wide-ranging pieces covering the current political situation, wartime conditions in England, literary gossip, attitudes to American soldiers and, of course, strongly expressed personal opinions about everything'.

Orwell's journalistic output is massive: Gillian Fenwick (1998) records more than 400 contributions to periodicals during the war alone (186–218) while Peter Davison (2014: 2) calculates that his journalism corpus includes 379 reviews of some 700 books, plays and films. This is an extraordinarily prolific output given his poor health and burning desire to write novels.

Often, he writes either for little financial reward or nothing. The main intention is that of the political activist: to promote the democratic left. For instance, his substantial seven-part reflection 'Looking back on the Spanish civil war' is written in 1942 entirely free for the tiny circulation, anarchist journal *New Road*, edited by Alex Comfort (Orwell 1980 [1942]: 595–608). His celebrated essay of 1946, 'Why I write' is published by *Gangrel*. Marks describes it as 'an obscure journal whose fleeting existence in 1945–6 went largely unnoticed' (op cit: 167). Its editor J. B. Pick (1921–2015) was a Quaker and conscientious objector during the Second World War. Significantly, Orwell writes in this essay:

> Every line of serious work that I have written since 1936 [and thus his experiences fighting in the Spanish civil war and heightened political awareness] has been written, directly or indirectly, against totalitarianism and for democratic Socialism as I understand it. ... What I have most wanted to do throughout the past ten years is to make political writing into an art. My starting point is always a feeling of partisanship, a sense of injustice (Orwell 1970 [1946]: 28).

Orwell – and the problems of always matching principles with practice

Just as Orwell has a low opinion of his journalism (describing it as 'mere pamphleteering') so at times he can be downbeat about the overall impact of the left press to which he devotes so much of his energies. For instance, in 1948, he contributes an essay 'Britain's left wing press' to the obscure Wisconsin journal, *Progressive* (see Woloch 2016: 248). Surprisingly, he lists just six papers – the *Daily Herald, Reynold's News*, the *New Statesman and Nation, Tribune, Forward* and the *Daily Worker* – as the only ones 'of any consequence'.

And while he is constantly critical of the performance of Fleet Street, occasionally he is prepared to work for it: in 1946, for instance, he writes a number of short articles on popular culture for the London *Evening Standard*: they include 'A nice cup of tea' (in which he considers the perfect brew), 'The Moon Under Water' (where he ponders the perfect pub) and 'Just junk: But who could resist it?' (where he debates the most attractive junk shop in London).

Orwell's most important involvement with the corporate press, however, follows his meeting in 1941 with fellow old-Etonian David Astor, whose family owns the *Observer* and who is to be its distinguished editor from 1948 to 1975. The two become friends immediately and so from March 1942, Orwell makes regular contributions to the *Observer* such as profiles and book reviews until his death in January 1950 (Heawood 2003; Keeble 2019). Astor also introduces Orwell to the world of intelligence and thus his trip to the continent to report the final months of the Second World War for the *Observer* and *Manchester Evening News* may well be the cover for some kind of intelligence mission (see Keeble 2015a and Chapter 3). Orwell constantly highlights the ways in which the power of the proprietors constrains press freedom. Clearly, in this instance, another principle – that friendship is all important – takes precedence.

In any case, as Chris Atton (2004: 10) warns, there is a danger of presenting a polarised vision of the mainstream and alternative spheres, positing a 'hegemonic approach' that 'suggests a complexity of relationships between radical and mainstream that previous binary models have been unable to identify'. Robert Hackett (2007) highlights the space within the dominant media in which progressive journalists can operate autonomously. And such approaches can help us further contextualise Orwell's occasional involvement with the mainstream.

Conclusions: Writing as a way of life

One of the most perceptive analyses of Orwell's *oeuvre* is provided by Lynette Hunter (1984). She argues that his ambivalences, contradictions and inconsistences emerge from his essential approach to writing and learning:

> The assumption that one can absolutely define Orwell in biographical terms is parallel to the assumption that his writing and message or interpretation are equally clear and fixed. But the very attempt to define and fix into stasis is part of a world view that Orwell rejected. If this is not recognized then the outcome is often the suggestion that Orwell is being inconsistent, hence untrustworthy and deceitful.

Orwell's approach is always questioning and educational as he invites his readers to join him in his quest for learning. This is particularly relevant to Orwell's journalism where he is able to bring together his political engagement, voracious reading – and political, social and cultural observations. As Hunter argues:

> All too often there is an unwillingness to accept that Orwell might learn, come to appreciate different things and change his mind, and to recognize that this apparent inconsistency overlays a fundamentally consistent belief in the need to evaluate actively, never to assume the quality of axioms and fixed standards (ibid).

Orwell's literary voice, above all, according to Hunter, 'does not impose opinion on others but invites discussion' (ibid: 11).

Similarly, David Dwan (2019: 206) says Orwell's overall *oeuvre* 'raises troubling questions about his own inconsistencies and doubletalk'. He adds:

> Contrary to what many have assumed, Orwell provides few solutions to our political difficulties, although this was never his job. As Hilary Putnam once suggested, the writer's task is not to deliver solutions but to engage in the 'imaginative re-creation of moral perplexities'.

Orwell's writings take in a vast range of genres: memoir, novels (though, interestingly, no short stories), war reporting, radio plays and commentaries, column writing, book, film and theatre reviewing, essays, political analysis and polemic, poetry, press analysis, investigative reporting, profiles, humorous sketches, social documentaries, letters, diaries and so on. Yet these genres are forever overlapping. As Hunter stresses: 'The divisions between subject and object, fiction and fact, novel and documentary and the whole field of static genre became subordinate to stance' (Hunter 1984: 3).

Journalism, then, is not to be seen as a discreet activity but one element of his *life as a writer*. Yet, as this chapter argues, it is crucially important for him. Significantly, his reflections on the press culminate in the creation of Winston Smith, the anti-hero of his dystopian masterpiece *Nineteen Eighty-Four* – published in 1949 just months before he died. For Winston is a media worker at the Ministry of Truth altering the records of *The Times* to conform to the current dogma. So Orwell's damning critique of the press persists to the very end.

Acknowledgements

I would like to thank Prof. Tim Crook, joint editor of *George Orwell Studies*, for his comments on an early draft of this essay. Any factual errors are my responsibility alone.

References

Anderson, Paul (2006) *Orwell in Tribune*, London: Politico's

Atton, Chris (2004) *An Alternative Internet: Radical Media, Politics and Creativity*, Edinburgh: Edinburgh University Press

Beddoe, Deirdre (1984) Hindrance and help-meets: Women in the writings of George Orwell, Norris, Christopher (ed.) *Inside the Myth: Orwell – Views from the Left*, London: Lawrence & Wishart pp 139–154

Bowker, Gordon (2003) *George Orwell*, London: Little, Brown

Campbell, Beatrix (1984) Orwell: Paterfamilias or Big Brother?, Norris, Christopher (ed.) *Inside the Myth: Orwell – Views from the Left*, London: Lawrence & Wishart pp 128–136

Crick, Bernard (1972) How the essay came to be written, *Times Literary Supplement*, 15 September pp 1039–1040

Crick, Bernard (1980) *George Orwell: A Life*, Harmondsworth, Middlesex: Penguin

Davison, Peter (ed.) (2010) *George Orwell's Diaries*, London: Penguin

Davison, Peter (2014) Introduction, *Seeing Things as They Are: George Orwell's Selected Journalism and Other Writings*, Davison, Peter (ed.) London: Harvill Secker pp 1–8

Dulley, Paul Richard (2015) *In Front of Your Nose: The Existentialism of George Orwell*. PhD thesis, University of Sussex. Available online at http://sro.sussex.ac.uk/id/eprint/56743/

Dwan, David (2019) *Liberty, Equality and Humbug: Orwell's Political Ideals*, Oxford: Oxford University Press

Fenwick, Gillian (1998) *George Orwell: A Bibliography*, Winchester: St Paul's Bibliographies

Hackett, Robert A. (2007) Is Peace Journalism possible? Shinar, Dove and Kempf, Wilhelm (eds) *Peace Journalism: The State of the Art*, Berlin: Regener pp 75–94

Heawood, Jonathan (ed.) (2003) *Orwell: The Observer Years*, London: Atlantic Books

Hitchens, Christopher (2002) *Orwell's Victory*, London: Allen Lane, The Penguin Press

Hunter, Lynette (1984) *George Orwell: The Search for a Voice*, Milton Keynes: Open University Press

Keeble, Richard (2007) Introduction, Keeble, Richard and Wheeler, Sharon (eds) *The Journalistic Imagination: Literary Journalists from Defoe to Capote and Carter*, London: Routledge pp 1–14

Keeble, Richard Lance (2012) Orwell, *Nineteen Eighty-Four* and the spooks, Keeble, Richard Lance (ed.) *Orwell Today*, Bury St Edmunds: Abramis pp 151–163

Keeble, Richard Lance (2015a) Orwell and the war reporter's imagination, Keeble, Richard Lance (ed.) *George Orwell Now!*, New York: Peter Lang pp 209–224

Keeble, Richard Lance (2015b) 'There is always room for one more custard pie': Orwell's humour, Keeble, Richard Lance and Swick, David (eds) *Pleasures of the Prose: Journalism and Humour*, Bury St Edmunds: Abramis pp 10–25

Keeble, Richard Lance (2019) Orwell, Astor and the making of *Nineteen Eighty-Four*, *orwellsocietyblog*, 3 June. Available online at https://orwellsocietyblog.wordpress.com/2019/06/03/orwell-astor-1984/

Marks, Peter (2011) *George Orwell the Essayist: Literature, Politics and the Periodical Culture*, London: Continuum

Marks, Peter (2016) *George Orwell the Essayist: Literature, Politics and the Periodical Culture*, London and New York: Continuum

Newsinger, John (1999) *Orwell's Politics*, London: Palgrave Macmillan

Newsinger, John (2018) *Hope Lies in the Proles: George Orwell and the Left*, London: Pluto Press

Orwell, George (1970 [1928]) A farthing newspaper, Orwell, Sonia and Angus, Ian (eds) *The Collected Essays, Journalism and Letters*, Vol. 1: *An Age Like This, 1920–1940*, Harmondsworth, Middlesex: Penguin pp 34–37; *G. K.'s Weekly*, 29 December

Orwell, George (1962 [1938]) *Homage to Catalonia*, Harmondsworth, Middlesex: Penguin

Orwell, George (1970 [1941a]) The Lion and the Unicorn, *The Collected Essays, Journalism and Letters*, Vol. 2: *My Country Right or Left 1940–1942*, Harmondsworth, Middlesex: Penguin pp 74–134; February 1941

Orwell, George (1970 [1941b]) London Letter to *Partisan Review*, Orwell, Sonia and Angus, Ian (eds) *The Collected Essays, Journalism and Letters*, Vol. 2: *My Country Right or Left, 1940–1942*, Harmondsworth, Middlesex: Penguin pp 137–149; 15 April

Orwell, George (1980 [1942]) *Complete and Unabridged*, London: Secker & Warburg

Orwell, George (1970 [1943]) Looking back on the Spanish War, Orwell, Sonia and Angus, Ian (eds) *The Collected Essays, Journalism and Letters*, Vol. 2: *My Country Right or Left, 1940–1942*, Harmondsworth, Middlesex: Penguin pp 286–306; Sections I, II, III and VII in *New Road*

Orwell, George (1998 [1944a]) As I Please, Davison, Peter (ed.) *Complete Works of George Orwell*, Vol 16: *I Have Tried to Tell The Truth, 1943–1944*, London: Secker & Warburg pp 145–148; *Tribune*, 7 April

Orwell, George (1998 [1944b]) As I Please, Davison, Peter (ed.) *Complete Works of George Orwell*, Vol 16: *I Have Tried to Tell The Truth, 1943–1944*, London: Secker & Warburg pp 164–166; *Tribune*, 21 April

Orwell, George (1998 [1944c]) As I Please, Davison, Peter (ed.) *Complete Works of George Orwell*, Vol 16: *I Have Tried to Tell The Truth, 1943–1944*, London: Secker & Warburg pp 251–253; *Tribune*, 9 June

Orwell, George (1998 [1944d]) As I Please, Davison, Peter (ed.) *Complete Works of George Orwell*, Vol 16: *I Have Tried to Tell The Truth, 1943–1944*, London: Secker & Warburg pp 276–277; *Tribune*, 7 July

Orwell, George (1998 [1944e]) As I Please, Davison, Peter (ed.) *Complete Works of George Orwell*, Vol 16: *I Have Tried to Tell The Truth, 1943–1944*, London: Secker & Warburg pp 251–253; *Tribune*, 28 July

Orwell, George (1998 [1944f] As I Please, Davison, Peter (ed.) *Complete Works of George Orwell*, Vol 16: *I Have Tried to Tell The Truth, 1943–1944*, London: Secker & Warburg pp 423–425; *Tribune*, 6 October

Orwell, George (1998 [1944g]) As I Please, Davison, Peter (ed.) *Complete Works of George Orwell*, Vol 16: *I Have Tried to Tell The Truth, 1943–1944*, London: Secker & Warburg pp 463–465; *Tribune*, 17 November

Orwell, George (1976 [1945]) *Animal Farm*, London: Secker & Warburg pp 13–66

Orwell, George (1970 [1946a]) Why I write, Orwell, Sonia and Angus, Ian (eds) *The Collected Essays, Journalism and Letters*, Vol. 1, Harmondsworth, Middlesex: Penguin pp 23–30; first published *Gangrel*, No. 4.

Orwell, George (1998 [1946b]) As I Please, Davison, Peter (ed.) *Complete Works of George Orwell*, Vol. 17: *Smothered Under Journalism, 1946*, London: Secker & Warburg pp 497–500; *Tribune*, 22 November

Orwell, George (1998 [1946c]) As I Please, Davison, Peter (ed.) *Complete Works of George Orwell*, Vol. 17: *Smothered Under Journalism, 1946*, London: Secker & Warburg pp 471–472; *Tribune*, 8 November

Orwell, George (1998 [1947]) *The English People*, Davison, Peter (ed.) *Complete Works of George Orwell*, Vol 16: *I Have Tried to Tell the Truth, 1943–1944*, London: Secker & Warburg pp 199–228

Orwell, George (1972) The freedom of the press, *Times Literary Supplement*, 15 September pp 1037–1040

Patai, Daphne (1984) *The Orwell Mystique: A Study in Male Ideology*, Amherst: University of Massachusetts Press

Smith, James (2013) *British Writers and MI5 Surveillance, 1930–1960*, Cambridge: Cambridge University Press

Taylor, D. J. (2003) *Orwell: The Life*, London: Chatto & Windus

West, W. J. (ed.) (1985) *Orwell: The War Broadcasts*, London: Gerald Duckworth and Co.

Woloch, Alex (2016) *Or Orwell: Writing and Democratic Socialism*, Cambridge, MA: Harvard University Press

2

THE LASTING IN THE EPHEMERAL

Assessing George Orwell's 'As I Please' columns

From the BBC to *Tribune*

In November 1943, George Orwell, with great relief, quit his job at the BBC and began working as literary editor of the leftist weekly journal, *Tribune*. In the process he took a substantial wage cut – from £720 a year to £500 – and started on the novel which was to secure his international reputation, *Animal Farm*. Launched by Sir Stafford Cripps and George Strauss (both Labour MPs) in 1937, *Tribune* had become the leading voice of the left-wing of the Labour Party. By the time Orwell joined the staff, Aneurin 'Nye' Bevan was editor (controlling its political position and writing most of the leaders) with Jon Kimche, who had worked with Orwell in 1934 as an assistant at Booklover's Corner, Hampstead, doing most of the editing and commissioning.

One of Orwell's main contributions to *Tribune* as literary editor was the 'As I Please' column. A similar title had been used by Raymond Postgate in *Commentary* in 1939 while Walter Duranty, foreign correspondent for the *New York Times* (1913–1939), had written a book, *I Write as I Please* (1935). But Jon Kimche told Peter Davison (1998a: 3), editor of the 20-volume series of Orwell's collected writings, that he had suggested the title for the column. In all, Orwell contributed 80 'As I Please' columns, his last one appearing on 4 April 1947 by which time Michael Foot, MP (later leader of the Labour Party) had become managing director.

After his unhappy two years as talks producer at the Indian Section of the BBC's Eastern Service, where he was increasingly annoyed by the censorship and bureaucracy, Orwell clearly loved the new freedom at *Tribune*, all the more so because it was a journal with which he could totally identify. In his 'As I Please' column on 31 January 1947, he writes: 'It is the only existing weekly paper that makes a genuine effort to be both progressive and humane – that is, to combine a radical socialist policy with a respect for freedom of speech and a civilised attitude towards literature and the arts.'

Between February 1945 and November 1946, there is a gap in Orwell's 'As I Please' contributions with Jennie Lee (who married Bevan in 1935 and was later first minister for the arts from 1967 to 1970) taking over the role. For the first three months of this period he served as war correspondent for the *Observer* and *Manchester Evening News* on the continent. His 19 articles from the Continent represent the only time Orwell worked as a reporter to strict deadlines for mainstream newspapers. And yet they have been either ignored or usually damned as dull (Crick 1980: 480, Ingle 1993: 67, Meyers 2000: 232; but see Keeble 2001).[1]

Orwell's distress over 'ephemeral journalism'

In contrast, commentators are virtually unanimous in ruling his columns outstanding examples of his journalistic style. Yet until Paul Anderson's edited collection of Orwell's *Tribune* writing (published in 2006) there was no academic study of all the 80 columns. And Anderson concentrates on Orwell's politics as expressed through the columns rather than his journalistic strategies and writing styles.[2] Paradoxically, Orwell shared many of the academy's prejudices against journalism. Throughout his career he constantly downgraded his own writing as 'mere journalism' or 'pamphleteering' and looked up to literature which he thought of as higher form.

In his celebrated 'Why I write' essay (Orwell and Angus 1970, Vol. 1: 26) of 1946 he confesses: 'In a peaceful age I might have written ornate or merely descriptive books and might have remained almost unaware of my political loyalties. As it is I have been forced into becoming a sort of pamphleteer.' Hilary Spurling, in her affectionate biography of Orwell's second wife, Sonia, records how Orwell confided to her, just before he died, how dissatisfied he felt with his overall output, feeling he had wasted too much time on 'ephemeral journalism' (Spurling 2002: 100).

Orwell and the tradition of 'personal journalism'

For Christopher Silvester (1997) Orwell's columns have to be considered in the context of a tradition of 'personal journalism' which emerged out of the 19th century's Romantic movement and its focus on the contemplation of the self. In addition, Silvester stresses the financial pressures on the new mass-selling newspapers in the United States and Britain which needed to vary their diet of straight, hard news with 'human interest' news, features and comment to maintain reader interest. T. H. White's 'Lakeside Musings' for the *Chicago Tribune* and the twice-weekly columns by J. M. Barrie, the creator of Peter Pan, in the *Nottingham Guardian*, in the mid-1880s, created a new genre of regularly appearing, well-crafted columns of commentary – both serious and whimsical.

In the early years of the 20th century – with the role of editor and proprietor now completely separated – editorials take on a more formal tone while the column becomes the site of vigorous, splenetic opinion, sometimes even going against the editorial line of the title in which it runs (ibid: xiii). By the 1930s columnists such as Walter Lippmann (whose thrice-weekly political analyses were syndicated out of the *New York Herald Tribune*) and the Broadway diarist Walter Winchell (syndicated out of the *New York Daily Mirror*) were becoming media celebrities. In Britain, syndication never caught on. But, as Silvester stresses, the 1930s proved to be a golden era for columnists in the mainstream press – with Tom Driberg's William Hickey gossip column and J. B. Morton's Beachcomber column in the *Daily Express*, D. B. Wyndham Lewis's witty columns in the *Daily Mail* and the anti-fascist rhetoric of Cassandra (William Connor) in the *Daily Mirror*.

Gordon Bowker (2003: 306) rather highlights the way in which Orwell's columns follow in the long tradition of Hazlitt, Lamb, Stevenson, Belloc and Chesterton. 'It was a form of good-humoured prose rumination practised in Orwell's day at Eton in the *College Chronicle* and in Butler's *Written Sketches* which he so enjoyed.' According to Orwell's biographer Jeffrey Meyers (2000: 226):

> His column transformed a humble genre into significant literary works. He not only promoted socialist ideas and put contemporary political events in historical perspective but also (gloomy as he was) cheered people up with entertaining subjects and – in an intimate tone of voice – combined public issues with personal feelings.

And for Scott Lucas (2003: 70), the column was crucial in establishing Orwell as 'an English cultural icon'.

Orwell: Making the personal political

According to Colin Sparks (1992: 39–40), the media's stress on the personal 'becomes the explanatory framework within which the social order is presented as transparent. … [T]he "personal" obliterates the "political" as an explanatory factor in human behaviour'. And he argues that the media's highly personalised representations of reality deny consumers the means to recognise the structural basis of power relations in society. In many ways, the current obsessions with sex, celebrity, randy royals and reality TV stars reflect a profound de-politicisation of the culture. Yet in his 'As I Please' columns, Orwell shows how the personal does not necessarily obliterate the political.

He does not cover the normal beat of a political columnist: elections, the personal squabbles of politicians, ministerial changes, legislation, parliament. But as Paul Anderson (2006) stresses: 'It would be wrong to suggest that his columns were not political. They were intensely so – even, paradoxically, when they appeared to have nothing to do with politics' (3).

Orwell's writing bursts with original ideas and yet is *distinctly journalistic* in that it is never obscured by abstraction and endless referencing.[3] The 'I' voice of the column is perfectly suited to his style, even though he feels typically ambivalent about this subjectivity. At the end of 'Why I write' (Orwell and Angus 1970, Vol. 1: 29–30) he asserts: 'One can write nothing readable unless one constantly strives to efface one's own personality. Good prose is like a window pane.' Yet, as Orwell's long-time friend and literary editor Cyril Connolly says of him: 'He was a man … whose personality shines out in everything he said or wrote.' Richard Filloy (1998: 49) resolves this apparent paradox by suggesting that self-effacement was the important persuasive strategy for Orwell.

> By making his reports those of an ordinary person rather than those of a great man, he allowed his audience to put themselves in his position without imagining the impossible. … By offering us a character who is ordinary, Orwell not only allows the reader to share the perceptions of the writer, he also disarms our suspicion of an ethos which is so good and so intelligent that our training tells us to mistrust it. After all, we are not in the presence of an especially superior person, merely another poor soul like ourselves (ibid: 52).

His 'persuasive rhetoric of personality' (ibid: 47–63) is most apparent in the columns which feature surprisingly idiosyncratic, 'ordinary' subject matter, deliberately far distant in tone and style from the heavy diet of political polemic and policy analysis that fills the rest of the pages of *Tribune* (Anderson op cit: 26). His column of 28 January 1944 (Davison 1998a: 80–83) is typical of the genre in blending together four very different topics drawn imaginatively from four contrasting sources: a news item, a letter from a reader, a barmaid's comment and a book he has just reviewed for the *Manchester Evening News*. In the first section, Orwell responds to a news item about an Indian journalist being arrested for refusing military service with argumentative gusto.

> By behaviour of this kind you antagonise the entire Indian community in Britain – for no Indian, whatever his views, admits that Britain had the right to declare war on India's behalf or has the right to impose compulsory service on Indians.

Next he answers a correspondent defending Ezra Pound, the American poet who had become a fervent propagandist for Mussolini in Rome. Basing his judgment on a concept of 'ordinary decency', Orwell argues that any writer's political opinions should not interfere with the critical assessment of their work. 'Personally I admire several writers (Céline, for instance) who have gone over to the Fascists and many others whose political outlook I strongly object to. But one has the right to expect ordinary decency even of a poet.' And he ends succinctly. Agreeing with the correspondent that the Americans should not shoot Pound, he quips: 'It would establish his reputation so thoroughly that it might be a hundred years before anyone could determine dispassionately whether Pound's much-debated poems are any good or not.'

His next section is particularly idiosyncratic as he expands on a passing comment by a barmaid (an archetypically 'ordinary' source) that 'if you pour beer into a damp glass it goes flat much more quickly'. From seemingly nothing Orwell conjures a fascinating list of 'those superstitions which are able to keep alive because they have the air of being scientific truths'. For this he draws on his childhood memories of fallacies taught to him 'not as an old wives' tale but as a scientific fact'. His favourites include: that a swan can break your leg with a blow of its wing; that bulls become furious at the sight of red and that powered glass is poisonous. He ends drolly: 'As for the third, it is so widespread that in India, for instance, people are constantly trying to poison one another with powered glass, with disappointing results.' And in the final section he argues the case for a new international language.

In another quirky column on 4 February 1944 (Davison 1998a: 89), Orwell responds to a Board of Trade announcement ending the ban on turned-up trouserends. He sees a tailor's advertisement, hailing this as 'a first instalment of the freedom for which we are fighting'. Orwell's close identification with his readers is sealed as he addresses them as 'we'. He continues: 'If we were really fighting for turned-up trouser ends, I should be inclined to be pro-Axis. Turn-ups have no function except to collect dust and no virtue except that when you clean them out you occasionally find a sixpence there.' From this specific news-driven point he moves on to make a general political and social comment about 'clothes snobbery'. 'The sooner we are able to stop food rationing the better I shall be pleased but I would like to see clothes' rationing continue till the moths have devoured the last dinner jacket and even the undertakers have shed their top hats.'

Orwell's factional voice

The 'As I Please' column (No. 22) of 28 April 1944 (see Anderson 2006: 130–133) captures many of the elements of Orwell's style. At the start he focuses on the 'when', 'who' and 'what' of the typical introductory section (the 'intro' in the jargon) of a news article together with a stress on his personal involvement in the event:

> On the night in 1940 when the big ack-ack barrage was fired over London for the first time, I was in Piccadilly Circus when the guns opened up, and I fled into the Café Royal to take cover. Among the crowd inside a good-looking, well-made youth of about twenty-five was making somewhat of a nuisance of himself with a copy of *Peace News*.

While rooted in news writing routines, the column has no specific newsiness (the event happened four years ago). Orwell is more concerned about the issues raised in his conversation with the youth. He says his account is not completely accurate (it 'went something like this') and with the 'youth' remaining anonymous Orwell's 'factional' strategy leaves him free to blend fact and fiction.

The 'youth' claims that a necessary 'compromise peace' with the Germans will help him 'remain alive' and allow him to get on with his work as a painter. In response, Orwell argues it is a fallacy 'to believe that under a dictatorial government you can be free *inside*' (his emphasis). And so emerges the central theme (the fate of the individual's spirit in the face of the Big Brother, totalitarian state) which is later to dominate his novel *Nineteen Eighty-Four* (1949).

Orwell moves from a snatch of conversation four years ago to an exploration of major political, cultural, philosophical issues: the importance of freedom of speech, the survival of creative inspiration and the threats posed by 'totalitarianism' which, he says, is 'on the up-grade in every part of the world'. 'Out in the street the loudspeakers bellow, the flags flutter from the rooftops, the police with their tommy guns prowl to and fro, the face of the Leader, four feet wide, glares from every hoarding.' But take away freedom of speech 'and the creative faculties dry up'. Anticipating Winston Smith with his secret diary in *Nineteen Eighty-Four*, Orwell here argues that 'little worth-while writing of any kind – even such things as diaries, for instance – has been produced in secret under the dictators'.

Orwell as proto-blogger: Building the community of the left

Tim Holmes (2006: 160–168) identifies four categories in a practical taxonomy of column writing[4]: community building, oppositional viewpoint, unofficial extension of predominant ideology and commercial advantage. Most writers fulfil one of these categories. Orwell somehow manages to achieve all of them in his columns.

According to Holmes (ibid: 162): 'Ever since 1693, when John Dunton [founder of the *Ladies' Mercury*] identified the market for a title aimed specifically at women, magazines have flourished on building communities around particular interests and offering particular approaches to those interests.' Holmes stresses that within the mainstream, 'community' is a 'commercial concept not a social ideal'. But for Orwell, deliberately working away from the mainstream, his enormous commitment is towards the social ideal of building up the community of the left.

Since travelling to Spain in 1936 to fight alongside the Republicans against Franco's fascists and witnessing both socialism in action and the ruthless attempts by the communists to suppress it (graphically captured in *Homage to Catalonia*, of 1938), Orwell's commitment to the left was sealed. As Taylor (2003: 2001) comments: 'Spain, it can be safely said, was the defining experience of Orwell's life.' Significantly, Orwell stressed in his famous essay 'Why I write', published in the totally obscure journal *Gangrel* in the summer of 1946 (Orwell and Angus 1970, Vol. 1: 23–32): 'Every line of serious work that I have written since 1936 has been written, directly or indirectly, against totalitarianism and for democratic socialism as I understand it.' This might suggest an emphasis on the rhetorical, propagandistic, 'journalistic' aspects of writing. Yet Orwell goes on to assert that he wanted to 'make political writing into an art', thus resolving the aesthetics versus politics dilemma by combining the two.

Orwell uses essentially two strategies to promote his notion of 'the community of the left': firstly through columns focusing on political, cultural, social or literary issues; and, secondly, and most imaginatively, through developing a close relationship with his readers. This relationship is crucial to the flowering of Orwell's journalistic imagination. While he realises mainstream journalism is basically propaganda for wealthy newspaper proprietors, at *Tribune* he is engaging in the crucial political debate with people who matter to him. They are an authentic audience compared with what Stuart Allan (2004: 85) calls the 'implied reader or imagined community of readers' of the mainstream media.

Often Orwell speaks directly to fellow socialists. For instance, in his fourth column of 24 December 1943, Orwell moves from commenting on the influence of T. E. Hulme (1883–1917) on many of the writers grouped around the journal *Criterion* (such as Wyndham Lewis, T. S. Eliot, Aldous Huxley, Malcolm Muggeridge, Evelyn Waugh and Graham Greene) to a gentle warning to the 'socialist movement' not to ignore the influence of this 'neo-reactionary school of writers'.

In the close relationship he instinctively develops with his readers, Orwell can, in many ways, be seen as a proto-blogger, responding to letters sent to him directly or sent to *Tribune*, inviting letters, asking readers to answer queries or to point him towards a book, pamphlet or quotation he's looking for, running a competition for a short story or giving them a quirky brain teaser to answer.[5] Not only does Orwell respond to letters but also, as Peter Davison's *Collected Works* show, his columns often provoke many letters, both critical and supportive, from readers. For instance, following his criticisms of newspapers carrying pictures of French Nazi collaborators on 8 September 1944 a reader comments: 'How much longer must your readers be affronted by the quite patently pro-Fascist, neo-Jesuit posturing of George Orwell. He writes in the wrong periodical.'

Oppositional viewpoint (licensed contradiction): Orwell as socialist dissident

According to Holmes (op cit: 165), a newspaper may wish to be seen to encourage debate and hire columnists who are licensed to disagree with the dominant editorial line. 'Culturally this establishes a tone of diversity, and commercially it hedges its bets with the readership.' Orwell performed this role perfectly – promoting socialism and yet, in his *Tribune* columns and elsewhere, constantly raising questions about the movement's ideas and strategies.

For the historian E. P. Thompson, Orwell betrayed the left with his constant critiques. While discussing Orwell's *Inside the Whale* of 1940 (in which he examines the writings of Henry Miller in the context of the main literary tradition of the 1920s and 1930s), he says: 'He is sensitive – sometimes obsessively so – to the least insincerity upon his left, but the inhumanity of the right rarely provoked him to a paragraph of polemic' (cited in Hitchens 2002: 26). Scott Lucas (2000) also argues firmly that 'Orwell was not a socialist'. His socialism 'consisted primarily of bashing other socialists' (ibid: 49). 'Orwell banged away in a negative key, his positive melody reduced to vestiges of Englishness – the perfect cup of tea, the consummate pub, the common toads – and the mantra of "freedom".' In contrast, John Rodden (1998: 177–178) stresses:

> … his criticism was almost always directed at social*ists*, not social*ism*: he railed at socialists because he wanted socialist intellectuals to be worthy of socialism. A 'conscience of the left' does criticize from within; and though Orwell may sometimes have been guilty of being the excessively scrupulous 'wintry conscience of his generation', he flayed the left intelligentsia in order to fortify it, not to weaken or abandon it.

A typical Orwellian 'imaginative provocation' appears in his column on 21 January 1944 (Davison 1998a: 76–79). Responding to a correspondent who reproaches him for being 'negative', he says he, in fact, likes praising 'things'. After an opening section on the pros and cons of the BBC output, he suddenly shifts focus and writes in praise of the Woolworth rose. The following week a reader accuses Orwell of 'bourgeois nostalgia'. Michael Foot later wrote that Bevan was 'the only editor who, in those days before Orwell's reputation was sure, would have given him complete freedom to offend all readers and lash all hypocrisies, including socialist hypocrisies' (see Taylor 2003: 326).

Thus, on 10 December 1943 he moves from discussing a pamphlet *The Negro: His Future in America* to highlighting the problems of securing class solidarity across racial lines. And he is quick to criticise fellow socialists for failing to confront the issues (Davison 1998a: 23–24).

> An English working-man spends on cigarettes about the same sum as an Indian peasant has for his entire income. It is not easy for socialists to admit this, or at any rate to emphasise it. … In Asiatic eyes the European class struggle is a sham. The socialist movement has never gained a foothold in Asia or Africa, or even among the American Negroes: it is everywhere side-tracked by nationalism and race-hatred.

Significantly, Alok Rai (1988: 63) suggests that the anti-imperialism which lay at the core of Orwell's critique of contemporary socialists emerged from his years in Burma (1922–1927) as a member of the Imperial Indian Police.

> The history of Orwell's relations with that highly differentiated entity, the 'left' is determined and bedevilled by a variety of factors: but it is clear at any rate that his colonial experience gives Orwell and air of superiority which he is often not greatly at pains to conceal.

In a similar vein, on 11 February 1944, Orwell uses his column to criticise the left's weak response to anti-Semitism (Davison op cit: 91–92). Reporting on how his recent *Observer* review of books dealing with the persecution of Jews in Europe has provoked 'the usual wad of anti-Semitic letters', he suggests the left's response is too rationalistic.

> The official left-wing view of anti-Semitism is that it is something 'got up' by the ruling classes in order to divert attention away from the real evils of society. The Jews, in fact, are scapegoats. This is no doubt correct, but it is quite useless as an argument. One does not dispose of a belief by showing that it is irrational.

Instead, he calls for a detailed inquiry into the causes of anti-Semitism and the main charges made against the Jews, whether anti-Semitism is actually on the increase and to what extent it has been aggravated by the influx of refugees since 1938.

And it is difficult for him to avoid making a jibe at fellow writers.

> Without even getting up from this table to consult a book I can think of passages in Villon, Shakespeare, Smollett, Thackeray, H. G. Wells, Aldous Huxley, T. S. Eliot and many another which would be called anti-Semitic if they had been written since Hitler came to power.

In his column of 3 March 1944 (Davison op cit: 111–115), he takes up the criticisms of a Catholic correspondent to explore, with rhetorical panache, the relevance of flying saints to socialism, linking it to the left's inadequate response to the decline in the belief in personal immortality. He achieves the shift to metaphysical, ethical debate with ease mixing vernacular slang with erudite argument. One moment he is talking about the 'wishy-washy metaphorical sense' of Christian doctrine; at another time he criticises the Catholic intellectual for playing a 'sort of handy-pandy game, repeating the articles of the Creed in exactly the same terms as his forefathers, while defending himself from the charge of superstition by explaining that he is speaking in parables'.

Along with criticising socialists went a critique of left-wing newspapers. For instance, on 10 December 1943 while examining the 'horrors of the colour war', he criticises the left press for using insulting nicknames:

> It is an astonishing thing that few journalists, even in the left-wing press, bother to find out which names are and which are not resented by members of other races. The word 'native' which makes an Asiatic boil with rage, and which has been dropped even by British officials in India these ten years past, is flung about all over the place.

On 17 January 1947 (Davison 1998d: 18–19), the *Daily Herald*, 49 per cent of its shares owned by the Trades Union Congress, comes under attack from Orwell for describing Indians who broadcast on German radio as 'collaborators'. Highlighting his own contacts with Indians in London, he argues: 'They were citizens of an occupied country, hitting back at the occupying power in the way that seemed to them best.' And he deplores a serious inaccuracy in a caption to a photograph. 'And this happens not in the *Daily Graphic* [6] but in Britain's sole Labour newspaper.'

Unofficial extension of predominant ideology: Orwell and Marxism

According to Holmes (op cit: 166), comment pieces also allow a publication to run articles which express more extreme versions of its own ideology. Significantly Orwell's columns fulfil this role too. Orwell's politics, literary criticism and social observations are never Marxist in the strictest sense and he maintains a longstanding suspicion of leftist ideological abstractions. Terry Eagleton (2003: 8) is blunt when he says:

> Orwell's commitment to decency makes him a mainstream English moralist like Cobbett, Leavis and Tawney; where the Continentals had Marxism, we English had moralism. Outside Catalonia, Orwell's contact with Marx did not extend much further than his poodle, who was named after him.

Yet Orwell does occasionally extend beyond *Tribune*'s predominant, non-communist Labour left ideology in his columns to embrace Karl Marx's theories.

For instance, in his column of 24 December 1943 (Davison 1998a: 34–35), he highlights the refusal of 'pessimists' such as Pétain, Sorel, Berdyaev, or the columnist 'Beachcomber delivering side-kicks at Beveridge in the *Express*' to believe that human society can be 'fundamentally improved'. The real answer, he argues, is to dissociate socialism from Utopianism. And with his argument flowing concisely and elegantly, he concludes:

> ...any thinking socialist will concede to the Catholic that when economic justice has been righted, the fundamental problem of man's place in the universe will still remain. But what the socialist does claim is that the problem cannot be dealt with while the average human being's preoccupations are necessarily economic. It is all summed up in Marx's saying that after socialism has arrived, human history can begin.

Again, on 25 February 1944 (see Davison ibid: 103–105), discussing G. K. Chesterton's comment 'There are no new ideas' in his introduction to Charles Dickens's *Hard Times*, he writes:

> Where your treasure is there will be your heart. But before Marx developed it what force had that saying? Who had paid attention to it? Who had inferred from it – what it certainly implies – that laws, religions, and moral codes are all a superstructure built over existing property relations? It was Christ, according to the Gospel, who uttered the text but it was Marx who brought it to life.

And on 17 November 1944 (ibid: 463–469), in responding to a correspondent who has sent him a copy of a pamphlet by a reactionary Conservative MP, he is keen to defend Marx against misrepresentation. According to the pamphleteer, Marxism regarded individual acquisitiveness as the motive force of history. But Orwell stresses: 'Marx not only did not say this, he said almost the opposite of it.'

Orwell and *Tribune*'s survival

Holmes argues that newspapers often use star columnists strategically as circulation boosters (op cit: 163–164). As a newspaper of the left, *Tribune*'s primary concerns were political agitation and education and not profit: hence its appeal to Orwell. Yet the contribution of Orwell to the survival of *Tribune* was significant. Under the editorship of H. J. Hartshorn, from 1938–1940, *Tribune* adopted the pro-Soviet line of the Communist Party of Great Britain opposing the war as an imperialist adventure (Anderson op cit: 13–16).

But this had disastrous consequences for the newspaper. As circulation dipped Hartshorn was sacked and in February 1940 journalist Raymond Postgate became editor with a new policy to back the war and take the paper upmarket to compete against the *New Statesman*. And so the revival of the newspaper began. Then under Bevan, with Orwell controlling a third of *Tribune*'s pages and occupying its most prominent by-lined space, it at last 'found real success despite a doubling of price to sixpence' (ibid: 23). While it would be wrong to say Orwell single-handedly rescued *Tribune* from oblivion, his contribution to the journal at a time when its survival appeared under threat was crucial.

The range of subject matter

According to Stephen Glover (1999), founding editor of the *Independent*, the columnist's skill is 'in writing about matters of which one is ignorant' (290–291). Orwell, on the other hand, demonstrates the opposite gliding confidently over a vast range of subjects: shifting tone from the polemical, the subversively witty, the campaigning, the poetic, the belligerent, the socially compassionate, the intellectually discursive, the analytical, to the personally intimate and revealing. One moment he is generalising provocatively; the next he is virtually inventing cultural studies, examining in precise details the front page of a newspaper or the advertisements in a women's fashion magazine, *Vogue*.[7]

As Paul Anderson (2006: 27) comments:

> The columns reverberate with reflections on the relationship between politics and literature and with observations of public opinion and political culture – the unreported rise of popular anti-Americanism, the impact of official pro-Russia propaganda, the effects of rationing and shortage, the influence of the flying bombs on morale, and attitudes to the treatment of war criminals.

For George Woodcock (1984: 18), too,

> ... he rarely failed to find a subject – a popular song, an aspect of propaganda, the first toad of spring[8] – on which there was something fresh to say in prose that, for all its ease and apparent casualness, was penetrating and direct.

Here's an overview of his subjects: views on writers and writing (86); critiques of the mainstream press (17); war effort (12); language (10); personal reminiscence and experiences (10); media censorship/promotion of free speech (9); idiosyncratic likes and dislikes (9); BBC (8); post-war reconstruction (8); racism/anti-racism/anti-Semitism (7); love of nature (5); socialism (4); critiques of socialism (5); ruling classes (5); social issues (5); social observations (4); handling of collaborators (3); promotion of *Tribune* competition (3); capitalism/anti-capitalism/imperialism (3); critique of foreign media (2); critiques of pessimists (2); nationalism (2); women's issues (2); critiques of left-wing press (2); training of journalists (2); architecture (1); national anthem (1); nature of history (1); problems of geography (1); definition of fascism (1); globalisation (1); British intelligentsia (1); plight of the writer (1); jingoistic ballad (1); costs of books (1); the poor (1); superstition (1) and the law of libel (1).

Keith Waterhouse (1995), the eminent *Mirror* columnist, advises: 'Every columnist needs a good half-dozen hobbyhorses. But do not ride them to death.' Orwell's hobbyhorse was clearly literature and the range of his reading is very broad, particularly given that at the same time he was writing the column he was acting as literary editor of *Tribune*, contributing regular columns to the American-based *Partisan Review* (see Newsinger 1999) and reviewing for the *Observer* and *Manchester Evening News*. His reading is eclectic: pamphlets, novels, journals, philosophy, newspapers, a book of cartoons, biographies and autobiographies, literary criticism, history, memoirs, children's stories, a preface to play: from *Chronological Tablets, exhibiting every remarkable occurrence from the creation of the world down to the present time* (printed by J. D. Dewick of Aldersgate Street in 1801 which pronounced the creation of the world as happening in September 4004 BC) to *Old Moore's Almanac*.[9]

Orwell and the journalistic imagination

Yet Orwell's journalistic imagination is so rich he never ceases to surprise in his columns. For instance, on 8 November 1946 (Davison 1998c: 471–472), he examines an American women's magazine sent to him and goes on to examine its representation of beauty. But Orwell does not simply stay with what's presented; he highlights what's missing:

> A fairly discreet search through the magazine reveals two discreet allusions to grey hair but if there is anywhere a direct mention of fatness or middle age I have not found it. Birth and death are not mentioned either: nor is work

except that a few recipes for breakfast dishes are given. The male sex enters directly or indirectly into perhaps one advertisement in twenty and photographs of dogs and kittens appear here and there. On only two pictures out of about three hundred, is a child represented.

This is hardly the writing of a typical anti-feminist.

Orwell is often linked with pessimism and defeat and gloom. For instance, according to Raymond Williams, Orwell was, like George Gissing, a spokesman of despair born of social and political disillusion (cited in Hitchens 2002: 35; see also Rai 1988). D. S. Savage (1983: 143) comments: 'From childhood onwards an embittered fatalist, Orwell yet struggled fitfully against his crippling despondency in vain attempts to escape into some freer, happier ambiance.' But in these columns it's his playfulness, optimism and lightness of spirit that so impresses. He appears to be a man at the peak of his powers, playing with the genre, switching from subject matter and tone effortlessly; one moment he is deconstructing the front page of a morning newspaper, the next he is constructing a mini-play about a family determined to drink their tea in the face of a V bomb attack, recounting a racist conversation overheard in a Scottish hotel, campaigning for communal washing up service or admitting a mistake over the authorship of a poem.

Elsewhere Orwell uses his column to chew over ideas touched on in book reviews or later developed into longer essays and books. For instance, his obsession with language, which culminated in the essay, 'Politics and the English Language' (in Cyril Connolly's *Horizon* of April 1946), and in his depiction of newspeak, oldspeak and doublethink in *Nineteen Eighty-Four* (1949), is reflected in many of his 'As I Please' columns. In another column, he describes the radio as a kind of Big Brother telescreen: 'a sort of totalitarian world of its own, braying propaganda night and day to people who can listen to nothing else' (see Lynskey 2019: 119).

His optimistic, campaigning stance is particularly striking throughout. Humour is always around the corner (see Keeble 2015: 15–16). For instance, on 7 January 1944, he writes:

> Looking through the photographs in the New Years Honours List I am struck (as usual) by the quite exceptional ugliness and vulgarity of the faces displayed there. It seems to be almost the rule that the kind of person who earns the right to call himself Lord Percy de Falcontowers should look at best like an overfed publican and at worst a tax-collector with a duodenal ulcer (Davison 1998a: 55–58).

Conclusion: The redefinition of radical politics

After Eric Blair adopted the pen name George Orwell in 1932, writing became the means for creating this new personality. But while he constantly sought to represent his own personality as 'ordinary', his feelings, actions and writings, such as his 'As I Please' columns, were far from commonplace. As Filloy argues (op cit: 59):

They were the result of an exceptionally astute and sensitive observer of wide experience bringing a sophisticated intellect to bear on the situation. ... It took all of Orwell's literary craftmanship to bury his Eton education and intellectualism and to render his perceptions and thoughts ordinary.

Orwell was, in effect, through his contributions to *Tribune* from 1943 to 1947, defining a new kind of radical politics. It involved reducing the power of the press barons, facing up to racial intolerance, defending civil liberties. Yet it also incorporated an awareness of the power of language and propaganda, a celebration of the joys of nature and an acknowledgement of the cultural power of Christianity. Above all, in the face of the vast political, cultural, economic factors driving history, it recognised the extraordinary richness of the individual's experience – summed up in his idiosyncratic columns.

According to Andrew Marr (2004: 369) 'Writing a column is easy. ... But writing a *good* column is not easy. It is fantastically difficult and only a handful of people at any one time are able to manage it.' Orwell certainly managed it.

Acknowledgements

The author wishes to thank Paul Anderson, John Gilliver, Nol van der Loop and John Tulloch for their excellent critical comments on a draft of this chapter (though he remains entirely responsible for the final copy). The essay was originally published (with the same title) in *The Journalistic Imagination: Literary Journalists From Defoe to Capote and Carter* (a collection of essays jointly edited with Sharon Wheeler), Routledge: London, 2007 pp 100–115.

Notes

1 In 1945–1946, Orwell's essays were presented as discreet features and not as 'As I Please' columns (see Davison 1998b). Paul Anderson suggests that Jennie Lee 'who was notoriously touchy, had nabbed the title while Orwell was away and refused to give it back'. Between March and November 1946, Orwell took refuge on the remote Scottish island of Jura 'supposedly to write what became *Nineteen Eighty-Four* (though, in fact, he spent most of his time fishing and mucking about)'. Paul Anderson in an email to the author, 10 October 2006

2 Bernard Crick contributes an introduction to *Unwelcome Guerrilla* (1980), an anthology of Orwell's writing in the *New Statesman*, published by the magazine, but again only briefly covers Orwell's reviewing style. For instance, he describes Orwell as a 'working journalist': 'he tries to have something lively, amusing and provocative to say, even in unlikely contexts'

3 Indeed, it could be argued that Orwell's greatness as a writer is largely due to his never having had to endure (or enjoy) a university education

4 Holmes includes a fifth category, 'Elite reinforcement of preferred message' (ibid: 164–165) but this only applies to editorial columns

5 George Orwell: Journalist and proto-blogger, by Richard Lance Keeble. Available online at http://www.fifth-estate-online.co.uk/comment/georgeorwell.html, accessed on 26 December 2006

6 Owned by Lord Kelmsley, proprietor of *The Sunday Times* and a vast chain of provincial morning and evening titles

7 Orwell does not reveal to his readers how he has come to possess a copy of the journal: it was because it carried a short profile and photograph of him. It is such an unreal world, he writes, that he feels compelled to search for evidence that women are anything other than creatures endowed with eternal youth and beauty. See Shelden 1991: 456

8 Woodcock erred here. Orwell's essay 'Some thoughts on the common toad' was printed on 12 April 1946, but not as part of the 'As I Please' series. See Anderson (2006: 306–309)

9 In a review of *The Complete Works of George Orwell*, edited by Peter Davison (*Observer*, 23 August 1998), Paul Foot comments: 'He says somewhere he had 900 books, but he seems to have read seven or eight times that many'

References

Allan, Stuart (2004) *News Culture*, Maidenhead: Open University Press, second edition

Anderson, Paul (2006) *Orwell in Tribune*, London: Politico's

Bowker, Gordon (2003) *George Orwell*, London: Little, Brown

Crick, Bernard (1980) *George Orwell: A Life*, Harmondsworth: Penguin

Davison, Peter (ed.) (1998a) I Have Tried to Tell the Truth 1943–1944: *The Complete Works of George Orwell*, London: Secker & Warburg

Davison, Peter (ed.) (1998b) I Belong to the Left 1945: *The Complete Works of George Orwell*, London: Secker & Warburg

Davison, Peter (ed.) (1998c) Smothered under Journalism 1946: *The Complete Works of George Orwell*, London: Secker & Warburg

Davison, Peter (ed.) (1998d) It Is What I Think 1947–1948: *The Complete Works of George Orwell*, London: Secker & Warburg

Eagleton, Terry (2003) Reach-me-down romantic, *London Review of Books*, June 19 pp 6–9

Filloy, Richard (1998) Orwell's political persuasion, Holderness, Graham, Loughrey, Bryan and Yousaf, Nahem (eds) *George Orwell: Contemporary Critical Essays*, Houndmills, Basingstoke: Macmillan Press pp 47–63

Glover, Stephen (1999) What columnists are good for, Glover, Stephen (ed.) *Secrets of the Press: Journalists on Journalism*, London: Allen Lane/Penguin Press pp 289–298

Hitchens, Christopher (2002) *Orwell's Victory*, London: Allen Lane

Holmes, Tim (2006) Creating identities, building communities: Why comment? Keeble, Richard (ed.) *Print Journalism: A Critical Introduction*, London: Routledge pp 159–168

Ingle, Stephen (1993) *George Orwell: A Political Life*, Manchester: Manchester University Press

Keeble, Richard (2001) Orwell as war correspondent: A reassessment, *Journalism Studies*, Vol. 2, No. 3 pp 393–406

Keeble, Richard Lance (2015) 'There is always room for one more custard pie': Orwell's humour, Keeble, Richard Lance and Swick, David (eds) *Pleasures of the Prose: Journalism and Humour*, Bury St Edmunds: Abramis pp 10–25

Lynskey, Dorian (2019) *The Ministry of Truth: A Biography of George Orwell's 1984*, London: Picador

Lucas, Scott (2000) The socialist fallacy, *New Statesman*, 29 May pp 47–50

Lucas, Scott (2003) *Orwell*, London: Haus Publishing

Marr, Andrew (2004) *My Trade: A Short History of British Journalism*, London: Macmillan

Meyers, Jeffrey (2000) *Orwell: Wintry Conscience of a Generation*, New York and London: W.W. Norton and Company

Newsinger, John (1999) The American connection: George Orwell, 'Literary Trotskyism' and the New York intellectuals, *Labour History Review*, Vol. 64, No. 1 pp 23–43

Orwell, Sonia and Angus, Ian (eds) (1970) *The Collected Essays, Journalism and Letters*, Vol. 1: *An Age Like This 1920–1940*, Vol. 2: *My Country Right or Left 1943–1945*; Vol. 3: *As I Please*; Vol. 4: *In Front of Your Nose 1945–1950*, Harmondsworth, Middlesex: Penguin

Rai, Alok (1988) *Orwell and the Politics of Despair: A Critical Study of the Writings of George Orwell*, Cambridge: Cambridge University Press

Rodden, John (1998) Orwell and the London left intelligentsia, Holderness, Graham, Loughrey, Bryan and Yousaf, Nahem (eds) *George Orwell: Contemporary Critical Essays*, Houndmills, Basingstoke: Macmillan Press pp 161–181

Savage, D. S. (1983) The fatalism of George Orwell, Ford, Boris (ed.) *The New Pelican Guide to English Literature*, Vol. 8: *The Present*, Harmondsworth: Penguin pp 129–146

Shelden, Michael (1991) *Orwell: The Authorised Biography*, London: Heinemann

Silvester, Christopher (1997) *The Penguin Book of Columnists*, London: Penguin

Sparks, Colin (1992) Popular journalism: Theories and practice, Dahlgren, Peter and Sparks, Colin (eds) *Journalism and Popular Culture*, London: Sage pp 24–44

Spurling, Hilary (2002) *The Girl from the Fiction Department: A Portrait of Sonia Orwell*, London: Penguin

Waterhouse, Keith (1995) Talking of which…, *Guardian*, 6 March

Taylor, D. J. (2003) *Orwell: The Life*, London: Chatto & Windus

Woodcock, George (1984) *The Crystal Spirit: A Study of George Orwell*, London: Fourth Estate, second edition

Websites

www.orwellfoundation.com/ and www.orwellsociety.com/ contain substantial archives of Orwell-related material.

3

ORWELL AS WAR CORRESPONDENT

A reassessment

From 15 February to the end of May 1945, George Orwell served as a war correspondent on the continent for the *Observer* and *Manchester Evening News* (*MEN*). The assignment was interrupted briefly when Orwell became so ill he had to enter hospital in Cologne on 24 March. Then he suddenly had to quit the hospital to return to England following the death of his wife, Eileen, aged only 39, on 29 March. By 8 April he was back in Paris, moving on then to Nuremberg, Stuttgart and Austria. These were, indeed, traumatic times for Orwell, which makes his completion of the assignment all the more remarkable.

In all he despatched 14 articles (each roughly 1,000 words long) to the *Observer* (though the final two, of 27 May and 10 June, were composed on his return to London) and five to the *MEN*. In the many studies of Orwell's work, these articles are either ignored (as in, say, Woodcock 1967; Fyvel 1982; Lewis 1981; Hunter 1984; Wykes 1987; Meyers 1991) or dismissed as untypically drab. Bernard Crick, in his biography of Orwell (Crick 1980: 480), says the reports were 'not distinctly Orwell'. 'He earned his salt but he did not shine.' Similarly Stephen Ingle (1993: 67) comments: 'Indeed, it is true to say that, thoroughly competent though his reporting was, his few months in Europe produced no writing of any great note.' Jeffrey Meyers (2000: 232) follows the consensus and describes the war articles as 'curiously flat, lifeless and impersonal'. Significantly, the four-volume *Collected Essays, Journalism and Letters* (*CEJL*), edited by Sonia Orwell, his second wife, and Ian Angus and published by Penguin (first in 1968 then, in paperback, in 1970), fails to include any article from the 'war' series. Peter Davison (1996: 122–122) devotes two pages to the war coverage and Shelden (1991: 421–422) makes a brief reference to one of the articles but neither writer analyses the texts.

Does a close examination of the articles support these critical views? The assignment is particularly fascinating since, though Orwell had by 1945 made his name as a left-wing novelist, essayist, columnist, polemicist and BBC broadcaster, he had never reported for a mainstream Fleet Street newspaper to regular deadlines. To what extent was he able, then, within these constraints, to reproduce the distinctive features of his writing style and pursue some of his main political preoccupations? And, most intriguingly, why did Orwell take on the assignment when both he and his wife, having just adopted a baby, Richard Horatio, were so ill.

Background to the assignment

The Orwell/Astor friendship

The origins of the assignment lie in the extraordinary friendship that developed between Orwell and the millionaire *Observer* journalist and old-Etonian David Astor, whose father owned the paper and who was to be editor from 1948 to 1975. Both Crick (1980: 425–426) and Cockett (1991: 94) report that Astor had been determined to meet Orwell after reading his *Lion and the Unicorn* (Orwell 1941). And he finally secured an introduction to him through Cyril Connolly, an old-Etonian friend of Orwell, then editing the influential literary journal *Horizon* and filling in for the *Observer*'s literary editor (Lewis 2016: 113). They met in a café near the BBC off Portland Place, where Orwell was working on broadcasts to India. Cockett comments: 'They quickly became friends, recognising each other's directness and simplicity and David seeing him as an intellectual guide and companion.' Orwell went on to provide the first two anonymous articles in a new front page 'Forum' comment series that Astor launched in the *Observer* in 1942, and occasional book reviews.

Then, after the leaving the BBC in November 1943, Orwell planned to report for the *Observer* from Algiers and Sicily following the Allied landings, but the authorities turned him down on health grounds. Orwell then quickly acquired the post of literary editor at the leftist weekly *Tribune*, which he held until February 1945 when he resigned to take on the war reporting assignment. By the end of the month he was installed at the Hotel Scribe, in Paris – a popular place for journalists and authors in transit (Taylor 2003: 344).

The need for money?

Astor, who was serving in the Royal Marines at the time, recalled that Orwell told his news editor, Fred Tomlinson, he strongly desired to travel to the continent before the end of the war to see at first hand a totalitarian state.[1] Indeed, according to Astor, Orwell was working under a serious misapprehension. 'He wanted to pick up the atmosphere of a dictatorship. But by the time he arrived in Germany it had blown away. He was looking for something that wasn't there.' W. J. West (1992: 122–124), however, suggests that the main motive for Orwell taking on the assignment was to earn a 'large lump sum' to help pay for his family's move to the remote Scottish island of Jura. Davison (1996: 472) records that Orwell earned £500 (£100 a month) from the *Observer* for his assignment. But at £35 an article, he suggests, this was not particularly large.[2] The need for money also appeared to be behind Orwell's links with the *MEN*. John Beavan, London editor of the *Manchester Guardian*, told Fyvel that after adopting Richard, Orwell had declared his need for a regular income and so Beavan had arranged a weekly book-reviewing assignment for the *MEN*, the *Manchester Guardian*'s popular sister paper (Fyvel 1982: 128–129).

Was it an intelligence mission?

Two years earlier Orwell had been denied clearance to travel as a war correspondent to Africa; now he was given the all clear although his health was far worse. Crick (1980: 470) comments: 'He was dressed in the officer's uniform of a war correspondent, carried his typewriter and a single large suitcase. This time the requirement of an army medical seems to have been overlooked or waived.'

Could Orwell have been on an intelligence mission? He is known to have met in Paris two men working for British intelligence at the time. One of them was Malcolm Muggeridge, who introduced him to P. G. Wodehouse (Wolfe 1995: 215). Muggeridge had been assigned to keep watch on Wodehouse who was suspected of having Nazi sympathies following his broadcast in the summer of 1941 from Berlin for the American CBS network. Orwell had written an article in defence of Wodehouse in February just before leaving for France (though it was not published until July 1945 in the *Windmill* magazine) and may simply have wanted to express his admiration to the creator of Jeeves and Bertie Wooster. Orwell also met the philosopher (and old-Etonian) A. J. Ayer, in Paris for the Secret Intelligence Service (MI6) who were particularly concerned about the danger of a communist coup (Ayer 1978: 286–287; Rogers 1999: 192). Rogers records that the two found they shared a devotion to the works of Kipling and Dickens and immediately became friends.

Orwell also saw Ernest Hemingway whom he had previously met in Barcelona during the Spanish civil war in 1937, who was serving as a war correspondent and staying at the Paris Ritz. He had close links with members of the Office of Strategic Services (OSS – the forerunner of the CIA) and his son Jack was a member of the OSS (Whiting 1999: 104). Carlos Baker's (1972) account of the meeting in his biography of Hemingway (627–673), based on letter he wrote to the critic Harvey Briet on 16 April 1952, only adds to the mystery:

> Orwell looked nervous and worried. He said that he feared that the Communists were out to kill him and asked Hemingway for the loan of a pistol. Ernest lent him the .32 Colt that Paul Willerts had given him in June. Orwell departed like a pale ghost.

But Rodden and Rossi (2009), after reviewing the evidence in detail, express serious doubts the meeting ever happened.

Orwell's possible links with the security service (MI5) are explored in detail by West (1992: 162–165). West reports a 'retired CIA officer in Washington' asserting that Orwell worked for MI5 and suggests that he could have developed contacts with Maxwell Knight, head of MI5's Department B5(b) counter-subversion unit and a former pupil of Orwell's prep school, St Cyprian's, in Eastbourne. Yet neither Anthony Masters (1984) nor Henry Hemming (2017) make any reference to Orwell in their biographies of Knight. Speculation about Orwell's links with the secret services intensified in 1991 after Michael Shelden (1991: 467–469) reported in his biography of Orwell that he had drawn up a 'little list' of 38 people, briefly (and somewhat crudely) identifying their politics, religious affiliations, sexual preferences and possible communist sympathies (Saunders 2000: 298–301).[3] According to Paul Lashmar and James Oliver, Orwell supplied the list to his friend, the sister-in-law of the author Arthur Koestler, Celia Kirwan (née Paget) in 1949 when she was working as Robert Conquest's assistant for the secret state's propaganda unit, the Information Research Department (IRD), recently established by the Labour government (Lashmar and Oliver 1998: 97). Lucas (2003: 110) is unforgiving:

> Far from being a one-off indiscretion, Orwell's list is the culmination of his response to the left from the 1930s onwards. Not only could he not co-operate with many fellow writers and activists, not only did he denigrate them publicly and privately, but he maintained a watch on them as possible subversives.

James Smith (2013: 145) is similarly critical:

> There can be little doubt that Orwell's choice to provide information to the IRD was a gross miscalculation, whatever excuses are made about physical sickness clouding his judgement or the sincerity of his belief regarding the necessity of opposing totalitarian communism. … Little could be further from these principles than speculative lists of accusations passed to government contacts and given Orwell's wartime fears about the secret files being kept by police, it was hypocritical in the extreme for Orwell to then swell the secret files held by other agencies.

Yet Kirwan always denied that the list ever reached the Foreign Office.[4]

David Astor's intelligence ties went back as far as 1939, when he did 'secret service stuff', according to his cousin, Joyce Grenfell (Macintyre 2014: 2014). He served in the early part of the Second World War in naval intelligence alongside Ian Fleming (later author of the James Bond spy novels) (Cabell 2008: 12) and later with the covert Special Operation Executive (SOE).[5] Thereafter, he maintained close links with intelligence. Dorril (2000: 457) reports that in 1944 Astor was transferred to a unit liaising between SOE and the Resistance in France, helping the French underground in London spread the word to groups throughout Europe. While in Paris, perhaps inspired by Astor, Orwell attended the first conference of the Committee for European Federation, bringing together Resistance groups from around Europe. Astor was later adamant that Orwell had no intelligence links and Peter Davison commented: 'I do doubt if Orwell would be involved with intelligence – but that by no means says he wasn't.'[6]

Paradoxically, Orwell had been closely followed by the secret state since becoming a radical journalist in Paris in the late 1920s. Orwell's Special Branch file (MEPO 38/69), covering material from 1936 to 1942 and running to around 24 pages, and his MI5 file (KV 2/2699), spanning 1936 to 1951 and containing 38 pages, were released in 2005 and 2007 respectively (Keeble 2012). To what extent was Orwell aware of being followed? In Chapter 8 of *Down and Out in Paris and London* (Orwell 1933), he relates a curious story concerning his brush with a communist group in Paris 'and briefly alludes to his fear that the French police were watching him during 1929'. An SIS report dated 8 February 1929, noted that 'Blair apparently states that he is the Paris correspondent for the "Daily Herald", "Daily Express", "G. K.'s Weekly", but he makes no mention of the "Workers' Weekly"'(Smith 2013: 114).

According to Smith, the next sustained security investigation of Orwell occurred in 1936 when he travelled to the North of England for two months examining working class conditions for what was later published as *The Road to Wigan Pier*, in 1937. On 22 February 1936, a detective constable in Wigan reports his contacts with 'undesirable elements', noting that he was staying 'at an apartment house in a working class district in this Borough', that 'a member of the local Communist Party was instrumental in finding Blair accommodation' and that he 'attended a Communist meeting in this town addressed by Wal Hannington' (ibid: 115). A four-page report filed on 11 March 1936, according to Smith, provides a 'reasonably comprehensive overview of the major periods of Orwell's life', based on 'files of security and governmental agencies, as well as possibly from a human source with access to the discussions of the "intimate friends" of Orwell' (ibid: 116). After this burst of investigation in 1936, Orwell appears to have attracted only sporadic attention from the spooks before the Second World War. Just before the opening of hostilities, Orwell's house was raided by police and several books were confiscated on the basis that they came from a Parisian publisher noted for 'obscene' texts. Moreover, while he worked at the Eastern Division of the BBC from 1941–1943, he was closely watched by both Special Branch and MI5 (ibid).

The style: Was it 'un-Orwellian'?

The subjective voice

According to David Astor, Orwell 'didn't do well' on the assignment because, away from book reviewing and comment articles, he was unsure about straight reporting. Orwell's first article in the series for the *Observer*, dated 25 February 1945 and headlined: 'Paris puts a gay face on her anxieties,' is particularly revealing since it reflects the writer struggling to deal with his new challenge, unsure in his subjective stance and uncertain about his relationship to his audience. First he is the generalised 'every newcomer'. Then he shifts to the 'I' voice which he had developed to such effect in his 'As I Please' column, reporting that 'in several ways of wandering to and fro in all kinds of quarters I have not seen a barefooted person and not many who were conspicuously ragged'. Next he speaks as an impersonal 'one' ('When a pale tree on the sidewalk is lopped one sees elegantly dressed women waiting to collect bundles of twigs.'). He moves on to speak through the 'you' voice ('On the Metro they eye your foreign uniform.'); then shifts back to 'one' ('One is not even asked for cigarettes.') and finally returns to the 'I'.

Yet Orwell achieves some kind of resolution in the final section. Here his individual voice emerges confidently. The reader accompanies Orwell around the French capital, comparing, in meticulous detail, the sites with those he had known during his previous stay – in 1937 on his way back from the Spanish civil war.

> Almost as soon as I set foot in Paris I returned, as anyone would, to the quarters I had known best in the days before the war. Round Notre Dame it was almost the same as ever. The little bookstalls along the river were just the same, the print sellers were even selling the same prints; the innumerable anglers were still catching nothing, the minders of mattresses were as busy as ever on the quays.

Next he observes: 'In the big Montparnasse Café, instead of a cosmopolitan mob of artists there sat middle class French families thriftily sipping at glasses of fruit wine.' Through the build-up of details, the reader is drawn into Orwell's travels which concluded in 'delight'. He writes wittily:

> Then to my delight, I came upon a little bistro which I used to know and which had not changed hands. The proprietor welcomed me with open arms, refused to take more than half the cigarettes I offered him and bought a bottle of something that was very drinkable though it was not what its label declared it to be.

Then Orwell suddenly shifts focus and tone. From a feeling of 'delight' he becomes aware of the appalling suffering behind the Parisian façade and ends:

> Across the street the tiny hotel where I used once to live was boarded up and partly ruinous. It appeared empty. But as I came away from behind the broken window pane of what used to be my own room I saw two hungry-looking children peeping out at me just like wild animals.

This is hardly dull prose.

Afterwards Orwell only occasionally returns to the 'I' voice. On 15 April, for instance, in his *Observer* article on the food crisis in Germany, he begins by stressing his own viewpoint:

When only a few weeks ago I visited a camp of 14,000 Displaced Persons in the Rhineland I was struck by the sensible manner in which the American officers in charge were handling the job and the obvious delight of the Displaced Persons at getting out of German hands.

Later, the human miseries he witnessed in Stuttgart provoke him into a sustained use of the 'I': 'I had entered the town to the sound of rifle shots and stray shots were still reverberating when I left two days later though all the pockets of resistance had long since been cleared out.' As he observes German prisoners being rounded up, he writes:

'Just like us in 1940' was a comment I heard several times. Some of these people even seemed to get a grim satisfaction in contemplating the ruin wrought by the bombs. I could not feel anything of the kind myself.

Otherwise, Orwell adheres to the journalistic convention of eliminating the 'I' from his pieces, though they remain full of personal comments, analysis and description.

The 'newcomer' stance

More problematic is Orwell's repeated reference to being a 'newcomer'. In one respect, it follows from his position, outlined in his essay 'Why I write' of 1946 (Orwell and Angus 1970, Vol. 1: 23–30), in which he challenges the notion of objectivity by emphasising the importance for the writer to acknowledge bias and subjectivity: 'The more one is conscious of one's political bias, the more chance one has of acting politically without sacrificing one's aesthetic and intellectual integrity' (ibid: 28). Here he makes no pretence of being the omniscient observer. He sees with the fresh and somewhat innocent eye of the outsider.[7]

Yet, on the other hand, the references to 'newcomer' can be seen to represent a part of Orwell's troubled efforts to conform to dominant journalistic conventions. Significantly, he does not say 'I, the newcomer'. Rather, he becomes the generalised newcomer and so distances himself from his observations. In effect, he is laying claim to some kind of objectivity. In his first article for the *Observer*, of 25 February, he writes: '... the first remark of every newcomer is that Paris manages to put on a very good face upon its miseries'. And in his 28 February *MEN* piece, he reports: 'A newcomer notes how alike all the papers are.' In his 4 March *Observer* article, he writes: 'One of the first things that strikes a newcomer is that almost any Frenchman has a far tougher attitude towards Germany than almost any Englishman.' Then, in his first report from Austria, on 20 May, he comments: 'In some places a newcomer must get the impression that Austria is being occupied not by the Allies but by the Germans.' Generalising can be an important aspect of journalistic writing – as a strategy largely to overcome insecurity – but it tends to oversimplify and to be over-emphatic.

The eye-witness reporter

His first article from Paris is archetypal Orwell. Just as when he returned to England in 1927 from his five-year service with the Indian Imperial Police in Burma, Orwell sought out the poor in Paris and London, so now his first moves are to explore the poorest areas. He observes in precise detail, his writing laying claim to a quasi-objectivity:

> There are no taxis and the streets are only half-lit but the girls are so carefully made up as ever and the hat shops and jewellery stores have almost their ancient glitter. Out in the working class suburbs things are naturally worse. Glassless windows are common, many of the cafés are shut, the food shops have a miserable appearance.

He writes: '... even in the poorest quarters the surface aspect of things is less bad than I would have expected.' And as one who has lived with tramps (and recorded his experiences in the semi-fictional memoir *Down and Out in Paris and London*, 1933), Orwell writes, again over-emphatically: 'It is an interesting fact that there are almost no beggars – certainly far fewer than there were before the war.' This is not the observation of a typical Fleet Street correspondent whose voice presumes an apolitical (largely male and white) audience unconcerned about beggars.

Much of the dramatic tension of Orwell's writing in these articles comes from his highlighting striking contrasts, the unexpected, the tragic. In his descriptions of Cologne, for the *Observer* of 25 March, he compares past glories with the present ruins (scenes of a kind that were to revisited in the bombed-out, proletarian, London areas of *Nineteen Eighty-Four*):

> The whole central part of the city, once famous for its romanesque churches and its museums, is simply a chaos of jagged walls, overturned trams, shattered statues and enormous piles of rubble out of which iron girders thrust themselves like sticks of rhubarb.

From Nuremberg, on 22 April, he writes in precise detail of what he witnessed nearby:

> Just outside the village a smashed road block, a corpse or two, an abandoned truck and orchard cratered by mortar shells marked the spot where the Germans had tried to make a stand. The village itself had been shelled. Several houses were burning.

And in typical Orwell style, he notes the strength of people in coping with the horror of their surroundings:

To a surprising extent village life continues as normal, even in the middle of the fighting. The oxen still trudge slowly in front of the barrow while the guns echo from all the surrounding hillsides and most of the peasants seem more afraid of being attacked by wandering Displaced Persons – freed foreign workers – than of being hit by a stray shell.

From these striking observations, Orwell moves to raising deeper political and ethical issues:

As one drives through this peaceful countryside with its winding roads fringed by cherry trees, its terraced vineyards and its wayside shrines there is one question that raises itself over and over again. It is to what extent can these obviously simple and gentle peasants, who troop to church on Sunday mornings, in decent black be held responsible for the horrors of the Nazis?

The use of conversations rather than interviews

One of the most fascinating and problematic features of Orwell's war reporting centres on his use of sources. Most journalists base their reporting on eye-witness observations and interviews – very often on elite sources (McQuail 1987: 156–158). In these articles, Orwell rarely records interviews. Instead, he cites conversations, discussions and overheard comments. It could be argued that Orwell is simply following an editorial brief to sketch conditions of life on the continent, not to interview politicians. But he is too much of an individualist to follow any brief, whatever its bias. In journalism, as in life, Orwell follows his own instincts. Indeed, his concern is never with official spokespersons but always, instead, on the views of 'ordinary' people. Thus, in his 28 February *MEN* piece from Paris, he uses a generalised quotation drawn from conversations: 'Your objections [to the purge of collaborators] always get the same answer: "It's difficult for you in England. You can do things peacefully because there is no real division within the nation."'

Then, also on 4 March, Orwell records his views of French political thought drawn from 'random' and 'private' conversations. During his examination of the controversy over state funding of Catholic schools, he refers to 'private comment' stressing the importance of the issue. Charles de Gaulle's broadcast on the fighting in Indo-China, he reports on 17 March, caused 'much discussion'. Over a month later, on 29 April, Orwell mentions his conversations with Germans with whom he had been billeted in Stuttgart, and on 28 May he is concerned to report that following Hitler's death he did not overhear 'any spontaneous comments on it'. The only time Orwell uses a direct quotation is during his 21 April *Observer* article from Nuremberg when he records an American prisoner of war as saying of the Russians: 'The sole thing that has saved us from being in the same condition as those people there is our parcels from home,' but this could be a paraphrase drawn from a conversation rather than an interview.

One reason for Orwell's avoidance of interviews is possibly his lack of any reliable recording technique. In one respect, his emphasis on drawing information from conversations also fits with his more general political and journalistic ideas. The journalistic interview is a formalised event in which the reporter assumes a dominant, controlling position over the person being interviewed (Allan 1999: 131). The presence of a notebook emphasises its artificial and contrived elements. In contrast, the conversation, the chat over a meal, are more authentic with all the participants occupying equal status. Yet the use of overheard conversations is particularly problematic and can perhaps be best understood in the context of Orwell's troubled search for his journalistic stance. Intriguingly, the 'overhearing strategy' allows the reporter to disappear altogether. Instead of assuming the disguised presence of the investigative reporter/researcher (as during his experiences with tramps and hop pickers), Orwell operates here as an absence.

The newspaper as a source

Orwell's other most prominent sources are newspapers. Always fascinated by newspapers in their own right, he uses them as sources of information and as an indicator of political attitudes. In fact, mainstream newspapers provide him with the dominant, 'popular' perspectives; left-wing journals (generally ignored by Fleet Street) provided alternative, dissident views. Orwell is also acutely aware of the way in which mainstream newspapers, while pretending to promote open debate and diversity, in fact promote conformism through a narrow consensus. Interestingly, his first ever recorded piece of journalism, for Henri Barbusse's paper, *Monde*, on 6 October 1928, concerns censorship in England and his first British publication, for *G. K.'s Weekly*, of 29 December 1928 (Orwell and Angus 1970, Vol. 1: 34–37), focuses on the Parisian farthing newspaper *Ami du Peuple*.

Throughout his war reporting assignment, Orwell constantly records facts and attitudes drawn from newspapers and expresses concern over their propaganda role. His first report for the *MEN*, of 28 February, dissects the Parisian newspaper scene. And here Orwell seems secure in his voice as an essayist. Typically, he notes 'how alike' all the newspapers are. The basic cause is censorship both official and voluntary, the self-censorship 'resulting from the general desire for national unity and for the re-establishment of France as a Great Power' being 'partly responsible for the timidity of the daily Press in discussing major issues'. He proceeds to note how the dominant consensus effectively silences newspapers from covering important issues:

> No paper will express anything that could be described as opposition to General de Gaulle. No paper will utter any really searching criticism of present day French foreign policy. No paper will be overtly anti-British or anti-American and still less will any paper be anti-Russian. Necessarily this leads to a certain sameness throughout the Press and on the other hand to a hullabaloo about secondary matters which actually conceal larger political issues.

From his analysis of a mass of publications Orwell generalises – effectively identifying four main tendencies: newspapers loyal to de Gaulle, the communist papers, Catholic papers and left-wing socialist papers. And in his conclusion he is able to articulate concisely his own journalistic ideals: 'The occupation has produced in large numbers a new type of journalist – very young, idealistic and yet hardened by illegality and completely non-commercial in outlook – and these men are bound to make their influence felt in the post-war Press.' An illegal paper published by Trotskyites is mentioned in his astute article in the *Observer* of 4 March which examines the effects of the recent German occupation on French political thinking, and on 11 March he notes the 'acrimonious remarks in the press' over state funding of Catholic schools.

When reporting on de Gaulle's broadcast on the French forces fighting in Indo-China for the *Observer*, of 18 March, Orwell writes that the newspapers published it 'in full with big headlines though, in many cases, without commenting on it'. Returning to his concerns over the silencing role of the consensus within the mainstream media, he notes, with the assurance of his essayist voice:

> Except when something violent happens, the French overseas territories hardly find their way into the French press. It is only by dipping into quite obscure periodicals that one can learn, for instance, that in Algeria and Morocco, the Vichy apparatus is still largely functioning and the local Socialist and Communist Press is fighting for its life against heavily subsidised newspapers of reactionary tendency.

Orwell reinforces this point at the end when, in discussing the failure of the mainstream press to publish any Indo-China views on the matter, he remarks: 'Indeed, when such topics do get any discussion, it is usually not in the daily Press but in little struggling weeklies whose pages are all too often chequered by blank spaces bearing nothing but the dismal word, Censure.'

From Cologne on 24 March, Orwell reports the Allies producing a weekly paper in German and later shows how both British and Nazi propaganda has given a distorted view of the German character:

> It is queer to think that these are the people who once ruled Europe from the Channel to the Caspian Sea and might have conquered our own island if they had known how weak we were. Propaganda, and especially their own propaganda, has taught us to think of them as tall, blond and arrogant. What you actually see in Cologne is somebody smallish, dark-haired people obviously of the same racial stock as the Belgian across the border and in no way extraordinary.

This emphasis on the remarkable ordinariness of people is typical of Orwell. As Wykes (1987: 5) comments, he sought, essentially, to cut a slice through life to reveal 'its basic if surprising ordinariness'.

Similarly, in his report on the 'Uncertain fate of the Displaced Persons' for the *Observer* of 10 June, Orwell is concerned to correct erroneous reporting in the British mainstream press, focusing, in Orwellian fashion, on the misuse of language.

> To begin with the term 'slave labour' habitually used in the British press, is misleading. Some of these people – it might even be possible to determine the number with reasonable accuracy – were volunteers and the rest, though they could be described as slaves in the sense that they were departed against their wills, do not seem in most cases to have been badly treated.

And in his report on current French attitudes, for the *Observer* of 6 May, Orwell illustrates his point about the lack of political interest by again returning to the press as a social indicator: 'Among the noticeable things in Paris are the long cinema queues and the large proportion of the dwindled Press given over to sport.'

Comment and analysis

The range of subjects Orwell covered is impressively broad. He examines the political aims of the French Resistance (*MEN*, 7 March); French imperial policy (*Observer*, 18 March); the plight of Displaced Persons (*Observer*, 15 April); the dangers of separate Allied and Soviet occupation zones in Austria (*Observer*, 20 May), and Germany's post-war political, military and economic development (*Observer*, 27 May). One of the most sensitive issues he explores in depth is the purge of collaborators in liberated France. Thus, in his first article on this subject, in the *MEN* of 7 March, Orwell is concerned not to condemn but to understand the motivations of the French:

> From our side of the Channel, this attitude may appear somewhat distasteful but one has to remember not only the bitterness resulting from occupation but the fact that a real political division, amounting to almost latent civil war, has existed for decades past.

Moreover, at this point he is even prepared to side with people of the left who are calling for an intensification of the purge of collaborators, declaring that 'it is probably true that France's future cannot be safeguarded unless some thousands of people are killed or driven into exile or in some way rendered harmless'.

Orwell returns to the subject in his next article for the *Observer* (of 4 March) noting that the people demanding the purge 'are not reactionaries and not necessarily Communists: they may be thoughtful, sensitive people whose antecedents are liberal, Socialist or non-political'. Later, when describing German prisoners being rounded up in Stuttgart, he does not condemn but contextualises people's actions:

> It is above all when one watches German prisoners being rounded up that a gulf seems to open up between almost any Anglo-Saxon and almost any

Continental European. One may recognise fully the need to destroy the German army and to use no matter what means to do it but one has to have lived under German rule before one can get an actual pleasure out of these scenes of humiliation.

But though he had earlier sympathised with the demands for the purge of collaborators in France, he writes of being unable to harbour any feelings of revenge against the Germans (a view that he was later to explore in his 'Revenge is sour' essay in *Tribune*, 9 November 1945: Orwell and Angus 1970, Vol. 4: 19–22).

The creation of 'Saint Orwell'

Sonia Orwell (whom Orwell married on his death bed in October 1949) and Ian Angus, the *CEJL* editors, understandably selected the texts with the intention of showing Orwell in the best light. Peter Marks (1995) recalls Sonia as declaring that 'the mundane, material of inferior quality and the ephemeral' were cut. But views that did not conform to what Daphne Patai (1984) has described as the 'Orwell mystique' (namely his image as the archetypal 'decent, plain-speaking, truthful man') were also eliminated. This probably accounts for the exclusion of some of the war reports from the *Collected Works*. For example, in his 8 April *Observer* article,[8] Orwell writes that 'the many protests against indiscriminate bombing which have been uttered by pacifists and humanitarians have merely confused the issue'. He continues: 'Bombing is not especially inhumane. War itself is inhumane and the bombing plane, which is used to paralyse industry and transport rather than to kill human beings is a relatively civilised weapon.' Here, then, is an example of Orwell, with his talk of 'civilised weaponry' descending into the doublethink of *Nineteen Eighty-Four*. But in his 8 April piece, Orwell argues that it would be wrong to delay the reconstruction of Germany, because:

> After the last war, the impossibility of obtaining substantial money reparations – in short, of making the enemy pay for the war – was finally grasped but it was less generally realised that the impoverishment of any one country reacts unfavourably on the world as a whole. It would be no advantage to turn Germany into a kind of rural slum.

Later, in his 4 May *MEN* article, Orwell expresses concern over the mounting food crisis in Germany, asserting that discontent over food shortages 'is the likeliest starting point for German resistance'.

Conclusion: Orwell the troubled journalist

Orwell's ambivalence

Orwell's ambivalent attitude to journalism has certainly influenced critical responses. In his essay 'Why I write', he makes clear that ideally he would have written

'literature' ('enormous naturalistic novels') but his development of political awareness 'forced' him into becoming a 'sort of pamphleteer' (Orwell and Angus 1970,
Vol. 1: 26). He quotes approvingly a critic who says that by including a lot of
newspaper quotations in his defence of the Trotskyists in *Homage to Catalonia*
(Orwell 1938), the account of his experiences fighting in a Republican militia
during the Spanish civil war, he 'turned what might have been a good book into
journalism'. Since academia has also been slow to acknowledge journalism as a
rigorous, respectable literary genre, this also partly accounts for the lack of interest
in Orwell's war journalism.

Yet, in his search for authentic living, journalism provided him with many of the
answers. It provided the opportunity to extend his experience beyond the narrow
confines of his class; his experiences with tramps and Parisian dishwashers, his trips
to Wigan and the impoverished north of England and his involvement in the
Spanish civil war were all used for documentary purposes. Journalism seems to have
provided him with the space for self-exploration as well as the chance to write on
the political and cultural issues of his day. Life for Orwell was a process of self-
education and thus reviewing books was not only an intellectual challenge but also
an opportunity to learn more as a writer − and to share that new knowledge with
his audience (see Hunter 1984: 10–11).

The primary ethical/political decision

Most significantly, journalism also enabled Orwell to resolve some of the issues he
felt strongly about relating to communication and audience. Just as he realised
mainstream journalism was basically propaganda for wealthy newspaper proprietors,
so the novel also often presumed a middle class, privileged audience. Orwell's main
objective after his experiences in the Spanish civil war (1937) was to speak for and
to democratic socialists. He rarely wrote for the mainstream press; rather, he chose to
concentrate on writing for small scale, left-wing publications in both Britain and the
United States, thereby deliberately engaging in crucial political debate with the
people who mattered to him. Orwell never failed to criticise the left press (particularly over its reporting of the Spanish civil war and Soviet communism) and leftist
intellectuals even though he sympathised with them. They were an authentic audience compared to what Stuart Allan (1999: 92), drawing on the seminal work of
Benedict Anderson (2006 [1983]), calls the 'implied reader or imagined community
of readers' of the mainstream media. Most of Orwell's work was generally poorly
paid with such small-circulation, literary or left-wing publications such as *Aldelphi,
Windmill, Gangrel, New English Weekly, Time and Tide, Tribune, Left News, Controversy, Left Forum, Polemic, Contemporary Jewish Record*. In the United States, he
chose not to contribute to the prestigious *New York Times* but to the left-wing *Partisan Review* and *Politics* (Newsinger 1999).

Orwell was, then, straying from his normal practice in working for the *Observer*
and *MEN* (and also, earlier, for the *London Evening Standard*). And his consciousness
of moving into the field of mainstream propaganda might partly account for the

awkwardness in his war reporting. His friendship with Astor and his need for money have already been identified as major factors behind his decision. But there may have been yet another factor at work. As James Curran states (Curran and Seaton 1991: 80–83), wartime newsprint restrictions and the accompanying free-dom from commercial controls had the effect of radicalising the press in general. Moreover, adds Curran:

> Newsprint was rationed on a statutory basis from 1940 in order to husband a scarce resource and ensure its equitable distribution. An unintended effect of this control was to liberate the press from some of the economic pressures that had previously inhibited the development of radical journalism (ibid: 80).

Journalistic standards rose, not only in the *Observer* but throughout Fleet Street with the emergence of more public affairs reporting and a decline in entertain-ment-oriented stories. Within this climate, Orwell was prepared to compromise his journalistic principles.

The road to equality

Journalism also provided Orwell with the medium through which he could deal with fellow socialists on an equal footing. Equality for Orwell is always the ideal: authentic relationships, he argues, could not exist when individuals, races or classes presume superiority. Hence his contempt for the representatives of British imperialism he met in Burma (and satirised in his first novel, *Burmese Days*, 1934). Hence his loathing of middle-class intellectuals (as in *The Road to Wigan Pier*, 1937) whose rhetoric in support of the working classes masks their inner feelings of superiority and his delight at the egalitarian spirit he experiences in the tren-ches in Spain (celebrated in *Homage to Catalonia*). But though journalism provided him with a vehicle for speaking close to the experience of the tramps or Spanish volunteers, his role as a journalistic observer and eye-witness also helped him achieve the detachment he needed to realise his individual vision. But this was a sympathetic detachment rather than the superior, ironic stance of the conven-tional middle class writer.

Preoccupations with propaganda

It is not surprising, then, that journalists, journalism and concerns over propaganda in general (particularly following his service as a BBC producer/propagandist during the war, 1941–1943) feature prominently in Orwell's writing. Ravelston, the affluent, Marxist magazine editor, features prominently in *Keep the Aspidistra Flying* (1936); Squealer, of *Animal Farm* (1945) is the journalist, propagandist and spin doctor for Napoleon as he tightens his grip on power, ever-ready to rewrite history in the interests of the ruling clique. Indeed, all of Orwell's obsessive con-cerns with the power of propaganda and the corruption of language, explored in many of his essays (such as 'Politics and the English Language', 1946) culminate in the dystopian vision of the Ministry of Truth, newspeak and totalitarianism of *Nineteen Eighty-Four* (1949).

The struggle to find an appropriate voice

In fact, the best elements of the journalistic style – immediacy, clarity, a sense of urgency, an ability to highlight the most interesting, the paradoxical, the most tragic; a facility both to generalise effectively and to focus on the specific, relevant detail; an economy of language even within colourful, descriptive, eye-witness reportage; a political and moral stance; an openness to conflicting views – all these elements are apparent in Orwell's best writing and in the best of his war reporting. Yet this study has also emphasised Orwell's difficulties in finding an appropriate voice in his unaccustomed role as a mainstream reporter. As Phillip Knightley (2000), author of the seminal history of war reporting, comments:

> At that late stage of the war in Europe there were dozens of battle-hardened war correspondents covering the last days of the fight against Germany. They were confident about what they did. Orwell was feeling his way. He was troubled, diffident and insecure in his reporting. Should he allow his emotions free rein? Could he insert his political views? Could he refute the propaganda some of the others had been writing? He never found the answers.[9]

Yet Orwell's problems are important because they arise in the very nature of journalism: here he aims both to admit subjectivity and yet to acquire objectivity. The paradox seems to present him with an impasse which he attempts to bypass through assuming various quasi-objective personas: that of the newcomer, the eye-witness and the 'overhearer' of conversations. Or he emerges as the confident essayist, or secure in the first person. At other times he confronts the problems of the genre more directly by reporting on reporting, by analysing newspaper coverage and dealing with issues relating to propaganda and language.

Thus Orwell's voice emerges here as one of vitality and power – but also one that is uncertain and troubled. It is a voice that points ultimately to more general questions. What precisely is a journalist? What is the authentic voice of the genre? How far is the voice addressed to a declassed, implicit or idealised audience? These questions remain as pertinent today as they were in 1945 when Orwell completed his war reporting assignment.

Acknowledgements

This chapter is based on a paper with the same title published in *Journalism Studies*, Vol. 2, No. 3, 2001 pp 393–406. The author wishes to thank Professor Peter Davison, John Gilliver, Phillip Knightley and Nol van der Loop for their valuable comments (though he remains entirely responsible for the final copy). The research was conducted at Cambridge University Library during my sabbatical year from City, University of London (1999–2000), using the original *Observer* copies. They can all be accessed in *The Collected Works of George Orwell,* Vol. 17: *I Belong to the Left: 1945,* edited by Peter Davison, London: Secker & Warburg, 1998.

Notes

1 In a telephone conversation with the author, 21 December 1999
2 In a letter to the author, 16 December 1999
3 The original list contained 105 names. Intriguingly, the British government still refuses to open up the notebook to public view (Lucas 2003: 106). The known suspects include Labour MPs, the future Poet Laureate, Cecil Day-Lewis, authors J. B. Priestley and John Steinbeck, journalist Richard Crossman, actors Michael Redgrave, Charlie Chaplin and Paul Robeson, actor and director Orson Welles and the historians A. J. P. Taylor and Isaac Deutscher. See also Garton Ash (2003)
4 In a letter to the author from Peter Davison, 24 February 1999
5 Knightley (1986: 131) records that when in July 1939 Col. Count Gerhardt von Schwerin, of the German General Staff, arrived in the UK as a spokesman for the German opposition to Hitler, he was met by David Astor. Cabell (2008: 29; 49) records that Astor and Fleming worked alongside Dennis Wheatley (specialising in deception plans), later to become the occult/adventure novelist. Little mention is made to Astor's intelligence activities in the *Observer*'s substantial, three-page obituary, 'Observing David Astor', on 9 December 2001. Cabell also reports that Fleming may well have played a central role in luring Rudolf Hess to Scotland in May 1941 (ibid: 40–52). SOE was established by PM Winston Churchill and Hugh Dalton in July 1940 'to facilitate espionage and sabotage behind enemy lines' and serve as the nucleus of a resistance movement if Britain were invaded by the Axis Powers (ibid: 45). Other intellectuals/writers involved with intelligence during the war include A. P. Herbert, Arthur Koestler (who had previously served the Soviet Comintern while a journalist during the Spanish civil war), David Garnett, Elizabeth Bowen, Norman Lewis, Muriel Spark, Alec Waugh and his brother Evelyn Waugh, and Graham Greene (Bower 1995: 227)
6 In a letter to the author, 7 December 1999
7 Significantly, Orwell had given a lecture 'An Outsider Sees the Distressed Area' to the *Adelphi* Summer School, 4 August 1936 (see *Collected Works of George Orwell, Vol. 10*: 493)
8 Intriguingly, selected as the sole example of Orwell's *Observer* writings in a special edition of the newspaper's 'Life' magazine celebrating 100 years of reportage: 'Observing the 20th Century', 19 December 1999
9 In an email to the author, 12 November 2000

References

Allan, Stuart (1999) *News Culture*, Buckingham, UK/Philadelphia: Open University Press
Anderson, Benedict (2006 [1983]) *Imagined Communities: Reflections on the Origin and Spread of Nationalism*, London: Verso Books
Ayer, Alfred J. (1978) *Part of My Life*, Oxford/London: Oxford University Press
Baker, Carlos (1972) *Ernest Hemingway: A Life Story*, Harmondsworth: Penguin
Bower, Tom (1995) *The Perfect English Spy: Sir Dick White and the Secret War 1935–1990*, London: William Heinemann
Cabell, Craig (2008) *Ian Fleming's Secret War*, Barnsley, South Yorkshire: Pen and Sword Books
Cockett, Richard (1991) *David Astor and the Observer*, London: Deutsch

Crick, Bernard (1980) *George Orwell: A Life*, Harmondsworth: Penguin

Curran, James and Seaton, Jean (1991) *Power Without Responsibility: The Press and Broadcasting in Britain*, London: Routledge, fourth edition

Davison, Peter (1996) *George Orwell: A Literary Life*, Basingstoke: Macmillan

Dorril, Stephen (2000) *MI6: Fifty Years of Special Operations*, London: Fourth Estate

Fyvel, T. R. (1982) *George Orwell: A Personal Memoir*, London: Weidenfeld and Nicolson

Garton Ash, Timothy (2003) Orwell's list, *New York Review of Books*, 25 September. Available online at https://www.nybooks.com/articles/2003/09/25/orwells-list/

Hemming, Henry (2017) *Maxwell Knight, MI5's Greatest Spymaster*, London: Arrow Books

Hunter, Lynette (1984) *George Orwell: The Search for a Voice*, Milton Keynes: Open University Press

Ingle, Stephen (1993) *George Orwell: A Political Life*, Manchester: Manchester University Press

Keeble, Richard Lance (2012) Orwell, *Nineteen Eighty-Four* and the spooks, Keeble, Richard Lance (ed.) *Orwell Today*, Bury St Edmunds: Abramis pp 151–163

Knightley, Phillip (1986) *The Second Oldest Profession: The Spy as Bureaucrat, Patriot, Fantasist and Whore*, London: André Deutsch

Knightley, Phillip (2000) *The First Casualty: The War Correspondent as Hero and Myth-Maker from the Crimea to Kosovo*, London: Prion Books

Lashmar, Paul and Oliver, James (1998) *Britain's Secret Propaganda War 1948–1977*, Stroud: Sutton

Lewis, Jeremy (2016) *David Astor*, London: Jonathan Cape

Lewis, Peter (1981) *George Orwell: The Road to 1984*, London: Heinemann/Quixote Press

Lucas, Scott (2003) *Orwell*, London: Haus Publishing

Macintyre, Ben (2014) *A Spy Among Friends: Philby and the Great Betrayal*, London: Bloomsbury

Marks, Peter (1995) Where he wrote: Periodicals and the essays of George Orwell, *Twentieth Century Literature*, Winter

Masters, Anthony (1984) *The Man Who was M: The Life of Maxwell Knight*, Oxford: Blackwell

McQuail, Denis (1987) *Mass Communication*, London: Sage

Meyers, Jeffrey (2000) *Orwell: Wintry Conscience of a Generation*, New York and London: W. W. Norton

Meyers, Valerie (1991) *George Orwell*, Basingstoke: Macmillan

Newsinger, John (1999) The American connection: George Orwell, 'Literary Trotskyism' and the New York intellectuals, *Labour History Review*, Vol. 64, No. 1 pp 23–43

Orwell, George (1933) *Down and Out in Paris and London*, London: Gollancz

Orwell, George (1938) *Homage to Catalonia*, London: Secker & Warburg

Orwell, George (1941) *The Lion and the Unicorn*, London: Secker & Warburg

Orwell, George (1949) *Nineteen Eighty-Four*, London: Secker & Warburg

Orwell, Sonia and Angus, Ian (eds) (1970) *The Collected Essays, Journalism and Letters*: Vol. 1: *An Age Like This 1920–1940*, Vol. 2: *My Country Right or Left*; Vol. 3: *As I Please*; Vol. 4: *In Front of Your Nose 1945–1950*, Harmondsworth, Middlesex: Penguin

Patai, Daphne (1984) *The Orwell Mystique: A Study in Male Ideology*, Amherst: University of Massachusetts Press

Rodden, John and Rossi, John (2009) The mysterious (un)meeting of George Orwell and Ernest Hemingway, *Kenyon Review*, Fall, Vol. 31, No. 4. Available online at https://www.kenyonreview.org/journal/fall-2009/selections/john-rodden-and-john-rossi/, accessed on 14 May 2019

Rogers, Ben (1999) *A Life: A. J. Ayer*, London: Chatto & Windus

Saunders, Frances Stonor (2000) *Who Paid the Piper? The CIA and the Cultural Cold War*, London: Granta

Shelden, Michael (1991) *Orwell: The Authorised Biography*, London: Heinemann

Smith, James (2013) *British Writers and MI5 Surveillance 1930–1960*, Cambridge: Cambridge University Press

Taylor, D. J. (2003) *Orwell: The Life*, London: Chatto & Windus

West, W. J. (1992) *The Larger Evils: Nineteen Eighty-Four – The Truth Behind the Satire*, Edinburgh: Canongate Press

Whiting, Charles (1999) *Hemingway Goes to War*, Stroud: Sutton

Wolfe, Gregory (1995) *Malcolm Muggeridge: A Biography*, London: Hodder & Stoughton

Woodcock, George (1967) *The Crystal Spirit: A Study of George Orwell*, London: Fourth Estate

Wykes, David (1987) *A Preface to Orwell*, London/New York: Longman

PART II

Making journalism an art: Literary journalism today

4

LYNN (DEMON) BARBER

The pleasures and pitfalls of the celebrity profile

Introduction

Lynn Barber is one of the most celebrated interviewers in Britain today. In her short autobiography, *A Curious Career* (Barber 2014a), which includes a selection of her recent profiles and comments on the art of interviewing, she traces her rise in the profession: from Oxford University to the 'men's magazine' *Penthouse*, through motherhood to the *Sunday Express Magazine,* the *Independent on Sunday* (which she found 'an unhappy ship, riven by internal feuds and institutional sexism') and then on to *Vanity Fair,* the *Telegraph* and *Observer* before settling into her 'present home', *the Sunday Times* (ibid: 1–14).

While she has been dubbed 'Demon Barber' for the ruthlessness of her debunking of the pretensions of celebrity, the chapter will seek to establish to what extent that nickname is justified. Barber has written extensively on the skills and ethics of interviewing and so it will be interesting to consider those views alongside a critical analysis of her actual profiles. The chapter will, then, aim to identify the main elements of the Barber style, her leading themes – placing all of that in the context of a range of theories such as those relating to the 'celebritisation' of the media, the broader culture and political arena, conventional modes of celebrity interviewing, the 'confessional culture' and the manufacture of 'authenticity'. It will also explore her humorous style, the pleasure it provides – and her role as a sort of jester to the contemporary court of celebrity.

The 'demon' debate

In *The Sunday Times* magazine, of 20 April 2014, a seven-page profile (usefully plugging *A Curious Career* and their star profiler) began with this paragraph in large type:

The ST magazine's Lynn Barber is Britain's most fearless (and feared) interviewer. She has asked Salvador Dali, Marianne Faithfull and Rafa Nadal the questions nobody else dared – and it all started at *Penthouse* where she learnt to quiz people about sex (Barber 2014b).

But to what extent is this true? Barber, herself, questions this representation of her essential interviewing technique as 'fearlessly' confrontational. In the 'Introduction' to her 1998 collection of interviews, significantly titled *Demon Barber* (playing on the words of the 1973 book and later celebrated film, *Sweeney Todd and the Demon Barber of Fleet Street*), she comments:

> My reputation as the Demon Barber is a mystery to me – I think I bend over backwards to be fair. It's true I ask very blunt questions, but that's really just in order to save time. Recently I noticed that Lesley White of *The Sunday Times* asked Harriet Harman [then a New Labour cabinet minister] 'Would you call yourself an intellectual?' whereas I asked: 'Are you thick?' (Barber 1998: x).

Later, in the 'Introduction' to her biography, *My Curious Career* (2014a: 13), she reaffirms her position. She records how, in 1990, she joined the newly-launched *Independent on Sunday* where she wrote regular, long interviews (of around 5,000 words) 'which won a couple of press awards' and adds:

> But I also acquired the nickname 'Demon Barber' which was a pain for a long time. It gave the impression that I only wrote hatchet jobs, which was unfair – I probably only wrote one or two a year, but they tended to be the ones that stuck in people's memories (ibid).

The decision to title her collection of interviews *Demon Barber* essentially highlights her own ambivalence over the nickname (perhaps mirroring society's broader ambivalence towards the 'stars'). For whilst she acknowledges 'demon' hardly captures her essential style of interviewing, yet it usefully serves as a kind of personal 'branding' in the highly competitive marketplace of media celebrity, suggesting she is not simply reproducing glorified PR for the stars but challenging them to reveal intimate details and previously hidden aspects of their personality. In fact, as this chapter will argue, most of her profiles reflect her overall admiration of the stars and failure to confront any of the major myths underlying the celebrity culture. On her preference to interview celebrities, she writes:

> Everyone tells me off for interviewing stars – why don't I interview 'real' people. They always know a fishmonger in Kensal Rise who is a million times more interesting than Rupert Everett. Well, fine – but who would *read* it? … Of course, it's possible to do good, real-people interviews, but it's not my job, it's not my skill and quite frankly, I prefer stars (ibid, emphasis in the original).

Thus, in her most recent collection of interviews in *A Curious Career* (op cit), those profiled are Marianne Faithfull, Martin Clunes (of *Doc Martin* fame), tennis super-star Rafael Nadal, author and political commentator Christopher Hitchens, former Pogues lead singer Shane MacGowan, film director Michael Winner, Booker-award-winning author Hilary Mantel and artist Tracey Emin.[1] They are mostly men and all are white Westerners: thus, in her selection, it could be argued Barber reproduces uncritically dominant myths about identity. Barber explains her own selection this way:

> I take little joy in interviewing 'virgins' – newcomers to the media scene – and none at all in 'real people'. I love stars. I love the tension between the public image and the private person. … Why mostly men? Only because I seem to interview men better, perhaps because I am more cautious about them. I was an only child, educated at a girls' school, and hardly met any boys till I went to Oxford. When I did, I was so excited and intrigued I kept a notebook in which I jotted my observations of the species, much as I had kept bird-watching notes as a child... (Barber 1991: viii–ix).

But, as Barry King (2008: 121) comments on conventional news values and sour-cing routines: 'The process is rigged to reflect a pre-existent schema of fame.' Ordinary people only get access to the mainstream media as representatives of lar-gely negative stereotypes (e.g. trailer-park trash, single parents, substance abuse victims, misfits and an ever-ready queue of offenders of respectability). According to Nick Couldry (2003: 47–48), it is a media cliché that ordinary people are only interesting or entertaining because unfortunate or outlandish things have happened to them. King (op cit) continues:

> Stars and celebrities, by contrast, are treated as exceptional individuals, marked off by inherent talent and physical beauty. For such favoured beings the mundane accomplishments (or failures) of falling in and out of love, of achieving maturity and having a family are invested with great ritual weight such as eludes the average Joe or Jane who have the joy (or the pain) without the accolades of exceptional significance.

Yet Barry King (ibid: 122) also highlights a paradox: the more 'knowable' the celebrity becomes through revelation of mundane tastes and habits (the detailing tastes in food, fashion, art, literature and so on) the more mysterious his or her creativity seems by contrast.

The theatre of the confessional

One way in which stars – with all their extraordinary fame and wealth – attain 'ordinariness' is through the public act of confession. Indeed, it is important to see Barber's print-based profiles as part of a whole celebrity, confessional culture which crosses over all media platforms (broadcast, online) and into politics and the broader culture. As King argues (ibid: 115):

> The pressure to confess, or at least to engage in self-disclosure, is the centre-piece of talkshows. Reality television shows, irrespective of theme or setting, are also constructed around confessional 'crises' – those moments when stressed out contestants disclose their 'true' feelings.

Moreover, the need to confess, to be truthful and 'authentic', according to Peter Brooks (2000: 5) ought to be considered 'the true heritage of the Church, even if what is to be disclosed and the norms of truthfulness that are deployed have differed over time'. John Frow (1998), in a paper tantalisingly titled 'Is Elvis God?', concludes that he probably is given the way in which celebrity today has taken on the cultural functions previously associated with religion. Chris Rojek (2006) compares the 'spiritual' experiences of celebrity fans with those of congregations of believers. In *Fame Attack* he argues that 'religiosity permeates the production, exchange and consumption of celebrity culture' (Rojek 2012: 121). Thus, in Barber's interview with the broadcaster and novelist Melvyn Bragg, he reveals:

> There was a time between the age of thirteen and fifteen or sixteen when I had a sort of nervous breakdown, unacknowledged by myself or anyone else. It was a particular sort of private, locked-in desperation, and the next time I encountered it was about fifteen years later [when his wife committed suicide] and I never want to go through that pain again. It wasn't depression, it was *fear*: it was something that scared the living daylights out of me and I'm still nervous sometimes that it will come back (emphasis in the original) (Barber 1991: 82).

Indeed, Martin Conboy suggests that one of the social functions of the celebrity system is to provide a space in which difficult issues such as illness, depression and death (or, in the case of Bragg, nervous breakdown) can be opened up to public debate:

> It allows the mundane facts of illness and death a newsworthiness which gives readers an opportunity to read about issues which would not otherwise be covered in the paper unless they are associated with a well-known celebrity face and the language associated with the world of the stars (Conboy 2014: 179).

In a similar vein, David Marshall (2010) argues that celebrity culture is a crucial part of a process which is potentially 'widening the public sphere' (40).

Of Richard Adams, the author of *Watership Down*, Barber writes in her *Independent on Sunday* profile:

He seemed frail and small walking beside me; he turns seventy this week and admits to 'an almost Johnsonian fear of death'. He says the worst thing about being old is the physical infirmity, having a false hip and being short of breath (Barber 1991: 7).

During their meal in the dining room (along with his secretary, her husband and the gardener), Adams becomes extremely emotional when talking about the death of his friends in the war. '…and the tears splashed noisily into the meat pie'.

The confession, then, exposes the celebrity's vulnerability and ordinariness: in the profile there is the articulation and recognition of common traits between the psychology and culture of celebrities and fans. The portrait of Adams mixes put-down ('he seems a perfectly sweet old buffer') with admiration (his agent, Jacqueline Korn, says he is 'one of the kindest, most considerate and appreciative authors she has ever had to deal with'). But then, to remind us of his 'specialness', Barber slips in a mention of his wealth:

> The house is not particularly grand – it is only when he takes you to the library and starts showing you his first editions or casually mentions that, to enlarge the garden, they bought the next door cottage and knocked it down, that you remember just how colossal his worldwide royalties from *Watership Down* must be. In the eighteen years since publication, it has been translated into twenty languages and become a bestseller in countries where they don't even have rabbits or downs – many of the foreign dust-jackets show species of gerbil cavorting among sand dunes (ibid: 2).

Journalist Julie Burchill seems to enjoy taking the confessional to extremes in her interview: 'She enjoyed shocking me and I was happy to oblige,' writes Barber (1998: 33). So is the meeting performance, theatre, an authentic expression of emotion? It's hard to know. Perhaps a mix of all those… (see Rodden 2013). Burchill certainly cries a lot. And spends a lot of time confessing. Of her former lover, Charlotte Raven, she says:

> I know my own character, and I know that I'm a bitch and I know that when I'm in love, I'm treacherous, and no matter how much I love somebody, at some point I'm going to do something bad to them. When I did that thing to Charlotte, I couldn't stand it, because I was hurting a woman and so I think now – if I'm going to hurt people, I'd rather hurt men than women. So I'm going to keep away from women in future, completely (op cit: 34).

Did she actually leave Charlotte for her brother? 'Not really – in fact, it was worse than that – they were overlapping!' At which point Barber, witnessing the confessional with commendable scepticism, adds, in parenthesis (hence cleverly avoiding intruding with her own perspective on Burchill's 'performance'): 'She says this with such theatrical delight I am not sure I believe her' (ibid).

And artist Damien Hirst, for his part, confesses to having a drink problem. 'If I'm not working,' he says 'I'm too drunk' (ibid: 28). He continues: 'I think that if I didn't drink I probably would have had a nervous breakdown by now.'

Wealth – all part of a naturalised, depoliticised world

Enormous wealth usually accompanies celebrity. Barber's coverage of it in her profiles tends to highlight the glaring disparities in wealth in society – but without any critical dimension. For her, wealth is part of a naturalised, depoliticised world. So on zoo-keeper and gambler John Aspinall, she writes:

> ... he has done very well for himself as a twentieth-century Briton. Born the illegitimate son of an Indian Army officer in 1926, with no inherited money, he has made two great fortunes and kept one of them; he owns a town house in Knightsbridge, two magnificent country houses in Kent, an estate, De Goede Hoop in South Africa, and two zoos which are the envy of the zoo-keeping world. All this from the fruits of gambling (Barber 1991: 24).

This is 'conspicuous consumption', as Thorstein Veblen stressed in his *Theory of the Leisure Class* (Veblen 1899), with the wealthy simply 'displaying the fact that they are wealthy'. So for author, wit and seemingly ever-present broadcast personality Stephen Fry, she writes:

> He can afford to be insouciant about money because since 1984 he has enjoyed an extraordinary windfall: he was asked to re-write the book of the old Cockney musical *Me and My Girl* and has received 3 per cent of its hefty worldwide box office ever since. This is in addition to the £100,000 or more he earns from television and advertising work. Consequently, he owns large houses in Islington and Norfolk, and is able to indulge his taste for expensive technology ... (Barber 1991: 117).

In her interview with the reclusive, hyper-billionaire J. Paul Getty 11 (in conventional journalistic terms an impressive 'exclusive'), there is a certain witty, ironic stress on his eccentricities and nonchalant assertion of wealth. She notices a Gustave Moreau painting in the hall and comments: 'They are so rare I thought they were all in museums. The scent of money was by now overpowering' (ibid 134). But then she is kept waiting while he sits watching golf on the box:

> After ten minutes the strain of keeping silent proved too much for me. 'Is that a Moreau in your hall?' I blurted. 'Yes, and I've got another in my bedroom,' he replied. Then he switched his eyes back to the golf (ibid: 135).

For readers there is a definitive pleasure in being given a privileged peep into the lifestyle and home of the outrageously wealthy. So with Getty's lawyer, Vanni

Treves, our intrepid interviewer is taken on a tour of Getty's London flat over-looking Green Park.

> ... and we admired the many fine pre-Raphaelite paintings, the shelves of priceless books, the gorgeous Persian rugs, the vast collection of 78 rpm records of great opera singers, and a gleaming kitchen which, like the bedroom, looked unused.

But then Getty's nonchalance is almost matched by Barber's when she details uncritically, *en passant*, his vast wealth:

> When his father died in 1976, he inherited one quarter of the Getty trust, which was then worth at least $1.3bn. But at that stage the trust's money was all tied up in Getty Oil shares. The real bonanza came in 1984 when Paul's brother Gordon sold out Getty Oil to Texaco and released all the cash. Since then Getty's *income* has been around a million dollars every week (ibid: 136, emphasis in the original).

Barber (1998: 11) begins her profile of Alan Clark (MP famous for his witty, scurrilous *Diaries*) by recording how he had first asked if *he* was to be given a fee for the interview. And she slips in this detail: 'This from a man who owns a £12 million art collection, a moated castle, a 27,000-acre estate in Scotland, a set in Albany, a chalet in Gstaad and whose worth was recently estimated by *Business Age* at £33 million.'

Reinforcing 'family values'

Barber's reflections on the craft of interviewing are always interesting. Many of her profiles focus on the celebrity's childhood and families. She explains:

> After the clever question and the plug, I usually move swiftly on to asking about their childhood. Most people talk fairly easily about their childhood – they regard it as a 'safe' subject, safely distant, and they are often quite happy to describe what they were like as children, warts and all, whereas they'd be more wary of describing themselves today. But I believe that if you can understand someone's childhood you're three quarters of the way to understanding them now (Barber 1991: xv).

Indeed, Alberoni (1972) argues that one of the principal functions of the celebrity system is to satisfy the need of the general community for an avenue through which to discuss issues of morality – such as those relating to the family – that are insufficiently or ineffectively handled in the rational sphere of political power elites.

As in the coverage of celebrities' wealth, this focus tends to present individuals within a depoliticised world in which 'the family is the core of the private sphere, whose aim is not to link individuals to the public world but to avoid it as far as possible' (Tithecott 2006: 448). Yet, the promotion of 'family values' is, in essence, highly politicised being usually associated with anti-progressive ideologies. For instance, in analysing the right-wing shift of Tony Blair's New Labour government in the late 1990s, Lavalette and Mooney (1999) highlight the way in which blame for anti-social behaviour was directed at 'bad families'. And in the Green Paper on welfare reform of 1998, minister Frank Field stresses:

> The family is the bedrock of a decent, civilised and stable society. But it is under enormous strain. Divorce and separation have increased, lone parent-hood has risen and child poverty has worsened. The reasons for this may be varied, but the impact is clear: more instability, more crime, greater pressure on housing and social benefits (ibid).

Not surprisingly, all those interviewed by Barber dwell at some time on their families and childhoods. Often there is a rags-to-riches narrative underpinning the profile. For instance, on ballet dancer Rudolf Nureyev, she first stresses his wealth:

> … he has homes in Paris, Monte Carlo, New York, a farm in Virginia and an island off Ischia and is thinking of buying another in the Caribbean. He owns several great paintings, many valuable antiques, an important collection of textiles (Barber 1991: 227).

But then, moving on to his early memories, she writes:

> For him, the past is – literally – another country, and one he hates to recall. When he thinks of his childhood – the cold, the hunger, the nine people crammed into one room – it seems 'as strange to me as it would to you. Like it never happened; like I read it in a book' (ibid: 229–230).

The family/childhood obsession is particularly interesting when Barber on those rare occasions interviews politicians. (She says she 'can't cope with bores' who, for her, 'include most politicians'.) It appears, for instance, when she interviews Tony Benn, the former Labour minister and radical campaigning MP for Chesterfield (ibid: 36–46). Thus Barber records that his mother, Viscountess Stansgate, 'is still alive, aged ninety-three, and he visits her often' (ibid: 38). His father died in 1960 'but he still refers to him constantly' (ibid: 39). He is clearly 'a doting father' to three sons and one daughter: '"So much of their life was scarred by my work," he says, recounting how, as children, they often had to run the gauntlet of hostile journalists on their way to school' (ibid: 41).

Thereafter, the mood of the interview shifts. As Barber writes: 'At the first whiff of a critical question from me, his manner suddenly changes' (ibid). And from then on Barber is concerned to highlight aspects of his personality: how he is 'profoundly unclubbable', how Prime Minister Callaghan once called him 'devious', how his recently published fourth volume of diaries (*Conflicts of Interest 1977–80*) is 'curiously devoid of introspection' (ibid: 45) and how he is thought to be 'fanatical and humourless' (ibid). Significantly, no question tackles any aspect of his political ideas or activities. The interview was published on 30 September 1990 – just days after the Iraqi invasion of Kuwait and the highly controversial military response of the United States and its allies. As a constant critic of US imperial adventurism, Benn would have been keen to speak out on this subject (particularly since virtually all of Fleet Street at that time was representing war with Iraq – or rather 'Saddam Hussein' in the highly personalised propaganda – as inevitable). But Barber shows not a whiff of interest about this – nor any other political topic.

Indeed, much research focuses on the way in which the 'human interest' bias in the media serves the ideological function of 'depoliticising' the public sphere. The human interest bias has been built into the routines of Western journalists – certainly since the emergence of professionalism in the second half of the nineteenth century. John Taylor (1991: 2) sums up:

> The concept of news as human interest has remained stable because it has consistently sold newspapers. These stories are the most widely read in both tabloids and broadsheets. Their appeal carries across the differences between men and women, young and old, middle class and working class.

But as James Curran, Angus Douglas and Garry Whannel argue, human interest is not simply a neutral window on the world but embodies a particular way of seeing (Curran et al. 1980: 306). Accordingly, the possibility of basic structural inequalities is rejected while non-historical forces of 'luck, fate and chance' are represented as dominant within a given naturalised world. This view is reinforced by Colin Sparks (1992: 39) who argues: 'The popular conception of the personal becomes the explanatory framework within which the social order is presented as transparent.' The media fail to convey the 'social totality' comprising 'complex mediations of institutional structures, economic relations and so on'. Similarly Steve Chibnall (1977: 26) suggests that the personalisation of politics and the media is 'perhaps the most pervasive product of cultural fetishism of modern society'. Issues are defined and presented in terms of personalities 'catering for the public desire for identification fostered by the entertainment media' (ibid). Moreover, at times, the human interest story can serve overtly propaganda functions. For instance, after the Iraqi invasion of Kuwait in August 1990, the personality of Saddam Hussein became the prime focus of sensationalist press coverage.

> Hussein, in effect, became Iraq. In this way the human interest bias, which is deeply embedded in journalists' culture, served a crucial propaganda function, simplifying an enormously complex history, seriously distorting the

representation of the conflict and drawing attention away from other important social, political, geostrategic, religious and economic factors (Keeble 1998: 72).

In other words, Barber's profiling approach tends to reinforce the 'depoliticising' bias of the corporate media. Thus, her interview with former Conservative minister and MP Alan Clark focuses for quite a while on sex (Barber 1998: 10–20). He likes talking about it, apparently: 'He thinks it's what chaps do' (ibid: 13). And this provides her with the chance to pronounce (somewhat schoolmarmishly) on his personality:

> It is as if, as a teenager, he adopted some gruesome old buffer's view of what being 'a man of the world' entailed and has persisted in it ever since. He is like a little boy trying to pass for a grown-up but eternally getting it wrong (ibid).

There is next talk about the allegation that he exposed himself to a girl in her early teens (he denies it); about his alcoholic mother; about his claim to have seen his stepmother killing his father with poison mushroom (ibid: 17); about his claim in his *Diaries* to have made love to a woman on a train on 18 February 1984. So here is a former minister of employment and defence – but Barber never once asks about his political views.

Barber and the techniques of interviewing

Barber clearly enjoys commenting on the practicalities and ethics of interviewing in the Introductions to her two collections. There are many approaches to profiling: for instance, Kenneth Tynan, the celebrated *New Yorker/Observer* journalist, would 'immerse' himself into the lives of his subjects sometimes for many years: befriending them, visiting them in their homes, watching them give public lectures or play cricket, using extracts from letters written to him and so on (see Keeble 2014a). For Barber (1991: xii), it largely happens in a short face-to-face interview: 'Most FPs [her acronym for Famous People] are busy people; they rarely agree to be interviewed for much longer than an hour.'[2] And thus, implicit in all her profiles is the problematic assumption that in the somewhat artificial environment of a journalistic interview her subjects will 'reveal all'. She writes: 'Thus an interview is not a conversation; it is not even a dialogue; what I hope it will be is a monologue with only minimal questions by the way of prompt...' (ibid).

For Barber, the interview as a journalistic process itself is often a prominent subject in her profiles. 'A meeting with Richard Adams is not for the socially squeamish or easily embarrassed,' are her striking first words (ibid: 1). Early on in another profile, she writes (ibid: 17):

> Talking to Jeffery Archer, or at least trying to interview him, is quite an experience. He rattles out answers like a machine-gun, and when he makes a joke he tells you, 'That is a *joke!*' He tells you what you can say and what you

can quote him as saying, and what you can say in your own words but not in his (emphasis in the original).

On zoo-owner John Aspinall, she says (ibid: 29): 'He speaks; you listen ... he does not brook argument, or even interruption; the role of the interviewer – especially the female interviewer – is to listen in awe.' Rachel Whiteread, the artist, she says 'is not an easy interviewee: she tried to be co-operative, but she hates giving pieces of herself away' (Barber 1998: 141). Inevitably Barber encounters public relations officers along with the celebrities she interviews. As Chris Rojek (2001: 10) comments:

> No celebrity now acquires public recognition without the assistance of cultural intermediaries who operate to stage-manage celebrity presence in the eyes of the public. 'Cultural intermediaries' is the collective term for agents, publicists, marketing personnel, promoters, fitness trainers, ward-robe staff, cosmetics experts and personal assistants. Their task is to concoct the public presentation of celebrity personalities that will result in an enduring appeal for the audience of fans.

Barber is somewhat ambivalent about the public relations element of most of her interviews: on the one hand she is quite dismissive about it. As she points out:

> Another key point at the beginning of the interview is The Plug. Most FPs nowadays only give interviews when they have something to sell – a new film or a book or whatever – and they are fretful until they have done it. I therefore let them do their plug at length and generously at the beginning of the interview, to get it out of the way (Barber 1998: xiv).

Yet in her profiles, that PR, newsy dimension is often quite prominent. For instance, Peter Bogdanovich is in town for the showing of his *Texasville* at the London Film Festival (Barber 1991: 63); Margaret, Duchess of Argyll, has just had her book (*My Dinner Party Book*) published (ibid: 14); Roald Dahl's *Matilda* is published in paperback for the first time (ibid: 87); Prince Edward talks about his new book, *Knockout, the Grand Charity Tournament* (ibid: 103); Ben Elton talks about his new play, *Gasping*, opening at the Theatre Royal, Haymarket (ibid: 108); Sir Anthony Hopkins has his new film *August* to advertise (Barber 1998: 121) and so on.

Moreover, her contacts with the celebrity's PR team often feature in her profiles. For instance, her interview with Calvin Klein (ibid: 131–140) begins: 'There is some heavy PR flak before you get to see Calvin Klein.' She continues:

> Calvin Klein Inc occupies several floors of an office block on 'Fashion Avenue', the heat of the New York rag trade, and his PR, Noona, a six-foot sun-kissed Amazon who speaks fluent PRspeak in seven languages, insisted on showing me every floor (ibid: 132).

Sometimes celebrities arrive for the interview 'exhausted and emotionally fragile'. 'But still the PR sits there stony-faced, forcing these poor knackered ponies to jump through their publicity hoops' (Barber 2014b: 25). Yet she is keen to emphasise her independence from PR pressures: 'I remain adamantly opposed to "copy approval" – the practice of letting interviewees see the article before publication – but it is now routinely demanded by nearly all A-list stars along with "photo approval"' (ibid: 75).

Humour – and the pleasure in the text

Humour is a crucial ingredient of Barber's profiling technique. As she comments: 'My articles are written with the primary intention of being entertaining and, where possible, funny' (Barber 1991: xix). For instance, she meets the three Beverley Sisters in a 'dark bar at London's Hippodrome' (ibid: 47). Her writing is alive with witty narrative drive – ending with an unexpected simile. They sashay down a flight of stairs towards her going 'Mmmmm ho-ow-ow much is that doggie in the window.' She continues: 'Then the big one, Joy, stopped singing and cried: "Don't mind us, Lynn." And they all ran down the stairs and kissed me. Peck peck. Peck peck. Peck peck. It was like being nibbled to death by gerbils.' The humour is often accompanied by a gentle mockery and put-down. Of MP Alan Clark, she delights in stressing his vanity:

> He kept standing sideways-on in front of the window so that I could admire his slim waist and boyish figure, though I could never take my eyes off his skull, which is such an extraordinary shape, going back for miles, like a slice of Cheddar; it makes you believe in phrenology: behold a totally weird man with a totally weird-shaped head (ibid: 11).

Of former *Times* editor Lord Rees-Mogg, she writes:

> The fine grammatical sentences roll on and on, not as a torrent but as a smooth-flowing mature river. The effect is weirdly impersonal. At one point, talking about television censorship, he gives me a lecture about 'what mothers want' without apparently ever asking himself whether I might be a mother. It is as if he is talking about the Ancient Egyptians or the Kalahari Bushmen. I keep wondering, why am I here? (ibid: 51).

Of broadcaster Melvyn Bragg, she writes (1991: 77):

> But this real-life, twitchy, neurotic Melvyn is in my view infinitely more interesting than the smug bit of thinking woman's crumpet that fronts *The South Bank Show*. Is he vain? As soon as I mention his looks, he becomes defensive...'[3]

And when she interviewed Robert Redford about *The Horse Whisperer*: 'He couldn't bring himself to praise *any* of his fellow actors, not even the horse' (Barber 2014b: 25, emphasis in the original).

Her profile of actor Jeremy Irons (1992: 196), who arrives annoyingly and unapologetically late for the interview, begins: 'This is not an objective article. I don't want to give a cool appraisal of Jeremy Irons, or even to be snide. I just want to boil him in oil.' As Sharon Wheeler (2009: 58) comments: 'The intro leaves us in absolutely no doubt as to Barber's feelings about Irons. But the slightly overstated "I want to boil him in oil" retains a sense of humour beneath the annoyance and exasperation.'

Conclusions

How to explain and theorise Barber's mix of affection for FPs, humour, putdown and gentle mockery? Is it useful to understand her as a modern-day court jester? During the Middle Ages, one of the most important roles at courts throughout Europe (and in India, Persia and China) was occupied by the jester. Often known as 'licensed fools' their crucial function was to mock their employer. Queen Elizabeth the First (who ruled between 1558 and 1603) was said to have even rebuked one of her fools for not being severe enough in his mockery of her. Fools, clowns and jesters all appear in Shakespeare's plays: Feste, the jester in *Twelfth Night*, is even described as 'wise enough to play the fool' (Otto 2001).

All this tells us a lot about the importance of humour and mockery in societies. Elites know they will always be mocked and attacked – but clever are those elites who control the mockery. The court jester system did just that. Today, intriguingly, a modern version of the court jester system operates, in both the political and cultural spheres, and while there is no formal licensing, a subtler – and hence more powerful – unwritten licensing system helps define the limits of acceptable debate (see Keeble 2014b).[4] Continuing with the metaphor, Barber, as a prominent Fleet Street journalist, is clearly a member of the 'court' of the cultural elite and, as a result, her witty put-downs can be seen not only as providing pleasure and entertainment – but necessary features of the contemporary celebrity circus.

Acknowledgements

This essay is based on a chapter with the same title in Joseph, Sue and Keeble, Richard Lance (eds) *The Profiling Handbook*, Bury St Edmunds: Abramis, 2015 pp 67–93.

Notes

1 See Martin Clunes (*Sunday Times*, 1 April 2012) pp 58–68; Rafael Nadal (*Sunday Times*, 5 June 2011) pp 81–93; Christopher Hitchens (*Sunday Times*, 4 March 2011) pp 96–109;

Shane MacGowan (*Observer*, 11 March 2001) pp 116–128; Michael Winner (*Observer*, 4 November 2007) pp 135–143; Hilary Mantel (*Sunday Times*, 13 May 2012); Tracey Emin (*Observer*, 22 April 2001) pp 169–180. In *Mostly Men* (1991), perhaps not surprisingly, out of the 37 people interviewed just eight are women (Margaret, Duchess of Argyll pp 10–15; the three Beverley Sisters pp 47–53; Zsa Zsa Gabor pp 124–130; Muriel Spark pp 257–267; Baroness Thyssen (along with the Baron) pp 293–299. In *Demon Barber* (1998), out of the 38 interviewed just four are women (Julie Burchill pp 30–38; Rachel Whiteread pp 141–149; Felicity Kendal pp 221–229; Harriet Harman pp 265–273)

2 But then in *A Curious Career*, she writes: 'I wouldn't agree to interview anyone unless I had at least ninety minutes with them' (Barber 2014a: 202)

3 In her *Sunday Times* article (2014b: 27) Barber says her Bragg interview 'was not flattering'. She continues: 'Bragg retaliated by putting a hideously ugly woman interviewer into his next trashy novel.' So in this way celebrity gossip circulates...

4 Significantly, George Orwell (1970 [1943]: 371) describes the American novelist and journalist Mark Twain (1835–1910) as the 'licensed jester' after he became 'that dubious thing: a "public figure", flattered by passport officials and entertained by royalty'

References

Alberoni, Fransesco (1972) The powerless elite: Theory and sociological research on the phenomenon of the stars, McQuail, Denis (ed.) *Sociology of Mass Communications*, London: Penguin pp 75–98

Barber, Lynn (1991) *Mostly Men*, London: Viking

Barber, Lynn (1998) *Demon Barber*, London: Viking

Barber, Lynn (2014a) *A Curious Career*, London: Bloomsbury

Barber, Lynn (2014b) She has ways of making you talk, *Sunday Times Magazine*, 20 April pp 18–27

Brooks, Peter (2000) *Troubling Confessions: Speaking Guilt in Law and Literature*, Chicago: University of Chicago Press

Chibnall, Steve (1977) *Law and Order News*, London: Tavistock Publications

Conboy, Martin (2014) Celebrity journalism – an oxymoron: Forms and functions of a genre, *Journalism*, Vol. 15, No. 2 pp 171–185

Couldry, Nick (2003) *Media Rituals: A Critical Approach*, London: Routledge

Curran, James, Douglas, Angus and Whannel, Garry (1980) The political economy of the human interest story, Smith, Anthony (ed.) *Newspapers and Democracy: International Essays on a Changing Medium*, Cambridge, MA: MIT Press pp 288–316

Frow, John (1998) Is Elvis God?, *International Journal of Cultural Studies*, Vol. 1, No. 2 pp 197–210

Keeble, Richard (1998) The myth of Saddam Hussein, Kieran, Matthew (ed.) *Media Ethics*, London: Routledge pp 66–81

Keeble, Richard Lance (2014a) Intimate portraits: The profiles of Kenneth Tynan, *Journalism*, Vol. 15, No. 5 pp 547–559

Keeble, Richard Lance (2014b) Rajiv Chandrasekaran's *Imperial Life in the Emerald City*: Beyond the court jester? Keeble, Richard Lance and Tulloch, John (eds) *Global Literary Journalism: Exploring the Journalistic Imagination*, Vol. 2, New York: Peter Lang pp 139–151

King, Barry (2008) Stardom, celebrity and the para-confession, *Social Semiotics*, Vol. 18, No. 2 pp 115–132

Lavalette, Michael and Mooney, Gerry (1999) New Labour new moralism: The welfare politics and ideology of New Labour under Blair, *International Socialism Journal*, No. 85. Available online at http://pubs.socialistreviewindex.org.uk/isj85/lavalette.htm, accessed on 13 February 2015

Marshall, David P. (2010) The promotion and presentation of the self: Celebrity as marker of presentational media, *Celebrity Studies*, Vol. 1, No. 1 pp 35–48

Orwell, George (1970 [1943]) Mark Twain: The licensed jester, Orwell, Sonia and Angus, Ian (eds) *The Collected Essays, Journalism and Letters*, Vol. 2: *My Country Right or Left*, Harmondsworth, Middlesex: Penguin pp 369–374

Otto, Beatrice (2001) *Fools are Everywhere*, Chicago: University of Chicago Press

Rodden, John (2013) The literary interview as public performance, *Culture and Society*, Vol. 50 pp 402–406

Rojek, Chris (2001) *Celebrity*, London: Reaktion Books

Rojek, Chris (2006) Celebrity and religion, Marshall, David P. (ed.) *The Celebrity Culture Reader*, New York: Routledge pp 389–417

Rojek, Chris (2012) *Fame Attack: The Inflation of Celebrity and its Consequences*, London: Bloomsbury

Sparks, Colin (1992) Popular journalism: Theories and practice, Dahlgren, Peter and Sparks, Colin (eds) *Journalism and Popular Culture*, London: Sage pp 24–44

Taylor, John (1991) *War Photography: Realism in the British Press*, London: Routledge

Tithecott, Richard (2006) Investigating the serial killer, Marshall, David P. (ed.) *The Celebrity Culture Reader*, New York: Routledge pp 443–453

Veblen, Thorstein (1899) *The Theory of the Leisure Class: An Economic Study of Institutions*, New York: The Modern Library

Wheeler, Sharon (2009) *Feature Writing for Journalists*, London: Routledge

5

LARA PAWSON'S GENRE-BENDING MEMOIR

Gravitas and the celebration of unique cultural spaces

Like no other journalist's memoir

Lara Pawson's (2016) *This is The Place To Be* is like no other journalist's memoir. Pawson's background is conventional enough: she worked for the BBC World Service from 1998 to 2007, reporting from Mali, the Ivory Coast, and São Tomé and Príncipe. From 1998 to 2000, she was the BBC correspondent in Angola, covering the civil war. Her investigation into the little-known events of 27 May 1977, when a small demonstration against the MPLA, the ruling party of Angola, led to violent repression and the massacre of thousands, is covered in *In the Name of the People: Angola's Forgotten Massacre* (2014), which was longlisted for the Orwell Prize 2015.

Inspired by Édouard Levé's (2012 [2005]) *Autoportrait*, which was notable for saying things about a person that are not normally said, Pawson's memoir was written almost entirely in one session, its short paragraphs and scattered sentences deliberately avoiding conventional chronology. In terms of content and form, the memoir is entirely original. It mercilessly debunks the myth of the heroic journo. Her highly critical comments on news reporting are interspersed with the everyday minutiae, tragedy and joys of her own life, together with reflections on gender, family, identity, nostalgia, childhood and time. This chapter firstly locates *This is The Place To Be* in the context of previous research on women's memoirs and, in particular, autobiographies by women journalists. And while Pawson's memoir is examined in detail, the chapter does not consider it in isolation. The chapter then builds on Pierre Bourdieu's (1973, 1984) notion of cultural capital to propose the notion of the cultural space which incorporates the various cultural forms *inspired* by the text. Thus it explores some of the interviews and reviews linked to its publication, considering these paratextual elements essential to the cultural space occupied by the text.

Memoirs by women: From the margins to the mainstream

According to Smith and Watson (1998: 4), women's autobiographies were rarely taken seriously as a focus of study before the 1970s, considered not appropriately 'complex' for academic dissertations, criticism or the literary canon. Since then, the place of women's memoir in the academy has changed dramatically. 'If feminism has revolutionised literary and social theory, the texts and theories of women's autobiography have been pivotal for revising our concepts of women's life issues – growing up female, coming to voice, affiliation, sexuality and textuality, the life cycle' (ibid).

Mary McCarthy's *Memories of a Catholic Girlhood* (1957), the translation of Simone de Beauvoir's four-volume autobiography (in 1958, 1960, 1963 and 1964), Anaïs Nin's *Diaries* (1966, 1974 and 1976) combining self-exposure with literary experimentation, and Angela Davis's *Autobiography* (1974) (which not only exposed the depth of racism in the US but also critiqued misogyny amongst Black Power writers) are pivotal publishing moments in the development of the women's memoir. Increasingly, attention is directed at the extensive women's literary tradition that existed for centuries in the so-called 'marginal' genres: journals, diaries and the many forms of private, autobiographical writing.

In *The Female Imagination*, Patricia Meyer Spacks (1975) uses autobiographies to explore women's 'characteristic powers of self-perception'. And with the publication of Mason and Green's (1979) overview of women's autobiographies and James Olney's (1980) collection of essays on memoir a new stress is placed on the understanding of women's sense of identity as a relational rather than individuating process. As Smith and Watson comment (op cit: 10):

> To what extent is women's autobiography characterized by the frequency of nonlinear or 'oral' narrative strategies unlike the master narratives of auto-biography that seem to pose stable, coherent self-narratives? To what extent is it characterized by frequent digression, giving readers the impression of a fragmentary, shifting narrative voice or indeed a plurality of voices in dialogue? Is the subject in women's autobiography less firmly bounded, more 'fluid'?

Interestingly, as we shall see, Pawson takes this nonlinear and 'oral' narrative strategy to extremes.

Since the 1980s, the study and teaching of women's life writing has 'exploded' in both the UK, US and internationally with interest directed at both the history of the genre (from the early 1700s onwards) and 21st century texts (Jelinek 1980; Nussbaum 1989; Corbin 1990; Scott 1991; Stanley 1992; Peterson 1996; Smith and Watson 2001; Cook and Cullen 2012). Conferences, professorships and the production of academic journals on the subject (such as Taylor & Francis's *Life Writing*) reinforce its position in the academy. Pedagogical studies have also incorporated strategies for handling the supervision of students writing personal trauma narratives (e.g. Joseph 2013).

Memoir by women journos

Intriguingly, Howard Good (1993), in one of the first studies of journalists' memoir, includes close analyses of the work of three women alongside those of five men. Under the chapter title 'Stunt girls and sob sisters', Good examines the memoirs of Elizabeth Jordan (editor of *Harper's Bazaar*, 1900–1913), Joan Lowell (a film actor and newspaper reporter in Boston, Massachusetts, in the 1930s) and Agness Underwood (journalist on the *Los Angeles Record* from 1928–1935, on the *Herald Express* from 1935–1962 and the *Herald Examiner* from 1962–1968). Good (ibid: 82) cites the work of Susan Stanford Friedman (1988) who, drawing on the concepts of female identity suggested by Sheila Rowbotham (1973) and Nancy Chodorow (1978), argues that the 'self, self-criticism and self-consciousness are profoundly different for women' than for men:

> The male autobiographer is psychologically and culturally grooved to present himself as separate from others, unique, an isolated being playing out on a dramatic scale his individual destiny. By contrast, the female autobiographer, Friedman wrote, 'does not feel herself to exist outside of others, and still less against others, but very much with others in an independent existence that asserts its rhythms everywhere in the community'.

Calvin L. Hall (2009) includes Jill Nelson and Patricia Raybon (along with Jake Lamarr and Nathan McCall) in his study of the autobiographies of African American print journalists. He argues (ibid: x) that they turn their memoirs into 'quasi political documents that challenge the status quo in journalism by illuminating through lived experience newsroom practices that have been detrimental to the kind of diversity that allows journalism to fully inform citizens'. Linda Steiner (1997) also incorporates a long list of US women journalist memoir-writers in her annotated bibliography. And an online bibliography on 'women as journalists, editors and authors' has 445 entries.[1]

But in a list of the top 30 journalism books in *Press Gazette*, the UK industry's magazine, Camilla Turner (2012) could manage to name only four by women.[2] The substantial *Encyclopedia of American Journalism*, edited by Stephen L. Vaughn (2009) has sections on 'Women journalists' (pp 590–594) and 'Women journalists, African American' (pp 594–600) yet memoir gets no mention at all.

Origins and inspiration for *This is The Place To Be*

In a 3,636-word interview (via email) with Rebekah Weikal for *3ammagazine.com*,[3] Pawson explains the background to the book's publication:

> It started life as a 20,000-word performance piece, a monologue that was experienced as a sound installation called 'Non Correspondence'. The installation was first put on at the Battersea Arts Centre in 2014. You'd walk into a

room, which had three armchairs in it, and a coffee table. On the coffee table was a radio. A woman's voice was being broadcast. She was speaking the text. I didn't tell any friends or family about it because I was strangely embarrassed. It's a very personal piece of work. I didn't want people I know to hear it.

Afterwards, she was persuaded to publish it as a book which then grew to 35,000 words. On her writing technique, she says:

> I was writing under constraint, yes, in so far as I didn't allow myself to go back and edit the text. I forced myself to keep going, to keep writing down each association that came into my head. I did self censor a tiny bit – around stuff to do with my family which I felt was too private and too likely to cause upset – but apart from that I made myself stick tight to the honesty of the process. Even when I expanded it by 15,000 words or so, I did that by going through the text all over again from scratch. Each time I had another thought I wrote it down. I didn't want to shape it deliberately or plan it. I tried to stick to the constraint of my spontaneous associative thoughts. It was hard because I had so many: I could have written 100,000 words or more. But I wanted to keep it a short, sharp shot in the arm.[4]

Pawson lists four 'main prompts' (all of them male). Firstly, there was Édouard Levé's *Autoportrait* (Levé 2012 [2005]), a series of seemingly random declarative sentences about the author. As Scott Esposito (2012) writes:

> They seem to include every genre of thing that could be said about a person, ranging from the factual ('I have never filed a complaint with the police') to the oddly pointless ('I do not foresee making love with an animal') to the philosophical ('I wonder whether the landscape is shaped by the road, or the road by the landscape') to the bizarre ('On the internet I become telepathic') to the psychoanalytic ('Whether it's because I was tired of looking at them, or for lack of space, I felt a great relief when I burned my paintings') to the comic and confessional ('On the street I checked my watch while I was holding a can of Coke in my left hand, I poured part of it down my pants, by chance nobody saw, I have told no one').

Levé also touches on a vast range of topics: including art, childhood, politics, sex, death, depression, fears, hopes, reading, walking, nature, sartorial preferences, Spanish cafés, scruples about talking too much, rubber boots and the fear that one's vocabulary is shrinking. Born in 1965, Levé was a business school graduate before turning to painting in 1991. A few years later, after a long stay in India, he destroyed most of his work and reinvented himself as a conceptual photographer and writer – influenced particularly by the work of Raymond Roussel (1877–1933) and other practitioners of 'constrained writing' techniques. His first publication, *Oeuvres* (2002) comprised a list of more than 500 imaginary conceptual projects. One was brought to fruition in *Amérique* (2006), photographs of small American towns named after great world cities (Berlin, Delhi, Rio, etc.). His final work, *Suicide* (2008) – its seemingly random structure intended to imitate the operations of human memory – was delivered to his publisher just days before he took his own life.

The second influence on Pawson was *Je Me Souviens* (Hachette, Paris, 1978) comprising 480 numbered statements, all beginning identically with 'I remember' by the French writer, Georges Perec (1936–1982). As Nicole Rudick (2014) comments:

> They were written between January 1973 and June 1977 but are pulled from the time when Perec was between ten- and twenty-five-years-old. His aim was to unearth memories that were 'almost forgotten, inessential, banal, common, if not to everyone, at least to many'.

At the same time, he never suggests that all his statements are true: 'When I evoke memories from before the war, they refer for me to a period belonging to the realm of myth: this explains how a memory can be "objectively" false.'

Perec was influenced himself by the *I Remember* series (1970–1975) by Joe Brainard (1942–1994), the American writer whose work includes assemblages, collages, drawings and paintings as well as designs for book and album covers, theatrical sets and costumes. The memoir deliberately challenges the conventions mixing the banal with the revelatory. As the website *poets.org* comments on *I Remember*:

> Painterly in its vivid details and collagist in its hands-off juxtaposition, it is an accumulative, oblique biography, a portrait of the artist as a young man. It is much, much greater than the mere sum of its parts. ... It has that sweet, playful self-possession that pervades Brainard's work.[5]

The final influence was the long poem, 'The alphabet', composed by the American Ron Silliman (1946–) between 1979 and 2004 which grew to 26 volumes, beginning with 'Albany' in 1979–1980. This is how it starts:

> If the function of writing is to 'express the world' My father withheld child support, forcing my mother to live with her parents, my brother and I to be raised together in a small room. Grandfather called them niggers. I can't afford an automobile.

As John Herbert Cunningham writes:

> 'Albany' opens with a sentence fragment, a dependent clause shorn of dependency through the omission of that on which it should be dependent. The clause is then followed by a sentence that has no relation to what has gone

before or what comes after – as do all the other sentences, which are assembled in a process best described ... as montage.[6]

Pawson's radical transformation of the genre

Given these influences, it is perhaps not surprising that at the core of Pawson's memoir is a deliberate debunking (through both content and format) of the myth of the heroic war correspondent.[7] There are no chapters. There is no logical or chronological structuring of the text which is deliberately fragmented. One short paragraph simply follows another – separated only by space. One sentence, such as (Pawson 2016: 37) 'That evening, in that cramped north London flat, something got unlocked', can be enough. Memories, reflections on reporting and the horrors of war, discussions about objectivity and journalistic ethics, explorations of class, race, gender and identity, confessions, insecurities, fears, blunt revelations about her own sexuality, celebrations of the land of Angola – all tumble out one after another in a process of instantaneous association. As Pawson comments:

> Everything is relevant. Everything matters. I'm not sure that one experience trumps another because they all feed into each other, bouncing off each other to form the constellation of one's life. I think what I really love about the book is precisely that it goes everywhere. The freedom is fantastic.[8]

The critique of journalism

The critique goes so deep she even questions the right to report. She writes:

> Working in different parts of the African continent for the mainstream media, particularly as a white British foreign correspondent, I worried a lot about what I should report and what I should not. Sometimes I asked myself what right had I to report at all (Pawson 2016: 9).

Pawson constantly questions conventional notions about journalistic objectivity. As she writes (ibid: 12–13):

> When I started out as a journalist I thought I understood the meaning of objectivity. But within a few months of reporting from Angola, I lost that faith and ceased to believe in objectivity even as a possibility. Yes, you can give a voice to as many sides as possible – but that's not objectivity. Today, I don't even believe that objectivity is a useful goal. It's false and it's a lie and it doesn't help people to mentally engage in events taking place around the world.

By the time she was reporting in the Ivory Coast in 2004, she had begun to question the relationship between the real and the imagination. 'And I began to engage more fully with the importance of doubt. This was the period when I started to think that perhaps the news world was not for me. It's the insistence on certainty that I most dislike' (ibid: 115). In the end, she voluntarily left the BBC: 'I couldn't carry on working in the mainstream media. I felt I was doing more harm than good and I was increasingly depressed about it' (ibid: 38).

She is constantly concerned to debunk the myth of the heroic war journo. For instance, at one point she admits to being 'a coward':

> When I was living in Abidjan, I saw a man being beaten by government soldiers. I think he was being beaten close to death. I was standing on the other side of the road with five other journalists, all men. We could hear the man screaming, the whip coming down on his back. And we did nothing (ibid: 50).

On war reporting, she comments:

> I can remember well the first time someone described me as a war correspondent. I felt like a fake. I dislike the label because it implies that war is something distinct from the rest of the news – that it is out of the ordinary. Yet, the whole point of war, I think, is that it is intrinsic to life. It is what we are. Britain has been at war continuously, somewhere in the world for over a century (ibid: 74).

Pawson is, indeed, keen to highlight in her narratives how the worlds of 'warfare' and 'peace' overlap. She recounts, how on two occasions, for instance, she was threatened by men with knives – once in 1992 in Johannesburg and once on the Jubilee Tube line, in London, in 1995 (ibid: 68).

Pawson also breaks with conventional journalistic practice (that requires a certain detachment) by often responding very emotionally to events. When she worked in Angola, she says, other journalists would sometimes laugh at her because she expressed her emotions so openly: 'I lost it with Peter Hain, the British minister for Africa – the so-called son of Africa if you remember – when he visited Luanda. And he voiced his support for a military solution to the conflict' (ibid: 10). A BBC inquiry later cleared her but she ends: 'Just writing this paragraph I feel the fury flooding back' (ibid: 11).

Speaking frankly: On war and sex

Along with the fragmentary, free-form style of writing goes a bluntness. Pawson is clearly determined to break taboos and to shock – both when talking about the horrors of warfare and her own sexuality.

She remembers a soldier from M'banza Kongo, the capital of Angola's northwestern Zaire Province. She writes: 'We heard a gunshot. We ran with the crowds. There he was, on the stump of a tree. Sitting and staring. A rifle at his feet.

His brains blown out through the back of his head' (ibid: 3). Later on she describes a Russian Antonov plane crashing into a Luandan slum: 'I saw part of someone's leg being dropped like a piece of wood onto a trailer' (ibid: 9). And 'Once, I saw a woman cut in half by an articulated lorry which was carrying food aid for the UN World Food Programme' (ibid: 81).

Sexual subjects are handled with similar frankness throughout. For instance, she writes: 'I'm now in my forties. I've had an abortion, two miscarriages and no children' (ibid: 8). Later, she remembers:

> I was promiscuous in those days. ... Another journalist, a man I thought of as a friend, locked me in his car. He began to cry and begged me to suck him off. Just once, please, just once. There is something awkwardly comic about this memory because I couldn't understand what he was asking me to do...
>
> I have had sex against my will twice in my life. Don't assume, as others have that I'm talking about somewhere in Africa because I'm talking about some-where in Europe. Somewhere called London.
>
> On another occasion, a soldier held an automatic rifle to my chest and told me he was going to fuck me. When I said No you aren't! he lowered the gun and walked away (ibid: 27–28).

She even talks about tampons: 'The first time I used a tampon, I felt like I was trying to reinsert an expanded cork into a bottle of wine. We were in the south of France. I didn't have a clue. And the whole thing made me hate being female' (ibid: 99).

This is The Place To Be – and cultural spaces

The French theorist Pierre Bourdieu is celebrated for introducing the notion of cultural capital (Bourdieu 1973, 1984). Accordingly, cultural capital operates as a social-relation within an economy of practices, comprising all of the material and symbolic goods which are considered rare and worth acquiring. The notion of cultural space (theorised here for the first time) is very different – focusing on the many cultural manifestations (past, present and future) that are associated with any cultural object. Thus, for any memoir to be understood fully, the cultural space it occupies needs to be considered, including not only bibliographies relating to memoirs, autobiographies, life writing and bibliographies in particular of women and women journalists, but also reviews of the text and interviews with the author. It might also incorporate films, art works, plays, social media follow-ups and so on, based on the text. Even this chapter (originally published in an academic journal) can be considered part of the text's cultural space. The political/economic under-pinnings of the cultural forms also need to be acknowledged – particularly in relation to the ownership and organisational structures of the corporate/alternative media in question (Murdock and Golding 2005).

Reviews – worth celebrating

The memoir received a particularly sensitive review by Cristina Rios in *Peace News* (Rios 2017). *PN* was established in 1936 as a voice for the pacifist Peace Pledge Union and continues today (on both on- and off-line platforms) – promoting non-violent revolution and critiquing corporate media coverage of conflict.[9] After briefly outlining Pawson's journalistic career, Rios comments: 'Indeed, not only does Pawson refuse to sensationalise her experiences, she also shows how violence surrounds us on a daily basis.' From the general, Rios moves to the specific:

> Shortly after describing a man being almost beaten to death by government soldiers in Abidjan, Pawson confesses a desire to assault or humiliate a nazi sympathiser she encounters years later on a train from London to Liverpool. The normalisation and ordinariness of violence, in conflict and in everyday life, is peppered throughout the text to great effect, making this a discerning and incisive reflection on its nature (ibid).

Next Rios highlights, concisely and elegantly, the memoir's distinct originality in terms of both form and content:

> Pawson's comments on conflict and her African sojourn are interspersed with the everyday minutiae, tragedy and joys of her own life, and combined with reflections on gender, family, identity, nostalgia, childhood and time. Written in short bursts – paragraphs and scattered sentences – which Pawson wrote almost entirely in one session, it eschews a conventional chronology in order to merge these diverse strands (ibid).

The reviewer is also perceptive in her response to Pawson's clear love for Angola: 'Her longing for Angola challenges our preconceptions of it, but Pawson is at all times nuanced in her depiction of the complexities and contradictions of life there and elsewhere' (ibid). And the final paragraph in the short review has a conclusive/coda-esque feel:

> Through its chronological irreverence and its melding of themes, *This Is The Place To Be* succeeds in pondering life and its horrors – ordinary and extraordinary – in an unexpected and unique manner. Its ideas and images linger with the reader long after (ibid).

Such a well-composed, thoughtful review in the revolutionary pacifist *Peace News* constitutes an important element of the cultural space occupied by Pawson's memoir. There is nothing flippant or clichéd about the comments: indeed, they add to the *gravitas* of the space.

Another fascinating review (all of 1,267 words) appears on the website of the *Los Angeles Review of Books* (not to be confused with the mainstream *Los Angeles Times* book reviews section), which describes itself as 'a non-profit organization dedicated to promoting and disseminating rigorous, incisive, and engaging writing on every aspect of literature, culture, and art'.[10] Houman Barekat (2017) begins by dwelling on the addictions of the novelist Graham Greene and war correspondent Anthony Loyd to seeking out danger (and the attendant adrenaline rushes) before citing Pawson on covering the Angolan civil war:

> It was an incredibly intense experience, one that influenced me radically. For a long time, I tried to work out how I could retrieve it. I wanted a repeat, like that absurd sensation you get when you first take certain class-A drugs (ibid).

This sort of admission 'normally takes the form of a fleeting disclosure, duly followed by a vague sense of shame and a swift changing of the subject'. But here 'the theme resurfaces again and again in the many disparate fragments' (ibid):

> Pawson recalls feeling 'a sort of lightness of being' after 9/11; later, she recalls how 'an overwhelming vigour definitely swept through me' when watching some people being killed. 'It was the same when I saw a group of children,' she writes, 'scrambling like rabbits into holes in the ground to hide from incoming shells' (ibid).

Barekat next highlights a central theme of the memoir, following it up with an astute psychological observation:

> Pawson is no latter-day Marinetti when she opines: 'The whole point of war … is that it's intrinsic to life'; the observation is all the more troubling precisely because it comes from someone whose approach to existence brims with humanity and compassion (ibid).

The review then shifts to consider the memoir's important reflections on journalistic professionalism, as Pawson 'bemoans the suffocating compromises of professional journalism, the necessity of reducing everything to a hackneyed sound bite and the impossibility of transcending the limits of the format'. Her questioning of BBC claims to objectivity, according to Barekat, is particularly apposite given the corporation's 'bending over backward to be seen as impartial' in its coverage of the rising tide of racist populism in Western politics 'a policy exemplified by its decision to carry a lengthy interview with the leader of the French far right, Marine Le Pen, back in November – on Remembrance Sunday, no less' (ibid).

Pawson's misgivings about the inherently exploitative nature of war journalism lead Barekat to consider the fate of the Pulitzer Prize-winning South African photojournalist Kevin Carter who took his own life at 33, apparently haunted by the horrors he witnessed in Sudan. And he makes this important political point:

Western correspondents working anywhere in the Global South are necessarily implicated, at least to some extent, in the structures of socio-economic and geo-political inequality that sustain the privations they are recording, and even someone who has embraced an adopted culture with pure and sincere motives is not entirely free from the taint of appropriation (ibid).

Pawson's 'ruminative vignettes are sporadically punctuated by moments of disarmingly jovial whimsy'. For instance, of the Cuban doctor who sucked on a cigar while telling her she had to quit smoking immediately, she comments: 'If anything, this made me take him more seriously.' Moreover, the memoir's oddness – its nonlinear, fragmentary form – 'gives it a kind of oneiric quality redolent of experimental fiction' (ibid). The effect is heightened by an occasional riffing on the unreliability of memory:

> We are invited, by implication, to speculate as to how much else was fill-in, and to reflect in turn on the authenticity of our own narratives. For all its personal candour, the spare laconicism of Pawson's prose — even when recalling harrowing acts of violence — militates against any sense of intrusiveness or therapeutic excess (ibid).

Barekat ends with a deliberately contentious, slightly whimsical generalisation: 'This is particularly important to an English readership, for we are delicate in the face of earnestness and cannot handle too much of it. Give it to us by stealth, though, and we will gladly have it.' But it's a surprising conclusion given that he imagines his audience as primarily English when the reach of the internet is global. All the same, a progressive political aesthetic underlies the piece. It performs the essential function of a review, comprising a well-structured, original, thoughtful and colourfully written reflection on the text but at the same carrying enough *gravitas* to interest the general reader who may not go on to acquire/read Pawson's work. As Keeble (2006: 246) stresses in his book on newspaper writing skills:

> The review must exist as a piece of writing in its own right. It must entice in the reader through the quality and colour of its prose. It must entertain, though different newspapers have different conceptions of what entertainment means.

In her *Times Literary Supplement* review, Lara Feigel (2016) considers Pawson's work alongside the posthumously published *The War on Women*, by the former BBC correspondent, Sue Lloyd-Roberts. She sums up the background concisely:

> For twenty years until her death from leukaemia last year at the age of sixty-four, Lloyd-Roberts made impassioned, angry films for the BBC documenting global injustice and suffering. In the lead-up to her death, she became aware that a striking number of the cases that she'd investigated had involved

violence aimed specifically at women. *The War on Women* documents a series of these, taking us from Gambia to Ireland, Kashmir to Bradford, asking for increased pressure to be put on governments around the world to stop turning a blind eye to the violation of basic human rights.

She moves on to consider some of the (often harrowing) cases Lloyd-Roberts champions. On Pawson, she first considers her as both a 'willing and unwilling outsider': 'Often mistaken for a boy when she was younger, she moved to Walthamstow from Hackney when it became too yuppified and left an enviable job at the BBC when she found the insider status it gave her too untenable' (ibid).

Feigel describes *This is The Place To Be* as Pawson's 'fragmentary inquiry into herself that uses her own experiences as a lens through which to investigate many things, but most crucially race, sexuality and violence' (ibid).

> If there is a narrative here, then it's about Pawson's relationship to Angola – a country that she had never heard of as a child, and that she came to think of as home. She lived in Luanda while reporting on the war there in the late 1990s and her distrust of the phrase 'war correspondent' stems from this time because she came to see that war wasn't distinct from ordinary life.

The centrality of Pawson's meditations on violence (picked up by the other reviewers) is also captured here. Feigel writes that the memoir is principally a meditation 'on whether the violence of war can be separated from a strain of violence that seems more endemic to human life'. And she elegantly links Pawson with Lloyd-Roberts, suggesting that both women insisted:

> … that the West cannot get away with separating itself from barbarity. She mentions that her only two experiences of sexual violence have happened in Britain rather than Africa, and describes fights with potential attackers that have taken place in her own London neighbourhood (ibid).

Pawson's incredibly intense experiences while reporting the Angolan war, highlighted by other reviewers, are also considered here. But Feigel challenges Pawson when she states that no one who has witnessed a war – 'who has seen the damage it does to people mentally and physically' – would ever wish for more hostility of this kind.

> But this is a statement belied in recent decades by the regimes that have perpetuated continual conflict. It is belied all around us now and indeed is contradicted by many of Pawson's own reflections in a book whose strength is that contrary observations frequently coexist.

The review ends comparing, again, aspects of the two texts: Feigel suggests there is a danger that on reading Pawson 'we will take refuge in inaction; that exposure to complication on this scale results in a kind of existential sense of the impossibility of agency. It is no coincidence that one of her favourite writers is Samuel Beckett' (ibid). In contrast, 'Sue Lloyd-Roberts can awaken us out of that torpor. Though her book is unrelenting, it is also unignorable'.

The *TLS* review, then, usefully highlights the way in which the cultural space of a text can cross both corporate and alternative sectors – and how progressive political, aesthetic ideas can appear in the mainstream. Indeed, while the essential function of the corporate media is to propagandise in the interests of dominant political, economic, ideological and military interests (Herman and Chomsky 1988), this does not operate one-dimensionally (the system is sufficiently strong enough to incorporate challenges). Significant spaces do appear in the political and cultural sphere in which dominant ideas and interests can be challenged. And such challenges, endowed with *gravitas*, are worth celebrating.

Interviews – and the pleasures of the text

The interview can be another important feature of the cultural space of a text. It helps expand the reception of the text across media and can introduce new perspectives, new psychological depth (*gravitas*) and new 'facts'. It can help in understanding and add to the aesthetic and intellectual pleasure of the text. On his blog *rhystranter.com*, Rhys Tranter (2016) begins an interview with Pawson by asking what motivates her to write. Until ten years or so ago, she says, she was inspired by a desire to persuade people to care about events and people around the world. More recently, her attitude has changed:

> I am much less certain of why I write and often uncertain of what I am writing until it's finished. The difference is that I accept that uncertainty. I indulge it. Doubt is neither comfortable nor comforting, but it is a good creative intellectual and emotional space. Perhaps digging into doubt is my real motivation (ibid).

After they discuss the origins of the memoir (indicated earlier in this paper), the focus turns to its fragmentary nature. Pawson says she began by writing a series of spontaneous associations about her times reporting wars in Angola and the Ivory Coast but then these spilled into other parts of her life. Pawson next acknowledges her debt to Levé, Perec, Brainard and Silliman (all men). But, interestingly, she goes on to highlight other writers who have influenced her: Kathy Acker,[11] Jean Améry,[12] Sven Lindqvist,[13] Mina Loy,[14] Claudia Rankine[15] and Derek Walcott.[16] Unfortunately, Tranter does not follow up by asking precisely how these authors impacted on her memoir. It would have been fascinating to know.

Pawson says that people who have read *This is The Place To Be* often comment to her on how it reminds them of the work of Marguerite Duras[17] and so she began to read Duras – with great interest.

The long interview by Rebekah Weikal for *3ammagazine.com* [18] is particularly useful for highlighting aspects of the text nowhere else considered. For instance, in response to an early question about how her work in radio influenced her writing, Pawson responds:

> I'd say that writing for radio is all about rhythm. For several years, I was writing day in day out for BBC World Service radio. I would always read my scripts aloud, repeatedly. You have to keep the language very tight. I'd be listening to the rhythm of each report, which often were less than a minute each – the length of a poem, if you like. I think the rhythm of my reports mattered as much to me as the content. It influences listeners even if they aren't aware of it. [19]

Weikal cleverly integrates her own subjectivity into the discussion which covers quite intimate issues – and it helps build trust with the interviewee – saying that one of her favourite parts of the book is when Pawson reveals she has only recently begun to think of gender 'outside the binary'. Pawson responds frankly:

> I am certainly surprised that it's taken me so long to move through and hopefully beyond the binary. I felt very old when I realised this, but immediately freed as well, as if I was shedding a thick layer of skin. The crumbling of gender binaries is one of the very few aspects of life at the moment that I feel excited about, even optimistic. I'm not sure if this is to do with the book more than the people I have been lucky enough to meet and to call my friends. So much else leaves me afraid and pessimistic. [20]

The intimacy quickly established between interviewer and interviewee means that Pawson is often quite open about her deepest feelings. For instance, she adds:

> I think it's a cathartic addendum to some of my turmoil around class, race, sexuality and identity. Spending time in two countries with war has obviously influenced me hugely, but no more than growing up in south west London as a privileged child who was sent to private school. [21]

When the discussion moves on to the ethics of journalism, Pawson mentions a number of reporters whom she admires: Sola Odunfa,[22] Ebrima Sillah,[23] Elizabeth Ohene,[24] Gray Phombeah,[25] Justin Pearce,[26] Robin White[27] and Obi Anyadike.[28] And she says she is inspired by many others in the profession, among them Lindsey Hilsum,[29] Anthony Loyd,[30] Gary Younge,[31] Rasna Warah.[32] She is next asked when she realised she could not keep her emotions out of her reporting:

> There was the time when I described the Angolan President, José Eduardo dos Santos, as 'predictably paranoid' in a report. The producer in London said it was partisan and had to be taken out. I refused. They probably deleted it from

the recording. Another time, I was reporting on a demonstration against the regime and I couldn't stop myself joining in the chanting with the protesters. It was a wonderful moment, being part of this courageous group of activists. I remember the elation.[33]

All this extra biographical information helps us understand the memoir more deeply. Pawson is asked to elaborate on her questioning, obsessively, 'the distinctions between fact and fiction, between the real and the imagination'. She replies, quoting from her memoir:

> With normal vision, and with perception of all kinds, there is a lot of unconscious guesswork that goes on. The brain knows what should be there and, to help us, it fills in for us, using unconscious processing and guesswork. So your eye is not the video camera you think it is. What we see is a simulation of reality (Pawson 2016: 80).

To support her argument, she quotes the case of Jean Charles de Menezes, the 27-year-old Brazilian shot dead by police on the London underground on 22 July 2005. Eyewitnesses reported seeing a man running away from police, vaulting over a ticket barrier and wearing a bulky jacket that concealed some sort of suicide bomb.

> In fact, when the truth eventually came out, we learned that Menezes had actually been wearing a light denim shirt, had walked through the ticket barriers and only ran when he saw his train pulling into the station. How could bystanders have got the facts so wrong?[34]

The discussion then moves on to travel, and Pawson reveals more of her constantly questioning, sceptical attitude to life (so much an integral element of the memoir):

> My earliest travel experiences, first in South Africa and then in Ghana, were extraordinary. Both countries seemed so different to the places I'd read about in texts by academics. They were almost unrecognisable. For several years, I wished I'd lived in them before studying them. To some extent, I felt that academic study had given me an illusion of knowledge that, as it turned out, I didn't really have at all. I realised how ignorant I was. But I think we always have to be cautious when we travel anywhere. First impressions are always superficial and usually unreliable. In fact, I think travel is unreliable, which is why, when I was working as a journalist, I preferred to live and work in a country, not to drop in and out. I think it's only by living in a place, by staying there and bedding down, that you start to understand it. Travel implies you are moving through a place. I'm not convinced it's a way to truly start to understand the world.

Pawson ends by saying she is currently working on a novel and travelling more in the UK:

> To survive life in London today, I try my hardest to observe it as if I were an outsider as well as an insider. This may sound a little contradictory but I also take solace from something I read by Hilary Mantel: 'When you find yourself at the centre, no longer part of the radical, start digging the ground beneath your feet.' This is what I'm trying to do at the moment – and I think it can be very radical.

Conclusion: On a personal note

I was first inspired to check out Pawson's memoir after seeing Rios's review of it in my favourite journal, *Peace News*. I was struck by the elegance of the writing, the sensitive, concise reflections on the text and by the memoir's form and content – as described by Rios. On securing the book I was amazed by its radicalism. And searching on the web, various other reviews and interviews appeared. I found all of them fascinating and well-constructed, sensitive to Pawson's aesthetic and underlying politics. Most of them appeared in alternative media – usually ignored by the academy. Investigating the writers/artists who inspired Pawson also led me down new, somewhat obscure and wonderfully stimulating intellectual avenues.

So around *This is The Place To Be* grew, for me, a host of cultural forms which helped deepen my appreciation and understanding of the text. Together, they seem to form a unique cultural space in which deeply important issues – sexuality, racism, professionalism, the blurred boundaries between reality and the imagined world and so on – are explored seriously – with *gravitas*, indeed. And I wanted both to celebrate and theorise this cultural space, building on Bourdieu's notions of cultural capital. Reviews and interviews are only occasionally considered alongside writings and yet (as this case study suggests) analysing them can help provide crucial new insights.

Acknowledgements

This chapter is based on a paper with the same title in *Ethical Space: The International Journal of Communication Ethics*, Vol. 15, Nos 3 and 4 pp 5–16.

Notes

1 See http://mupfc.marshall.edu/~rabe/women.htm, accessed on 9 August 2018
2 Similarly, In the *Independent*, of 24 March 2016, Lucy Scholes reviewed some 'classic newsroom books'. The first five are all by men (George Gissing, Jonathan Coe, Michael Frayn, Evelyn Waugh and Andrew Martin) – and the photograph illustrating the feature shows a busy, all-male newsroom. Tucked at the end are references to novels by three women (Annalena McAfee, Monica Dickens and F. E. Bailey) (Scholes 2016)

3 See http://www.3ammagazine.com/3am/place-interview-lara-pawson/, accessed on 2 July 2018

4 Ibid

5 See https://www.poets.org/poetsorg/text/joe-brainard-i-remember, accessed on 2 July 2018

6 See http://quarterlyconversation.com/the-alphabet-by-ron-silliman, accessed on 2 July 2018

7 See for instance, *Frontline*, by Clare Hollingworth (1990). The doyenne of war correspondents was 105 when she died in January 2017. Her great scoop was to witness the German invasion of Poland and the launch of the Second World War in 1939. The cover blurb says: 'She has been a distinguished and indefatigable frontline reporter for the *Guardian* and *Telegraph*, one of a rare species – a journalist always more interested in presenting the facts objectively than in promoting a cause or herself. She is self-reliant, brave, exhilarated under fire and immensely tenacious.' Typical of her writing style is the way she reports her first assignment in Poland: 'We came under machine-gun attack from German fighters strafing the roads, we rocked in and out of great pot-holes, we were covered in dust and after dusk we found ourselves driving without lights on an invisible road in an unknown country' (ibid: 210; see also Adie 2003; Bowen 2006; Hastings 2002; Leslie 2008; Sissons 2012). Phillip Knightley's (2000) seminal analysis of war reporting also succeeds in debunking many of the heroic myths. So too does the hilarious novel *Scoop* by Evelyn Waugh (1938)

8 http://www.3ammagazine.com/3am/place-interview-lara-pawson/, accessed on 2 July 2018

9 Editor Milan Rai (2010) writes: 'For *Peace News*, citizen journalism has meant activist journalism with self-reporting by large numbers of social movement activists through the years' (211). He adds that one of the purposes of *PN* is 'to search the output of the mass media with diligence and a sceptical eye, cutting through the mass of misrepresentation and fraud to discover nuggets that can help citizens to better understand – and more effectively alter – the world in which we are living and acting' (ibid: 217).

10 See https://lareviewofbooks.org/about/, accessed on 9 August 2018

11 Kathy Acker (1947–1997) American experimental novelist, punk poet, essayist, influenced by W. S. Burroughs, Marguerite Duras and by the Black Mountain School poets. In her fragmentary texts she blends memoir, sex, power and violence

12 Jean Améry (1912–1978) Austrian writer whose work was often influenced by his experiences in the Auschwitz concentration camp. He wrote *On Suicide: A Discourse on Voluntary Death* (1976). Améry killed himself in 1978

13 Sven Lindqvist (1932–) Swedish writer of over 30 books of essays, aphorisms, memoir, documentary prose, travel and reportage. His more recent works focus on the subjects of imperialism, racism, war and genocide. He has argued, controversially, that the Nazi application of the expansionist and racist principles of colonialism was significant because for the first time it was applied against fellow Europeans rather than against the distant and dehumanised peoples of the Third World

14 Mina Loy (1886–1966) English poet, artist, feminist, playwright, novelist and lampshade designer. In 1946, she became a naturalised citizen of the United States and in later life continued to work on her junk collages. See https://www.poetryfoundation. org/poets/mina-loy

15 Claudia Rankine (1963–) Born in Kingston, Jamaica, she is an essayist, poet and playwright. Her poems explore the unsettled territory between prose and poetry and the ways in which individuals are influenced by skin colour, economics and global corporate culture

16 Derek Walcott (1930–2017) Winner of the 1992 Nobel Prize for Literature, he was a poet, playwright and essayist, born in St Lucia. His book-length poem *Omeros*, loosely based on Homer's *The Iliad*, was published in 1990 to acclaim. It explores his dominant themes: the harsh legacy of colonialism, the beauty of the Caribbean islands, the difficulties of writing and living in two cultural worlds

17 Marguerite Duras (1914–1996) French novelist, journalist, playwright, experimental film-maker and active member of the French Communist Party. Her partly fictionalised autobiographical work *L'Amant* (*The Lover*) won the Goncourt Prize in 1984 and was turned into a highly successful film by Jean-Jacques Annaud in 1992. According to *britannica.com*, Duras turned regularly to a more abstract and synthetic mode, with fewer characters, less plot and narrative, and few of the other elements of traditional fiction (see https://www.britannica.com/biography/Marguerite-Duras)

18 See http://www.3ammagazine.com/3am/place-interview-lara-pawson/, accessed on 2 July 2018

19 Ibid

20 Ibid

21 Ibid

22 A freelance, Africa-based correspondent who often appears on the BBC. See http://frontierleaks.blogspot.com/2014/11/sola-odunfa-profile-of-one-of.html, accessed on 10 August 2018

23 Former BBC correspondent based in The Gambia, he was appointed director general of Gambia Radio and Television Services in February 2017. See http://thepoint.gm/africa/gambia/article/ebrima-sillah-is-new-grts-director-general, accessed on 10 August 2018

24 Ghanaian journalist and politician who has contributed to the BBC's *Letter from Africa*

25 A Kenyan-based journalist

26 Formerly a reporter in South Africa, Angola and the UK, he is currently a researcher at Cambridge University (see https://theconversation.com/profiles/justin-pearce-247414)

27 Born in Nottingham in 1944, MBE, he was for many years editor of the BBC's *Focus on Africa* and *Network Africa*

28 Editor at Large at *irinnnews.org* (covering aid, conflict, the environment, disasters and migration)

29 International editor at *Channel 4 News*. See https://www.channel4.com/news/by/lindsey-hilsum, accessed on 10 August 2018

30 Award-winning *Times* foreign correspondent. See https://www.thetimes.co.uk/article/anthony-loyd-dispatches-from-the-front-line-2kp0tm6sb, accessed on 10 August 2018

31 Editor at large at the *Guardian*. See https://www.theguardian.com/profile/garyyounge, accessed on 10 August 2018

32 A Kenyan writer and editor. See https://www.nation.co.ke/authors/1959272-1914582-my0lriz/index.html, accessed on 10 August 2018

33 http://www.3ammagazine.com/3am/place-interview-lara-pawson/, accessed on 2 July 2018

34 http://www.3ammagazine.com/3am/place-interview-lara-pawson/, accessed on 2 July 2018

References

Adie, Kate (2003) *The Kindness of Strangers*, London: Headline

Barekat, Houman (2017) The whole point about war: On Lara Pawson's *This is The Place to Be*, *Los Angeles Review of Books*, 27 February. Available online at https://lareviewofbooks.org/article/the-whole-point-about-war-on-lara-pawsons-this-is-the-place-to-be/#!, accessed on 9 August 2018

Bourdieu, Pierre (1973) Cultural reproduction and social reproduction, Brown, R. (ed.) *Knowledge, Education and Social Change: Papers in the Sociology of Education*, London: Tavistock Publications pp 71–112

Bourdieu, Pierre (1984) *Distinction: A Social Critique of the Judgment of Taste*, Cambridge MA: Harvard University Press

Bowen, Jeremy (2006) *War Stories*, London: Simon & Schuster

Chodorow, Nancy (1978) *The Reproduction of Mothering; Psychoanalysis and the Sociology of Gender*, Berkeley: University of California Press

Esposito, Scott (2012) Review of *Autoportrait*, *The Quarterly Conversation*, 5 March. Available online at http://quarterlyconversation.com/autoportrait-by-edouard-leve, accessed on 2 July 2018

Feigel, Lara (2016) Witnesses to the world, *Times Literary Supplement*, 26 October. Available online at https://www.the-tls.co.uk/articles/public/witnesses-to-the-world/, accessed on 9 August 2018

Friedman, Susan Stanford (1988) Women's autobiographical selves, Benstock, Shari (ed.) *The Private Self: Theory and Practice of Women's Autobiographical Writing*, Chapel Hill, NC: University of North Carolina Press pp 35–56

Good, Howard (1993) *The Journalist as Autobiographer*, New Jersey and London: The Scarecrow Press

Hall, Calvin L. (2009) *African American Journalists: Autobiography as Memoir and Manifesto*, Maryland, Toronto and Plymouth: Scarecrow Press

Hastings, Max (2002) *Editor*, London: Macmillan

Herman, Edward and Chomsky, Noam (1988) *Manufacturing Consent: The Political Economy of the Mass Media*, New York: Pantheon

Hollingworth, Clare (1990) *Frontline*, London: Jonathan Cape

Jelinek, Estelle C. (1980) *Women's Autobiography: Essays in Criticism*, Indiana: Indiana University Press

Joseph, Sue (2013) The lonely girl: Investigating the scholarly nexus of trauma life-writing and process in tertiary institutions, *Text*, Vol. 17, No. 1. Available online at http://www.textjournal.com.au/april13/joseph.htm, accessed on 2 July 2018

Keeble, Richard (2006) *The Newspapers Handbook*, London: Routledge, fourth edition

Knightley, Phillip (2000) *The First Casualty: The War Correspondent as Hero and Myth-Maker from the Crimea to Kosovo*, London: Prion Books

Leslie, Ann (2008) *Killing My Own Snakes*, London: Macmillan

Levé, Édouard (2012 [2005]) *Autoportrait* (trans, Stein, Lorin), Illinois: Dalkey Archive Press

Mason, Mary Grimley and Green, Carol Hurd (1979) *Journeys: Autobiographical Writings by Women*, Virginia: G. K. Hall

Murdock, Graham and Golding, Peter (2005) Culture, communications and political economy, Curran, James and Gurevitch, Michael (eds) *Mass Media and Society*, London: Hodder Arnold pp 60–83

Olney, James (ed.) (1980) *Autobiography: Essays Theoretical and Critical*, Princeton: Princeton University Press

Pawson, Lara (2016) *This is the Place to Be*, London: CB Editions

Rai, Milan (2010) Peace journalism in practice: *Peace News* for non-violent revolution, Keeble, Richard Lance, Tulloch, John and Zollmann, Florian (eds) *Peace Journalism, War and Conflict Resolution*, New York: Peter Lang pp 207–221

Rios, Christina (2017) Review of *This is The Place to Be*, *Peace News*, February–March. Available online at https://peacenews.info/node/8621/lara-pawson-place-be, accessed on 4 August 2018

Rowbotham, Sheila (1973) *Women's Consciousness, Man's World*, London: Penguin

Rudick, Nicole (2014) I remember Georges Perec, *Paris Review*, 30 July. Available online at https://www.theparisreview.org/blog/2014/07/30/i-remember-georges-perec/, accessed on 2 July 2018

Scholes, Lucy (2016) Classic newsroom books: A memorable saunter down the Street of Shame, *Independent*, 24 March. Available online at https://www.independent.co.uk/a

rts-entertainment/books/features/classic-newsroom-books-a-memorable-saunter-down-the-street-of-shame-a6950211.html, accessed on 12 July 2018

Sissons, Peter (2012) *When One Door Closes*, London: Biteback

Smith, Sidonie and Watson, Julia (1998) *Women, Autobiography, Theory*, Madison, WI and London: University of Wisconsin Press

Spacks, Patricia Meyer (1975) *The Female Imagination*, New York: Alfred A. Knopf

Steiner, Linda (1997) Autobiographies by women journalists: An annotated bibliography, *Journalism History*, Vol. 23, No. 1 pp 13–15

Tranter, Rhys (2016) Lara Pawson discusses her memoir, *This is the Place to Be, rhystranter. com*, 8 September. Available online at https://rhystranter.com/2016/09/08/lara-pa wson-memoir-this-is-the-place-to-be-interview/, accessed on 9 August 2018

Turner, Camilla (2012) List of top 30 journalism books, *Press Gazette*, 17 December. Available online at http://www.pressgazette.co.uk/press-gazettes-christmas-list-best-journalism -books/, accessed on 1 July 2018

Vaughn, Stephen L. (ed.) (2009*) Encyclopedia of American Journalism*, New York and London: Routledge

Waugh, Evelyn (1938) *Scoop*, London: Chapman & Hall

6

JOHN TULLOCH

On the importance of mischief-making

Introduction

The writings of John Tulloch, former Head of the School of Journalism at the University of Lincoln, spanned a vast range of topics: the ethics of literary journalism, media history, Indian newspapers, the coverage of the 'war on terror', the film reviewing of George Orwell, ethics and the teaching of journalism and media studies, the 'witchifying' of Rebekah Brooks, the history of the links between hacks and cops – and so on. Serious topics, he approached often idiosyncratically but always with tremendous literary flair and moral engagement. This chapter, by a friend and colleague and so unapologetically affectionate, focuses on some of John's major preoccupations and his wonderfully original analyses. Moreover, there was a cheeky side to his personality and writings which this chapter aims to highlight and celebrate.

Remembering John as friend and colleague

When I left City University to become Professor of Journalism at the University of Lincoln in 2003 I was stepping into the unknown – but how lucky I was to work then alongside John for the last ten years of my full-time academic career. I could not have hoped for a better colleague. He was extremely supportive of my personal interests – such as peace journalism, investigative reporting, literary journalism, the alternative, activist media – and we spent many hours thrashing out ideas late at night in his Lincoln digs just a stone's throw away from the beautiful cathedral.

John could be shy and self-effacing in his relations with people. But he had a massive intellect; he was an extraordinary polymath: history, Indian culture, military aircraft, literature, music – from Bach to Bessie Smith and just about everything in between – the media, robots, the arts, politics, travel, second hand bookshops were a few of his obsessions. Just chatting to him was an education in itself. He estimated he had something like 20,000 books crammed into his north London home, university office and the terrace house he rented in Lincoln. But these books did not merely furnish the rooms: John had read them and more to the point he remembered what he had read. John was driven by an extraordinary curiosity about life. He was the quintessential journo: looking closely, witnessing with an ever critical, intelligent eye, curious about everything. I always remember as we went walking through the streets of say New Delhi, Paris or London he appeared to know the histories of every building we passed.

His writings and conference presentations over the years covered a vast range of subjects: peace journalism, Indian newspaper history, press regulation, media coverage of the US 'war on terror', the BBC; investigative reporting, literary journalism, journalism education to name but a few. He wrote beautifully: his prose was bubbling with original ideas and wit. He was able to mix subtle theory, even sections of quantitative analysis, with elegant references to some of the many books he had read. Take for instance, his *Ethical Space* review of Robert Fisk's *The Age of the Warrior: Selected Writings* (Tulloch 2009) in which the author serenades his cat: John took the opportunity to slip in mention of other literary cats – of Keats, Christopher Smart and Dr Johnson, for instance, complete with apt quotations, of course. John could even include the word 'bullshit' in an academic essay and make it appear both apt and profound.

His cheeky side

Indeed, there was a cheeky side to his personality that came out in his writings: while constantly critical of the 'dumbing down' of the media he always wanted to celebrate the tabloids for their mischief-making. So he was quick to challenge John Lloyd's stress on the need for 'responsible journalism' writing (Tulloch 2005: 5):

> Don't we need a less solemn vision of journalism that has some space for active mischief-making, and scepticism and suspicion of the motives of the powerful, even if some of that mischief is damaging even to the body politic. Is a perch at the *Financial Times* an appropriate place to preach about the role of journalism in English culture? Where is the space in Lloyd's world for the engaged, radical and fundamentally critical intelligence of a Paul Foot?

John's contribution to the 2012 annual conference of the Institute of Communication Ethics (ICE) was so typical of the man. Amidst all the avalanche of media coverage of the Leveson Inquiry into press practices and ethics, John picked on what he called the 'witchifying' of Rebekah Brooks – who may otherwise have been so easily passed over as a Murdoch crony not worth any sympathy or academic attention. So he read carefully from his script (Tulloch 2013: 4):

Last year, Rebekah Brooks positively willed herself to be my subject. She is, as many have seen fit to tell us, hard to resist. Not the Cotswold-living lady who rides retired police horses, or the tabloid editor and compulsive chum of celebrities. … But the woman in the middle of the bizarre process that seems to happen regularly, when for a short period, they become a subject of press interest, are objectified and, not to be too dainty about it, monstered.

He continued:

Apart from the too tempting opportunities for portentous moralising, her case is fascinating for what it can tell us about contemporary media culture, the persistence of class-based attitudes and a sexism so engrained into our public life as to appear 'natural', old boy.

Notice the vitality and wit, the subtle shifts of tone and register of John's prose. How elegantly it mixes subtle theorising, journalese and witty vernacular. All of this crammed into just a few score words. John saw the 'witchifying' of Brooks being given an 'elegant start signal' by Charlotte Harris, a prominent lawyer representing alleged victims of phone hacking who described her as looking 'a little bit Salem' on the BBC2's *Newsnight* (ibid). Thereafter, the witch image, along with 'Medusa' went viral – including the front cover of *Private Eye* 'that reliable barometer of the British media climate' (ibid: 5). Next, John cleverly and ironically debunks the BBC Edward Stourton's celebration of Brooks' 'mystery and seemingly superhuman cleverness' by listing in impeccable detail his all-too-conventional CV. He is clearly 'one of us' (ibid).

John would always be seen walking around the University of Lincoln with two newspapers tucked under his arm: the *Guardian* and the *Daily Mail*. 'You have to read the *Mail* to understand the real temperature of Middle England,' he would say. So the *Mail* story under the headline 'Rebekah Brooks, the schmoozer hated by Murdoch's wife and daughter' receives a typically robust Tulloch critique: 'Of course, what is playing with some nuance and sensitivity by Edward Stourton turns into an exercise in the bleedin' obvious in the coarser tones of the *Daily Mail*' (and notice there the perfect injection of the vernacular).

John's dedication to serious academic research was often reflected in the listings and detailed quantitative analyses he included in his papers and conference presentations. Indeed, as an administrator he was always confident handling all the business of budgets, figures and audits (which for others might appear tedious and daunting). Here he meticulously lists eight ancient myths and theories on which the 'witchifying' coverage drew: for instance, the witch's background is mysterious – sired perhaps by the Devil; the witch threatens the patriarchal system with her special abilities; men can't compete with her intuitive qualities – and so on (ibid: 5). He concludes so elegantly: 'Harmless tabloid fun? Maybe. A defining feature of British tabloid culture is its tendency to create objects of hatred by a process of dehumanisation and the routine evocation of "evil" as an explanatory tool.'

More original takes on Leveson

John's idiosyncratic approach to the Leveson Inquiry into the practices and ethics of the press (2011–2012) (essentially overblown theatre and pantomime for mainstream journos and politicians) further demonstrates his 'cheeky' side and his stress on the importance of tabloid mischief-making. Scandal surrounded the alleged corrupt relationship between journalists and the police. John simply looks at the history of police and press relations and concludes that 'the essentially comforting proposition in the academic literature on crime and the media that payments to police for information by the press have been comparatively rare' is a myth (Tulloch 2012a: 309). He continues:

> Few things are more tedious than the historian's reflex of 'Nothing new…' But it can be argued that this phenomenon goes back to the birth of the popular press and that we simply have no reliable evidence to assess its scale. What can be inferred is that crime news was one of the basic staples in the rise of the press in the early nineteenth century, along with gambling, sexual scandal and sport. Along with sport, crime was commodified (ibid: 311).

Returning to his beloved Dickens, he suggests that it is likely 'he made payments to favourite police officers, as well as publicly hosting parties for detectives in his offices'. Bringing the historical overview up-to-date, John highlights reports in the *Guardian, Camden New Journal* and *Daily Telegraph* that testify to the ubiquity of the corrupt culture. But he doesn't then go on to conclude with a tediously moralistic condemnation of the practice. His concern, instead, is that efforts to stamp out payments between hacks and cops could lead to the death of popular journalism.

> Indeed, defending freedom of the press may require us to argue that we might tolerate a moderate level of corrupt payments to insiders to enable crime to be reported, especially the crimes of the powerful in the wider public interest. It doesn't lend itself to transparency, or ethical puritanism and it doesn't exactly meet any Kantian test. … But it may be a price worth paying, compared to a *Crimewatch* press (ibid: 317).

On the ethics of journalism

John was a regular attender at the annual conferences of the Institute of Communication Ethics, was books reviewer for its quarterly journal *Ethical Space* and (during his final years when suffering from cancer) he was always there in an email or at the end of the phone line with some wise words of advice for the ICE executive group. Indeed, ethical concerns lay at the heart of all his writing and teaching. Like one of his heroes, George Orwell, he used book reviewing as a way of expounding his theories about life and journalism and everything. So on Anthony Feinstein's *Journalists under Fire: The Psychological Hazards of Covering War* he writes:

The concept of the journalist as emotionless 'filter', devoid of social context, history, ideology jumps up like a claymore mine. Damn such 'filters'. Surely the appropriate professional filter for journalists about conflicts within which we are enmired *is* paranoia about authority, empathy for the victims, and anger at the stupidity, historical illiteracy, ambition and greed which brought this to pass. Held together, of course, by a steely effort to construct credible 'facts'. Patrick Cockburn, Robert Fisk, John Pilger and Ghaith Abdul-Ahad spring to mind (Tulloch 2007a: 42).

In his essay, 'What moral universe are you from? Everyday tragedies and the ethics of press intrusion into grief' published in *Ethical Space* (Tulloch 2004: 29), he outlines four essential journalistic ethical approaches:

- Firstly: the journalism is a 'rough old trade' argument: journalists are special and should not be subject to ordinary ethical codes. The PCC Code is primarily a public relations exercise, a deal with the political class to buy off political pressures.
- Secondly: the 'virtuous journalist' argument. Journalists should be subject to ordinary ethical codes but virtuous behaviour can only be based on the operation of individual conscience.
- Thirdly: the 'cultural meliorism' argument. Voluntary codes can 'improve the culture of journalism' gradually via training and contracts.
- And finally: the 'structural determinism' argument. Codes and conscience will count for little in a newspaper industry run by media combines to maximise profit.

He concludes: 'My own prejudice would be to support the virtuous journalist argument but this is only feasible if journalists establish a right to refuse instructions that breach the code.'

On the ethics of literary journalism

John was one of the leading international theorists of literary journalism, co-editing two texts on the subject and writing on a range of writers. And in writing about Charles Dickens in a chapter for a book I co-edited, *The Journalistic Imagination: Literary Journalists from Defoe to Capote and Carter*, he articulates his profound belief in the cultural and political value of journalism as literature.

One obvious reason for the low status of English journalism has been its perceived lack of creative control by the author compared to the control allegedly associated with the 'artist'. Arguably one of the malign effects of Romanticism in English culture was to define the 'true' artist's status as not having a patron but a soulful relationship to the audience that precluded writing for anything as vulgar as the market. Certainly, the issues of creative control and his relationship to the mass audience tantalized Dickens (Tulloch 2007b: 60).

He goes on to celebrate Dickens's journalism (often marginalised by critics who focus more on his great novels) stressing its moral engagement (ibid: 63):

> Just as in his novels, his journalism continues to return to, and to rework, certain themes. The continuity is remarkable as the growth, and the *flâneur* of the early *Sketches* [*by Boz*] may be fanciful but is not lightweight. He is morally engaged and never a lizard-like transplant from the boulevards. The later wanderer of the city streets may be subject to existential doubts but he retains an essential whimsicality and wit.

Another of his heroes was George Orwell. And in the 'Introduction' to *Global literary Journalists: Exploring the Journalistic Imagination Vol. 1* which we co-edited, John is very concerned to highlight Orwell's own, brilliantly perceptive analysis of Dickens (Tulloch 2012b: 1–19). He looks at his face and comments (ibid: 9):

> Well, in the case of Dickens I see a face that is not quite the face of Dickens's photographs, though it resembles it. It is the face of a man of about forty, with a small beard and a high colour. He is laughing, with a touch of anger in his laughter, but no triumph, no malignity. It is the face of a man who is always fighting against something, but who fights in the open and is not frightened, the face of a man who is generously angry...

John next goes on to examine in some detail Orwell's (1931) extraordinary account of witnessing a hanging and in a few words explore complex issues relating to truth, honesty, trust and emotional veracity (ibid: 10):

> Trust in the veracity of the voice (thus eliminating any doubts that Orwell actually witnessed the hanging) derives from accurate, precise observation and an emotional response which remains completely appropriate in relation to the facts of the case. Honesty – and the trust we feel for this voice – is *in* those details (italics in the original).

And John's take on the endless disputes on the precise definition of literary journalism is typically drawn from a vast store of subtle, morally informed reading (the writing, as always, with a Dickensian *élan*, originality and vitality) (ibid: 7):

> On a value-free level, we might argue that, rather than a stable genre or family of genres, literary journalism defines a field where different traditions and practices of writing intersect, a disputed terrain within which various overlapping practices of writing – among them the journalistic column, the memoir, the sketch, the essay, travel narratives, life writing, 'true crime'

narratives, 'popular' history, cultural reflection and other modes of writing – camp uneasily, disputing their neighbors' barricades and patching up temporary alliances.

John used his exploration of the writings of Gordon Burn in the same volume to extend the study of what we termed 'the fuzzy boundaries between fiction and reportage' (Tulloch 2012d). For instance, in some of his journalistic interviews, Burn, 'rather than creating a spurious aroma of authenticity' uses them to emphasise

> the fragility of our sense of the real and how tenuous are the signifiers – the plausible manner, an accretion of well-observed detail, an untidy shape to the unfolding narrative – which we accept as separating that reality from 'fiction'. But as we walk on uncertain ground, we are immensely enlivened by the level of attention and thought this writer demands of us (ibid: 53).

Moreover, John returns to his fascination with Orwell in a collection of essays I edited – focusing this time (originally) on his war-time film reviewing for the magazine *Time and Tide* ('the vaguely right of centre periodical edited by the eccentric Margaret, Lady Rhonda') from 5 October 1940 to 23 August 1941 (Tulloch 2012c). With typical attention to quantitative detail, John provides a tabulated list of the 43 films reviewed, its director, principal actors, date of publication plus some additional comments (ibid: 87–95). He concludes:

> Orwell wrote his film reviews while he constructed some of his most memorable essays, struggled to earn a living from other occasional journalism, and sought a meaningful role in defeating Nazism. He shared in many of the standard prejudices of the Thirties intellectual against film – it was a mass art, machine-made by capitalism producing low-grade rubbish for working class consumption. It is unsurprising that his reviews are less than original in their approach to the medium. ... Nevertheless, they contain some valuable insights and embody a developing vision of the possibilities of film, both in its degraded form as a mass-produced mechanism for propaganda and escapism and an agency through which contrary, humane perceptions can be articulated (ibid: 98).

John himself had a kind of Orwellian ability to use literary criticism as a way of exploring some of the most profound and complex issues facing humanity. Take, for instance, his essay on the writings of Geoffrey Moorhouse (Tulloch 2014). Of course, John has read closely all 28 of Moorhouse's books. In tracing Moorhouse's preoccupations with place, fear, faith and identity, he quotes his 'deceptively simple' underlying philosophy and journalistic approach (ibid: 213): '... my own point of view is that we're all essentially like each other. We all suffer the same things, we all laugh at the same things, and we all have to recognise this interdependence.'

John suggests that it is 'easy to caricature as a windy concept of common humanity'. He continues, with profound insight:

> But for the journalist it implies a fundamental trajectory: an attempt in every narrative to uncover the human significance of experience in all its intricate complexity and detail. This is not the 'human interest' beloved of the popular journalist, where events can be crammed, to multiple deadlines, into a set of handy packages – a limited range of 'stories' with interchangeable elements designed to be easily forgotten, so that the next day's 'product' can take its place. Rather, it is an understanding of the meaning of human experience in time. This implies a form of journalism that we might describe as 'slow' – certainly observant, patient and considered. It implies a journalism that is sensitive to the individuality of place and culture.

In many respects, those words sum up John's own approach to journalism.

Confronting evil: Literature and investigative journalism

In one of his most original studies, John engages in a critical, comparative analysis of the writings of Gitta Sereny and Gordon Burn (Tulloch 2011: 316–333). In the case of Sereny, who covered the Nuremberg trials in 1945 for the *Daily Telegraph* and later wrote a book about the Holocaust, John sees her main approach as placing herself 'fully in the story as a moral, observing being' (ibid: 323). In the case of such monstrous acts normal journalistic objectivity is impossible.

> Instead, Sereny attempts to establish a direct relationship with the reader as a sort of moral guide or commentator who reports on her complex states of feeling as the narrative unwinds. This space allows Sereny to admit to feelings of shock and repugnance as she confronts the material but also to feelings of empathy for her subject.

Gordon Burn's book on the so-called 'Yorkshire Ripper', Peter Sutcliffe (convicted in 1981 of murdering 13 women and attempting to murder seven others), *Somebody's Husband, Somebody's Son* (1984), is the focus of John's study here. While the style of the book owes much to the Normal Mailer of the *Executioner's Song* in its deliberate narrative flatness,

> its principal feature is a dense mesh of interlocking quotes, presented in an ostensibly non-judgmental framework. Ostensibly because, as the narrative progresses, Burn's skilful use of the unspoken, and of significant juxtapositions, releases a wealth of possible explanations for the evolution of a person into a mass murderer (ibid: 327).

John concludes, arguing that the crucial distinction between Sereny and Burn is the presence or absence of the persona of the writer within the narrative frame.

> In his study of Sutcliffe, Burn is punctilious in keeping himself outside the frame of the story, utilising a variety of links between factual information and actuality from his family sources to keep the narrative going and establish a consistent flow of verifiability. In contrast, Sereny figures strongly as a narrator in a posture that asks us to invest much in her truthfulness and reliability (ibid: 329).

John clearly prefers Burn's journalistic strategy. Yet he is able to finish on these generous, profound and moving words: 'But if there is reason for doubt as to her techniques, there is no reason to doubt Sereny's passionate and risk-taking commitment to the complexity of issues of good and evil and of being human' (ibid: 330).

Ethics of the media coverage of the 'war on terror'

Some of John's most morally engaged and original writing focused on the media coverage of 'the war on terror'. His study of the reporting of 'extraordinary rendition' (Tulloch 2007c) is massively detailed, drawing on some 77 references and a wide range of theoretical perspectives and primary sources: such as the *Guardian*, *Sunday Times*, *New Statesman*, radio and television programmes on the BBC and Channel 4, the *Sun*, *News of the World*, *Daily Express*, *Washington Post*, *Le Monde Diplomatique*. But beyond all the 'noise' of all the international mainstream media coverage, John perceives its many limitations (ibid: 37):

> Against the optimistic account of rendition as a triumph of journalistic exposure, it can be argued that most of what passed for investigative journalism in the uncovering of extraordinary rendition was questionable in originality of its research and in its relation to powerholders. ... In addition, it can be argued that much journalism was:
>
> - indebted to heavy and self-interested briefing by unnamed intelligence sources;
> - looked investigative but was heavily dependent on the painstaking research of a large band of human rights NGOs, academics and lawyers;
> - recycled stories of a handful of 'innocent' rendees and the efforts of their defence lawyers;
> - worked from the basis that the use of illegal methods and torture was essentially an 'extraordinary' departure by the authorities from civilised behaviour.

While critical of the overall reporting of rendition, John still admired enormously some of the brave journalists who specialised in the area – one of them being the freelance Stephen Grey whom John was at pains to interview (on 14 July 2006) for the academic quarterly *Journalism* (Tulloch 2007d). And while John was at home in the many esoteric theoretical debates in communication studies, the practicalities of the job never ceased to enthral him. Thus, in chatting to Grey it is the precise processes by which he arrived at his exclusive, involving a substantial degree of co-operation with European and American colleagues that fascinate him.

On ethics and the teaching of journalism

Ethics also lay at the heart of John's promotion over many years of journalism and media studies as academic disciplines. As far back as 1996, in the wake of an outburst of Fleet Street and Jeremy Paxman attacks on media studies, he writes:

> Media studies is not a discipline it itself but a field where a number of other disciplines meet – among them history, politics, economy, sociology and law. Far from being 'incoherent' in Paxman's ignorant formulation, this field is a key meeting place to gain an understanding of the forces which shape our lives. Mediawork is strong in all the fashionable transferable skills – teamwork, self-presentation, research, negotiation, communicating with different audiences – that we are asked to value in higher education (Tulloch 1996: 31).

On the Westminster part-time Master's in Journalism Studies, he said: 'We hope the theory provides a critique of current journalism and a forum for the discussion of ethical and political issues, encouraging students to be aware of the potential consequences of their activity.'

Having just arrived to head the journalism school at the University of Lincoln in 2004, John takes the opportunity of a feature in *Media Education Journal* (2005), being edited by Des Murphy, to outline, inspirationally, his seven wonderfully apt principles for journalism teaching. For instance,

1. it should provide 'a thorough and critical understanding of the political context in which journalism happens and, in particular, a sustained scrutiny of the relationship between journalism and the state';
2. it should 'promote a critical understanding of the history, politics and philosophy of human rights in the UK and around the world';
3. explores 'critically the available models of journalism and ground them in a factually based historical and social narrative';
4. values 'models of journalism and journalistic enterprise that are local, community-based, or otherwise non-metropolitan';
5. explores 'the conditions under which news media can have a meaningful understanding of and relationship with their audiences which is not merely manipulative nor profit driven';

6. avoids 'the condescension of the academy in exploring the various modes of popular journalism, and devises ways of meaningfully discriminating between positive and negative practices';
7. debates with students 'the proposition that the highest function of journalism is not entertainment but to tell truth to power' (ibid: 5).

Indeed, John played a crucial role in the development of journalism education in the UK and internationally over the last 40 years. Under his leadership from 2004 to 2012, the Lincoln School of Journalism rose to being one of the leading schools in the country, launching, for instance, innovative Master's programmes in peace journalism, science and arts journalism and the country's only BA in investigative journalism. He also played a crucial role in building up the LSJ's close links with the internationally acclaimed investigative journalist John Pilger. Significantly, when Pilger was awarded the Grierson Trust's Lifetime Achievement Award in 2011, he asked John Tulloch to give the welcome speech, which was much acclaimed. John Pilger commented: 'Whereas journalism is taught competently elsewhere, it was invested with its due ethical and inspirational quality by John Tulloch – both at Lincoln and abroad.'

Conclusion

John was very much part of the John Mair/Keeble book factory system (with the publishers Abramis, of Bury St Edmunds) which has produced many books over recent years. For John, it meant bashing out massively referenced chapters to very short deadlines – often late into the night. Significantly Ian Sinclair, the *Morning Star* and *Tribune* reviewer, always singled out John's chapters for special praise (see, for instance, http://www.tribu nemagazine.org/2012/09/power-prerogative-of-the-harlot-through-the-ages/).

And that was not surprising. Whether writing on trust in the media (for instance, see Tulloch 2008), or the ability of literary journalists such as Charles Dickens, George Orwell, Geoffrey Moorhouse, Gitta Sereny and Gordon Burn to confront some of the major dilemmas in being human, or on US and UK newspaper's coverage of torture and rendition John was always original and insightful – and so often exuberant and witty. His prose – the fruit of years of reading, reflection and pedagogic commitment – now lives on to remind us of his genius.

Acknowledgements

This chapter is based on a paper with the same title in *Ethical Space: The International Journal of Communication Ethics*, Vol. 12, No. 1 pp 23–29.

References

Orwell, George (1931) A hanging, *Adelphi*, August. Available online at https://www. orwellfoundation.com/the-orwell-foundation/orwell/essays-and-other-works/a-ha nging/, accessed on 12 June 2019

Tulloch, John (1996) Universities challenged, *20/20: The National Magazine for Photography and Media Education*, No. 4 pp 3–32

Tulloch, John (2004) 'What moral universe are you from?' Everyday tragedies and the ethics of press intrusion into grief, *Ethical Space: The International Journal of Communication Ethics*, Vol. 1, No. 3 pp 25–30

Tulloch, John (2005) Journalism: The myth of trust, *Media Education Journal*, No. 36 pp 4–5

Tulloch, John (2007a) Review of *Journalists under Fire: The Psychological Hazards of Covering War*, by Anthony Feinstein, *Ethical Space: The International Journal of Communication Ethics*, Vol. 4, No. 3 pp 41–42

Tulloch, John (2007b) Charles Dickens and the voices of journalism, Keeble, Richard and Wheeler, Sharon (eds) *The Journalistic Imagination: Literary Journalists from Defoe to Capote and Carter*, London: Routledge pp 58–73

Tulloch, John (2007c) Exploring legal black holes: Extraordinary rendition, investigative journalism and the moral imagination, Maltby, Sarah and Keeble, Richard (eds) *Communicating War: Memory, Media and Military*, Bury St Edmunds: Abramis pp 29–41

Tulloch, John (2007d) Hunting ghost planes: An interview with journalist Stephen Grey, *Journalism*, Vol. 8, No. 5 pp 493–498

Tulloch, John (2008) Picnics on Vesuvius: The media and the problem of trust, Mair, John and Keeble, Richard Lance (eds) *Beyond Trust: Hype and Hope in the British Media*, Bury St Edmunds: Abramispp 95–106

Tulloch, John (2009) Review of *The Age of the Warrior*, by Robert Fisk, *Ethical Space: The International Journal of Communication Ethics*, Vol. 6, No. 1 pp 54–56

Tulloch, John (2011) Confronting evil: Literature and investigative journalism, Mair, John and Keeble, Richard Lance (eds) *Investigative journalism: Dead or Alive?*, Bury St Edmunds: Abramis pp 318–333

Tulloch, John (2012a) 'The man believed to be a journalist, was arrested': Journalism, bribery and the detective police, Keeble, Richard Lance and Mair, John (eds) *The Phone Hacking Scandal: Journalism on Trial*, Bury St Edmunds: Abramis pp 308–320

Tulloch, John (2012b) Introduction – Mind the gap: On the fuzzy boundaries between the literary and the journalistic, Keeble, Richard Lance and Tulloch, John (eds) *Global literary journalism: Exploring the Journalistic Imagination*, New York: Peter Lang pp 1–22

Tulloch, John (2012c) Sceptic in the palace of dreams: Orwell as film reviewer, Keeble, Richard Lance (ed.) *Orwell Today*, Bury St Edmunds: Abramis pp 79–101

Tulloch, John (2012d) Journalism as a novel: The novel as journalism – The writing of Gordon Burn, Keeble, Richard Lance and Tulloch, John (eds) *Global Literary Journalism: Exploring the Journalistic Imagination*, Vol. 1, New York: Peter Lang pp 39–56

Tulloch, John (2013) 'A little bit of Salem': Rebekah Brooks, of News International, and the construction of a modern witch, *Ethical Space: The International Journal of Communication Ethics*, Vol. 10, No. 1 pp 4–7

Tulloch, John (2014) Journalism, imagination and the art of fact: The work of Geoffrey Moorhouse, Keeble, Richard Lance and Tulloch, John (eds) *Global Literary Journalism: Exploring the Journalistic Imagination*, Vol. 2, New York: Peter Lang pp 201–216

PART III

War, peace and the press: Yesterday and today

7

INFORMATION WARFARE IN AN AGE OF HYPER-MILITARISM

> The daily press and the telegraph, which in a moment spread inventions over the whole earth, fabricate more myths ... in one day than could have formerly been done in a century.
>
> *Karl Marx (1871)*

There was no war in the Gulf in 2003. Rather, a myth of heroic, spectacular warfare was manufactured, in large part, as a desperate measure to help provide a *raison d'être* for the (increasingly out-of-control) military–industrial complexes in the US and UK – and to hide the reality of a rout of a hopelessly overwhelmed 'enemy' army. The links between mainstream journalists and the intelligence services are crucial factors in the manufacture of the myth. But it is not essentially a massive elite conspiracy. Rather, the myth's origins lie deep within complex military, historical, ideological, and political forces which it is crucial to identify. Moreover, the manufacture of the 'war' myth has profound implications for any study of the political and military origins of the conflict and press representations.

The war problematic

The US/UK invasion was supposedly over Iraq's Weapons of Mass Destruction (WMD) – yet none were ever found. US and UK jets had been bombing Iraqi targets regularly since the end of the 1991 conflict so there was no clear start to the conflict. And with the president of the defeated state melting away into thin air there was no clear end. Casualties on both sides mounted as hostilities continued after the end of the so-called war. Thus the bombing of Baghdad on 20 March 2003 became the manufactured 'start' of the 'war' narrative; and there were two contrived endings: the symbolic toppling of the Saddam statue before the world's media on 9 April and the statement by President Bush before a gathering of US troops on 1 May that the 'major combat operations' were over.

The 'greatest battles since World War II' were predicted and celebrated in the press, just as during the 1991 Gulf conflict. But again there was no real warfare: no credible enemy. In a matter of days the world's mightiest military power inevitably crushed a ragtag army of conscripts and no-hopers. As defence expert John Keegan (2003) commented in the *Daily Telegraph* of 8 April: 'In truth, there has been almost no check to the unimpeded onrush of the coalition, particularly the dramatic American advance to Baghdad: nor have there been any major battles. This has been a collapse, not a war.' Agence France-Presse (AFP) photographer Cris Reeves, with the US marines, saw hardly any action at all. 'It was like two weeks of camping for me with 20-year-old marines. I was 48 so I was exhausted' (Guillot 2003).

War is about killing. We know precisely how many Americans and British soldiers died. Some 115 US troops were killed in combat and 23 in accidents and so-called friendly-fire incidents (though from 1 May to 1 November 2003 the toll was 221 as the 'war' dragged on); 19 British troops died in combat with 25 killed in 'non-hostile situations' (Beaumont and Graham 2003). All of these casualties were profiled and listed in 'rolls of honour' in the mainstream press (Epstein 2003). According to John Pilger (2003), as many as 10,000 Iraqi civilians were killed during the invasion – with thousands more injured. But the precise figure of how many thousands of Iraqis perished, were maimed or psychologically damaged (in the lead-up to the invasion, during the invasion, and in the aftermath) we will never know. So silence shrouds the essential horror.

The war's most heroic story, the saving of Private Jessica Lynch, turned out to be a completely manufactured drama (Kampfner 2003) while a Sky News 'exclusive' about a cruise missile launch from a Royal Navy submarine proved to be a hoax. The outrageous victory claims of the Iraqi minister of information, Mohammed Saeed al-Sahhaf (dubbed 'Comical Ali' by the Western media), as US troops captured Baghdad airport were only matched, given the scale of the slaughter, by the US/UK's fantastic claims over their supposedly precise weapons (Mayrhofer 2003).

The controversial comment of the French postmodern theorist, Jean Baudrillard (1991), about the 1991 Gulf conflict – 'there was no war'– appears equally relevant to the 2003 conflict. The mainstream media, in effect, manufactured the myth of war. Jack Lule (2002: 277) argues that myth is best understood as 'a societal story that expresses prevailing ideas, ideologies, values and belief'. Accordingly, a tidy narrative of quick and relatively easy 'warfare' (built around myths of national glory, macho heroism, monstrous villainy and 'precision weaponry') was manufactured in the British mainstream press while the reality was an illegal, unnecessary assertion of brute force (Mailer 2003).

Militarism 'out of control'

The war myth emerges from the fact that the force deployed by the US and UK bears no relation to the threat posed. The US and UK are essentially fighting phantoms of their own making: thus the threats are grossly exaggerated, fictionalised. The US budget plans for 2004 incorporated defence spending of more than $400 billion (alongside a record White House deficit of $455 billion) – and that did not include the extra billions expected for the occupation of Iraq. This represents more than all the military spending of the rest of the world and more than twice the spending of the next 15 of the world's powers. Moreover, the US has military bases in three-quarters of the countries of the world and 31 per cent of all wealth. Robert Harvey (2003: 13–36) talks of the 'United States of the World'. This is a military colossus (backed by the UK) of a kind never before seen since the Roman empire. As the late historian E. P. Thompson (1982) argued, there is a technological imperative driving the US and UK towards warfare and testing new military systems.

The boom in military spending, begun during the Korean War years of the 1950s, continued relentlessly during the Cold War. By 1990, more than 30,000 US companies were engaged in military production, roughly 3,275,000 jobs were in the defence industries and 70 per cent of all money spent on research and development was directed at defence work (Drucker 1993: 126). With the demise of the Soviet Union, the United States became desperate in its search for new enemies (Keeble 1997). Grenada (1983); Libya (1986); Panama (1989); Iraq (1991, 1993, 1998 and 2003); Somalia (1992–1993); Serbia (1999) (Hammond and Herman 2000); and Afghanistan (2001) were all puny powers rapidly crushed by the overwhelming firepower of the American colossus in a series of manufactured, media-hyped militarist adventures (Webster 2003).

In the UK, the arms industry at the turn of the century was worth more than £5 billion a year, amounting to 20 per cent of global weapons sales. It employed up to 150,000 people, the UK standing as the world's second largest manufacturer after the US with 32 per cent of the market. Yet arms deals remain remote from public scrutiny, being run by the Defence Export Services Organisation, 'a secretive group within the Ministry of Defence, controlled by the arms companies themselves and with a history of actively conniving at bribery' (Leigh 2003).

Thus the US/UK responses to the September 11 attacks, with the launch of the endless 'war on terrorism', the attacks on Afghanistan and Iraq, and the threats to the 'rogue' states, Syria, Iran, and North Korea, were not distinctly new strategies but accelerating long-standing strategies of military imperial adventurism (Curtis 2003a, 2003b). Al-Qaeda, blamed for the 11 September atrocities and a series of later attacks on Western interests, was a shadowy, elusive grouping against whom traditional, war fighting strategies (involving major battle confrontations) were inappropriate. And so the US/UK were left manufacturing a spectacle of traditional 'warfare'. As US novelist Don DeLillo comments:

I'm almost prepared to believe that the secret drive behind our eagerness to enter this war is technology itself – that has a will to be realised. And that the administration is essentially a Cold War administration looking for a clearly defined enemy which was not the case after September 11. Now there is a territorial entity with borders and soldiers in uniform.[1]

Moreover, given the integration of the media industries' interests with those of the military industrial complex and the importance of the media's role in supporting the state's militarism, it is worth identifying the media–military–industrial complex as another factor behind the manufacture of the 'war' myth (Keeble 1997: 26; McChesney 2002).

Secrecy feeds the myth-making

Secrecy also feeds the myth-making. Alongside the 'democratic' state in both the US and UK there exists a secret and highly centralised state occupied by the massively over-resourced intelligence and security services (MI5, MI6 and GCHQ, the Cheltenham-based signals spying centre), secret armies, and undercover police units. Since the 1980s a raft of legislation, such as the Official Secrets Act, the Regulation of Investigatory Powers Act, the Anti-Terrorism, Crime and Security Act 2001, has reinforced their growing powers (Morgan 2003). Mark Almond (2003), lecturer in modern history at Oriel College, Oxford, stresses the extent to which intelligence had reached into the heart of the Blair government:

> More than any predecessor, Blair has relied on a kitchen cabinet in Downing Street but one made up of a cabal of diplomats and intelligence officials rather than ambitious, if unelected party apparatchiks. Hence the focus on globalisation rather than domestic issues. Blair has liberated British politics from the influence of politicians.

Professor David Beetham (2003) similarly highlights the 'secret, warfare' state which had totally undermined the democratic system. But examining the activities of the intelligence services remains incredibly difficult.

Spooks and hacks: Close encounters of a strange kind

While it might be difficult to identify precisely the impact of the spooks (variously represented in the press as 'intelligence', 'security', 'Whitehall' or 'Home Office' sources) on mainstream politics and media, from the limited evidence it looks to be enormous. As Roy Greenslade, media specialist at the *Guardian*, comments: 'Most tabloid newspapers – or even newspapers in general – are playthings of MI5.'[2] Bloch and Fitzgerald (1983: 134–141) report the editor of 'one of Britain's most distinguished journals' as believing that more than half its foreign correspondents were on the MI6 payroll. In 1991, Richard Norton-Taylor revealed in the

Guardian that 500 prominent Britons paid by the CIA and the now defunct Bank of Commerce and Credit International, included 90 journalists (Pilger 1998: 496).

In their analysis of the contemporary secret state, Dorril and Ramsay (1991: x–xi) give the media a crucial role. The heart of the secret state they identify as the security services, the cabinet office and upper echelons of the Home and Commonwealth Offices, the armed forces and Ministry of Defence, the nuclear power industry and its satellite ministries, together with a network of senior civil servants. As 'satellites' of the secret state, their list includes 'agents of influence in the media, ranging from actual agents of the security services, conduits of official leaks, to senior journalists merely lusting after official praise and, perhaps, a knighthood at the end of their career'.

Following the passing of the 1989 Security Service Act, links between the media and MI5 and MI6 grew closer, according to James Adams (1994: 94–98). Phillip Knightley, author of a seminal history of the intelligence services, even claims that at least one intelligence agent is working on every Fleet Street newspaper.[3] During the controversy that erupted following the end of the 'war' and the death of the arms inspector Dr David Kelly (and the ensuing Hutton Inquiry) the spotlight fell on BBC reporter Andrew Gilligan and the claim by one of his sources that the government (in collusion with the intelligence services) had 'sexed up' a dossier justifying an attack on Iraq. The Hutton Inquiry, its every twist and turn massively covered in the mainstream media, was the archetypal media spectacle that drew attention from the real issue: why did the Bush and Blair governments invade Iraq in the face of massive global opposition? But those facts will be forever secret. Moreover while the Gilligan affair might appear to have reinforced the liberal notion of adversarial state-media relations, in fact, as Rogers (1997: 64) argues, 'this focus obscures the extent to which the media have actually supported and colluded with the secret state'. Significantly, the broader and more significant issue of mainstream journalists' links with the intelligence services was ignored by the inquiry.

During the Hutton period, a myth emerged that the 2003 invasion of Iraq was the first conflict to be justified on (dodgy) evidence supplied by the intelligence services. Yet even during the Vietnam conflict, intelligence on the strength of the Vietcong was faked to make the case for war more plausible (Ramsay 2003). Similarly, the US attack on Libya in 1986 – deliberately aimed to effect 'regime change' by assassinating President Gaddafi – was justified by President Reagan on dubious intelligence (dutifully reported in the mainstream media) of Libyan responsibility for the bombing of a disco in West Berlin, frequented by US servicemen. Intelligence misinformation before the 1991 Gulf massacres constantly 'over-sexed' Iraq's alleged nuclear capability since opinion polls in the States showed fears of President Saddam Hussein as a 'nuclear monster' were most likely to win support for the military option (Reich 2002). Even during the 1991 Iraqi conflict much of the reporting was based on intelligence-driven disinformation. For instance, while Iraqi soldiers were deserting in droves and succumbing to one massacre after another, all the British media highlighted intelligence predictions of the 'largest ground battle since the Second World War'. Images of enormous berms, sophisticated Iraqi defences and trenches of burning oil filled the media. But in the end there was nothing more than a 100-hour rout. Colin Powell, in his account of the 1991 war, estimated that 250,000 Iraqi soldiers were eliminated (Powell 1995).

Similarly immediately following the September 11 atrocities in the United States, the London- based mainstream media were awash with intelligence-inspired leaks stressing the dangers of terrorist attacks in Britain. Even the *Independent*, most critical of the US/UK rush to military action, gave credibility to dubious 'intelligence' sources. On 16 September 2001, for instance, Lashmar and Blackhurst reported that at least three terrorist cells linked to Osama bin Laden were at large in Britain. An 'intelligence source' is quoted as saying: 'There is no reason why what happened in America couldn't happen in Britain or any European country.' But how much is fiction? (Bright 2002). Similarly in September 2002 the *Daily Express* was awash in intelligence-inspired scare stories. 'Nuclear attack in just months,' it thundered on 9 September; 'Anthrax threat on our streets: Britain on alert for Saddam suicide squads' it reported the next day. A climate of fear is manufactured allowing the apparatus of the national security state (surveillance cameras, email snooping, arrest without trials and the demonisation of asylum seekers) to expand. On 15 September 2002, drawing on intelligence disinformation linking Iraq to nuclear weapons, the *Sunday Express* editorialised: 'War brings evil but we believe the country must not be frightened from doing what we pray will save the world from the greater evil of nuclear bombs. We see no alternative but to help demolish the Iraqi regime.' On 18 March 2003, before the major air assault on Baghdad began, the *Sun* typically reported: 'According to intelligence reports Republican Guard units have been equipped with chemical warfare shells to make a desperate last stand south of Baghdad. A source said: "They clearly have given some chemical capability to some forces."'

On 2 April, the *Sun* 'revealed' that Saddam Hussein had issued a coded chemical attack on US/UK troops. Coalition intelligence chiefs, it reported, interpreted a reference to 'catching breath' in a speech by Saddam Hussein 'as a signal for lethal chemicals or nerve gas to be unleashed against US forces massing south west of Baghdad'. There were similar reports throughout the mainstream press.

Intelligence, hyper myth and the epistemological implications

The problem with intelligence is that it can never be double-checked. By definition, it remains secret and exclusive. It could all be fiction (and often is). All too often journalists are seduced by the attractions of secret exclusive information. When politicians further doctor the evidence from the intelligence services, as appears to have happened before the Iraqi conflict, for their own warmongering purposes (with the creation of a new intelligence agency, the Office of Special Plans, by US Defense Secretary Donald Rumsfeld, to manufacture evidence of Iraqi possession of WMD) we have entered the realm of hyper myth. As Dorril (2003: 4) comments:

The reality is that intelligence is the area in which ministers, and the MI6 info ops staff behind them can say anything they like and get away with it. Intelligence with its psychological invite to a secret world and with its unique avoidance of verification, is the ideal means for flattering and deceiving journalists.

The former Foreign Secretary, Lord Howe, told the Scott arms-to-Iraq Inquiry (1992–1996):

In my early days I was naïve enough to get excited about intelligence reports. Many look, at first sight, to be important and interesting and significant and then when we check them they are not even straws in the wind. They are cornflakes in the wind (Norton-Taylor 2003).

Another problem with intelligence is that anyone attempting to highlight its significance is accused of lacking academic rigour and promoting 'conspiracy theory'. Certainly underlying the myth of 'warfare' lie complex cultural, military and ideological forces. But given the close links between politicians, journalists and the intelligence services some conspiratorial elements have to be acknowledged to be behind the mainstream media's coverage of the Iraqi crisis.

With the emphasis on intelligence, the focus of journalism shifts from objective, verifiable 'facts' to myth: in effect, there is a crucial epistemological shift. As General Richard Myers, chairman of the Joint Chiefs of Staff, admits: 'Intelligence doesn't mean something is true. You know, it's your best estimate of the situation. It doesn't mean it's a fact. I mean, that's not what intelligence is' (Stephen 2003). Similarly, the historian Timothy Garton Ash (2003) stresses: 'The trend in journalism as in politics, and probably now in the political use of intelligence, is away from the facts and towards a neo-Orwellian world of manufactured reality.' The assumption of Iraq possessing WMD was based entirely on unverifiable intelligence reports as is so much of the reporting of the 'war on terror'.

The crucial role of embedded journalists in the manufacture of the 'war' myth

Most of US/UK imperialism advances essentially in secret. Both countries have deployed forces virtually every year since 1945 – most of them away from the glare of the media (Peak 1982). But at various moments the US/UK chooses to fight overt, manufactured 'wars'. We, the viewers and readers, have to see the spectacle. It has to appear 'real'. During the first Gulf 'war', the pooling system was used to keep correspondents away from the action (Keeble 1997: 109–126; McLaughlin 2002: 88–93). And since most of the action was conducted over the 42 days from the air, with journalists denied access to planes, the reality of the horror was kept secret.

In contrast, during the 2003 conflict, journalists were given remarkable access to the 'frontlines'. And those frontline images and reports from journalists who were clearly risking their lives, aimed to seduce the viewer/reader with their facticity; the correspondents were amazed at their 'objectivity'. Yet beyond the view of the camera and the journalist's eye-witness, with the war unproblematised, the essential simulated, mythical nature of the conflict lies all the more subtly and effectively hidden. Moreover, military censorship regimes always serve essentially symbolic purposes – expressing the arbitrary power of the army over the conduct and representation of 'war'.

Significantly Defence Minister Geoff Hoon claimed: 'I think the coverage ... is more graphic, more real than any other coverage we have ever seen of a conflict.' Most of the critical mainstream coverage highlighted the information overload. But, as David Miller (2003) commented: 'It is certainly true to say that it is new to see footage of war so up-close but it is a key part of the propaganda war to claim that this makes it "real".'

Some 600 US and 128 UK journalists, including journalists from the *Western Daily Press, Scotsman, Manchester Evening News, Ipswich Evening Star* and *Eastern Daily Press*, and one from the music network MTV, were 'embedded' with military units. According to Phillip Knightley (2003):

> The idea was copied from the British system in World War I when six correspondents embedded with the army on the Western front produced the worst reporting of just about any war and were all knighted for their services. One of them, Sir Phillip Gibbs, had the honesty, when the war was over, to write: 'We identified ourselves absolutely with the armies in the field.' The modern embeds, too, soon lost all distinction between warrior and correspondent and wrote and talked about 'we' with boring repetition.

As *The Times* media commentator, Brian MacArthur (2003), reported: 'Embeds inevitably became adjuncts to the forces.' Audrey Gillan, with the Household Cavalry for the *Guardian*, was one of the few to accuse the military of censorship. She reported that soldiers complained of being like mushrooms – kept in the dark with you know what shovelled on top of them – but she could not use this phrase for fear of upsetting the brigade HQ (ibid).

Some 5,000 journalists were in the Gulf region to cover the hostilities. Two thousand were in Kuwait and on ships with the US and UK naval task forces in the Arabian Gulf; 290 were in Baghdad; 900 in northern Iraq with Kurdish fighters: the rest were in Jordan, Iran, Bahrain and at the Allied Central Command in Doha, Qatar (Milmo 2003). Here there was little consistent challenge to the dominant military agenda. On one occasion *New York* magazine writer Michael Wolff (2003) dared to break ranks and ask the provocative questions: 'Why are we here? Why should we stay? What's the value of what we're learning at this million-dollar press centre?' He was soon to pay the price for his daring. Fox TV attacked him for lacking patriotism and after right-wing commentator

Rush Limbaugh gave out his email address, in one day Wolff received 3,000 hate messages. Unprecedented access to the 'front lines' was the carrot, but the stick was always on hand. Fifteen non-Iraqi journalists were killed, two went missing and many unilateral non-embeds were intimidated by the military. Had there been the same death rate for journalists during the Vietnam war, there would have been 3,000 killed.[4]

As John Donvan (2003) argues, 'coalition forces saw unilaterals as having no business on their battlefield'. Unilateral Terry Lloyd, of ITN, was killed by Marines who fired at his car; Reuters camera operator Taras Protsyuk and José Couso, a cameraman for the Spanish television channel Telecino, died after an American tank fired at the fifteenth floor of the Palestine hotel in Baghdad while Tarek Ayoub, a cameraman for Al-Jazeera, died after a US jet bombed the channel's Baghdad office. Two journalists working for RTP Portuguese television, Luis Castro and Victor Silva, were held for four days, had their equipment, vehicle and video tapes confiscated and were then escorted out of Iraq by the 101st Airborne Division. How many Iraqi journalists perished in the slaughters we will never know. For most of the Western mainstream media they are non-people.

The nature of the Fleet Street consensus

For the 1991 conflict all Fleet Street newspapers backed the military response together with 95 per cent of columnists. For the 1993 and 1998 attacks on Iraq the consensus fractured with the *Guardian, Independent*, and *Express* coming out against the attacks. Then for the Nato attacks on Serbia in 1999 virtually all of Fleet Street backed the action, even calling for the deployment of ground troops (which not even the generals dared adopt as policy). There was one exception – the *Independent on Sunday* – and its editor, Kim Fletcher, left the paper just weeks after the end of the conflict. But there was far more debate among columnists. A survey I conducted showed 33 out of 99 prominent columnists opposed military action against Serbia. For the attacks on Afghanistan and the toppling of the Taliban in 2001, the whole of Fleet Street backed the action – but again there was a wide-ranging debate among columnists and letter writers (Keeble 2001).

In 2003, with significant opposition to the rush to war being expressed by politicians, lawyers, intelligence agents, celebrities, religious leaders, charities and human rights campaigners – together with massive street protests – both nationally and internationally, the breakdown in Fleet Street's consensus was inevitable. Yet still for the invasion of Iraq, the majority of Fleet Street backed the action (though columnists and letter writers were divided). The *Independents* (the daily and Sunday), carrying prominently the dissident views of foreign correspondent Robert Fisk, were the most hostile. Following the massive global street protests on 15 February, the *Independent on Sunday* editorialised: 'Millions show this is a war that mustn't happen.'

The *Guardian* did not criticise military action on principle but opposed the US/ UK rush to war and promoted a wide range of critical opinions. The *Mirror*s were also 'anti' in the run-up to the conflict (perhaps more for marketing reasons since the Murdoch press was always going to be firmly for the invasion) with the veteran dissident campaigning journalists John Pilger and Paul Foot given prominent coverage. But then, after editor-in-chief Piers Morgan claimed his newspaper's stance attracted thousands of protesting letters from readers, their opposition softened. And the *Mail*s managed to stand on the fence mixing both criticism of the rush to military action with fervent patriotic support for the troops during the conflict.

The demonisation of 'Saddam'

The media's focus on the 'monstrous', 'evil', global power of Saddam Hussein was from 1990 until his death in December 2006 an essential ingredient of the propaganda strategy to manufacture a credible enemy. The Iraqi president was clearly an appalling dictator – as critics had stressed since the 1970s (though the CIA played significant roles in the two coups that brought Hussein's Ba'athists to power in 1963 and 1968). But in the 1980s, when Iraq was closely allied to the West during its eight-year war with Iran, Fleet Street's coverage of Hussein was rare and generally positive. Even the reporting of the chemical bombing of Kurds in Halabja on 16 March 1988 was notable for its restraint. And the Iranians, not 'Saddam' were blamed (Casey 2003).

The demonisation of 'new Hitler', 'madman', 'monster' Saddam, the 'butcher of Baghdad' only began in earnest following the Iraqi invasion of Kuwait in August 1990. And this hyper-personalisation of the conflict remained a constant feature of the press coverage – even in newspapers critical of the US attacks of 1993, 1996, 1998 and 2003. It served to simplify an enormously complex history and direct all blame at one man.

During the 1991 massacres, Fleet Street constantly focused on Iraq's army as being '1 million-strong', the 'fourth largest in the world', 'full of battle-hardened fanatics' following the 1980–1988 war with Iran. In reality, the Iraqi army was war-weary, full of bare-footed conscripts desperate to surrender, and quickly destroyed in a massive 42-day assault. In this context, the stress on 'global terrorist' Saddam in the propaganda was crucial in the manufacture of the credible enemy (Keeble 1998).

By 2003, Iraq was a completely dysfunctional state, destroyed following more than a decade of UN sanctions and constant weekly bombings by the US/UK – hardly covered in the mainstream media – and with a profoundly unpopular regime. Thus, the focus on the demonised personality of 'Saddam' throughout the media was all the more important in the creation of the war myth. On 19 March, as Iraqis prepared to defend Baghdad, the *Sun* reported on Saddam Hussein: 'Fiend to unleash poisons.' Another report described him as a 'monster'. The following day the *Sun* reported Lt Tim Collins calling for 'Our boys to "rock the world" of Saddam's evil diehards.' Saddam was planning to poison Iraq's water system 'as a last act of savagery'. In the *Daily Star* of 28 March, the Iraqi president was described as 'an evil dictator', a 'brutal tyrant' while an unnamed military source is quoted as saying: 'There appear no depths to which Hussein will not stoop.' As the US troops approached Baghdad, on 4 April, the *Mirror* framed its coverage entirely around the personality of 'tyrant' Saddam. 'What will he do?' asked its front page headline. 'As US troops reach Baghdad, the world waits for Saddam to play his final, despotic card.' Significantly, the *Mail*'s logo for its coverage of the conflict was 'War on Saddam'. On 30 March, the *Sunday Telegraph* editorialised, highlighting his unique barbarism:

> Saddam's record means that the coalition forces must be ready for anything. This, after all, is a dictator who planned during the last Gulf War to chain American PoWs to the front of his tanks; a murderer who – uniquely in the history of depravity – has turned chemical weapons on his own people.

On 20 March, Julian Borger, in the *Guardian*, grappled with the contradictions. On the one hand, he reports: 'In terms of technology and sheer might, this coming conflict is likely to be one of the most unequal in history.' Yet, to reaffirm the myth of war, there is always the Saddam demonisation card to play. So Borger continues: 'But the Iraqi leader's proven readiness to embrace desperate and unconventional measures makes him potentially a far more dangerous foe than any the Pentagon has taken on in recent years.'

Significantly, the *Observer*, in outlining its support for military action in its leader of 19 January, frames its entire argument around the demonised personality of 'Saddam'. First it refers to the 'nature of Saddam Hussein's regime and the call by many Iraqi exiles and dissidents for him to be overthrown'. The war is not about oil. 'For the second motive for displacing Saddam is the danger he poses to the wider world.' And it concludes: 'If Saddam does not yield military action may eventually be the least awful necessity for Iraq.'

The manufacture of the precise, clean, humanitarian war

Central to the manufacture of the war myth is its representation as clean, precise and humanitarian. All the US/UK overt major military interventions since Vietnam, up to 2003 were largely risk-free, taking less than 1,000 US troops' lives. All resulted in appalling civilian and enemy soldier casualties. Yet the propaganda – in Orwellian style – has constantly stressed the precision of the weapons and claimed the raids were for peaceful purposes: to introduce democracy and freedom. Casualty figures were always covered up (or dubbed in the militaryspeak 'collateral damage'). According to Cummings (1992: 121), the 1991 conflict appeared not as 'blood and guts spilled in living colour on the living room rug' but through a 'radically distanced, technically controlled eminently "cool" post-modern optic'. Kellner (1992: 386) describes it ironically as 'the perfect war'. During the 'humanitarian' Nato attacks on Serbia in 1999, hundreds of civilians were killed

(Chomsky 1999; Hammond 2000). A leaked government report later revealed that only 40 per cent of RAF bombs hit their targets while the hit-rate for the high explosive, 1,000 lb bomb was just three out of 150, or 2 per cent (Plavsic 2000).

During the 2003 invasion of Iraq, the press constantly reaffirmed this same propaganda stress on precision, yet reached new heights of exaggeration. As the *Sun* of 20 March reported beneath the headline: 'The first "clean" war':

> A senior defence source said last night: 'Great attention to precision-guided weapons means we could have a war with zero casualties. We are a lot closer towards that ideal. We may be entering an era where it is possible to prosecute a humanitarian war.'

Even the *Guardian*, one of the most critical of the US/UK rush to invade Iraq, reported on 19 March:

> The last Gulf War may have marked the introduction of space age weapons – from laser-guided bombs to cruise missiles smart enough to know which set of Baghdad traffic lights to turn left at – but as collateral damage figures later proved, the technologies were still largely in their infancy.

Following the Ameriyya shelter bombing by an American Stealth jet during the Gulf massacres of 1991 (when hundreds of Iraqi women and children perished) most of Fleet Street blamed 'Saddam', described it as a propaganda coup for the Iraqi leader or claimed it was inevitable (Keeble 1997: 166–172). All of this was part of a strategy to deflect blame for the atrocity away from its perpetrators. Similar strategies appear during the 2003 invasion. For instance, after a bomb fell on a Baghdad market on 26 March most of Fleet Street follows the military agenda and questions whether the Iraqis (incredibly) fired the missile. In the *Mail* of 27 March, the headline focuses on 'the propaganda coup Saddam had hoped for' while correspondent Ross Benton reports: 'It was the first major incident of "collateral damage" since the war began but allied officials said they could not confirm that the bombs were dropped by US or British warplanes.' The *Sun* on the same day headlines 'Who's to blame?' and reports: 'If the market blasts were caused by off-target Allied bombs, it will be a propaganda gift to Saddam.' The *Guardian*, alongside a moving eye-witness account by Suzanne Goldenberg of the aftermath of the bombings, highlights US 'confusion over blame for raid'. But the *Mirror*, fiercely anti-war at the time, discounts US denials and condemns it as 'the worst civilian outrage since the war began a week ago'. No newspaper lists nor profiles the 14 Iraqis reported killed: they are the nameless victims of the carnage.

Even in those newspapers critical of the US/UK invasion, the dominant images reflect the military agenda of marginalising the reality of the slaughter. For instance, a special issue of the *Independent Review* of 9 April 2003 is devoted to images from the conflict. But out of 14 photographs, just three focus on Iraqi casualties while another shows blurred images of bodies on a road after a 'friendly fire' attack on a convoy of US and Kurdish forces. The pro-Blair *Times*'s section 2 issue of 10 April carries 49 images: out of these just five show casualties (but pictures of 24 British soldiers killed and the coffins of another six were also carried). Similarly the *Sun*'s '24-page souvenir' of 15 April displays 43 images – all of them predictably cele-brating US/UK military heroics, with no casualties shown and Iraqis almost invi-sible. Again pictures of 'the brave men who died for freedom' are carried. The *Observer* of 13 April carries an eight-page 'war in pictures' supplement: out of 50 images, just six focus on casualties. The unnamed dead are always Iraqi.

The manufacture of heroism in a post-heroic age

Modern war-fighting strategies have virtually eliminated the possibilities for heroic action. Technology has taken the place of men (and the occasional woman). Soldiers now largely press buttons and watch the consequences on a video. Electronics and space-based technologies are all-important. Luckham (1984: 2) comments: 'We are now entering a stage in which the manufacture of warfare is overtaking man and expropriating his culture. Automated warfare and the nuclear bomb have deprived man of his capacity to strive for glory, recogni-tion or safety through combat.'

Slaughtering thousands of conscripts, soldiers and civilians in appalling massacres is hardly heroic. Yet society desperately needs its heroes. So the spectacular 'war' pro-vides the perfect theatre for the manufacture of heroism. Thus, the patriotic pops are full of celebrations of 'Our boys' and their heroic deeds. Typically, the *Sun*'s leader of 21 March highlights Prime Minister Tony Blair's 'sombre and emotive' broadcast hailing the 'heroism of Our boys and girls'. On 24 March, it lists the 31 US and British soldiers killed under the headline: 'How the tragic heroes perished.'

During the 1991 Gulf massacres there was virtually no hand-to-hand combat, and so in an attempt to revive the heroic images of the Second World War, the press constantly used cartoon representations and photographs of troops in training. In 2003, no such devices are necessary. The 'frontline' shots are enough to pro-mote the myth of 'real' battle.

The most blatant manufacture of heroism surrounds the exploits of Private Jessica Lynch which gripped the world's media on 3 April 2003. Under the strapline, 'An incredible story of heroism as teenage PoW snatched back', the *Sun* reports on the 'daring midnight raid'. 'Army supply clerk Jessica, 19, was plucked to safety by US special forces from a hospital used as a base by Saddam Hussein's death squads.' And it goes on to quote Brigadier General Vince Brooks: 'America doesn't leave its heroes behind. Never has, never will.' Along with the rest of the mainstream media, the *Guardian* frames its coverage around the title of the Hollywood blockbuster *Saving Private Ryan*. Under the headline 'Saving Private Lynch: How special forces rescued captured colleague,' it reports on the 'daring midnight raid'. But in the end, all is found to be fiction. There was no gun battle – simply because there were no Iraqi soldiers in the hospital at the time, as Kampfner (2003) revealed in the *Guardian*.

Given the prominence of media hype in current conflicts it is inevitable that a few critical journalists will deconstruct certain events and expose their manufactured dimension. Even the *Sun*, on 15 April, exposes the story of the heroic 'Stay lucky' soldier pictured wearing a helmet riddled with bullet holes as a prank. But focusing on individual hoaxes is very different from highlighting the whole 'war' as a construct.

The essential task

A few months before his death in September, Edward Said (2003) identified the way in which the dominant discourse in the US/UK before the invasion of Iraq fabricated an 'arid landscape ready for American power to construct there an ersatz model of free market "democracy"'. But he concludes with typical optimism:

> Critical thought does not submit to commands to join in the ranks marching against another approved enemy. Rather than the manufactured clash of civilizations we need to concentrate on the slow-working together of cultures that overlap, borrow from each other and live together.

Indeed, while US/UK militarism appears out of control my analysis here argues that it is built on lies, misinformation and myth. And by exposing the lies and the myth, by joining with the global movement for peace and human rights, we can all help put a brake on the US/UK military juggernaut.

Acknowledgements

This essay is based on a chapter with the same title in *Reporting War: Journalism in Wartime*, edited by Stuart Allan and Barbie Zelizer, London: Routledge, 2004 pp 43–58.

Notes

1 Quoted in Notes from New York, a profile of DeLillo, by Duncan Campbell, *Observer*, 4 May 2003
2 Quoted in Seamus Milne (1994) *The Enemy Within: The Secret War Against the Miners*, London: Verso; reprinted by Pan in 1995: 262
3 Phillip Knightley interviewed London, 25 September 2003
4 Christiane Amanpour, chief international correspondent for CNN, quoted in Jessica Hodgson (2003) Mother of all war journos, *Observer*, 2 November

References

Adams, James (1994) *Secret Armies: The Full Story of SAS, Delta Force and Spetsnaz*, London: Hutchinson
Almond, Mark (2003) So how will he be judged?, *Guardian*, 15 May

Baudrillard, Jean (1991) The reality gulf, *Guardian*, 11 January

Beaumont, Peter and Graham, Patrick (2003) Iraq terror spirals out of control as US intelligence loses the plot, *Observer*, 2 November

Beetham, David (2003) The warfare state, *Red Pepper*, June

Bloch, Jonathan and Fitzgerald, Patrick (1983) *British Intelligence and Covert Action*, London: Junction Books

Bright, Martin (2002) Terror, security and the media, *Observer* online, 21 July. Available online at http://observer.guardian.co.uk/libertywatch/story/0,1373,758265,00.html, accessed on 22 July

Casey, Leo (2003) Questioning Halabja: Genocide and the expedient political lie, *Dissent*, New York, summer pp 61–65

Chomsky, Noam (1999) *Lessons from Kosovo: The New Military Humanism*, London: Pluto

Cummings, Bruce (1992) *War and Television*, London: Verso

Curtis, Mark (2003a) Partners in imperialism: Britain's support for US invasion, *www.zmag. org*, 10 May, accessed on 11 May 2003

Curtis, Mark (2003b) *Web of Deceit: Britain's Real Role in the World*, London: Vintage

Donvan, John (2003) For the unilaterals, no neutral ground, *Columbia Journalism Review*, May/June. Available online at www.cjr.org/year/03/3/donvan.asp, accessed on 12 July 2003

Dorril, Stephen (2003) *Spies and Lies*, Free Press, April

Dorril, Stephen and Ramsay, Robin (1991) *Smear*, London: Fourth Estate

Drucker, Peter E. (1993) *Post-Capitalist Society*, Oxford: Butterworth-Heinemann

Epstein, Edward (2003) How many Iraqis died? We may never know, *San Francisco Chronicle*, 3 May

Garton Ash, Timothy (2003) Fight the matrix, *Guardian*, 5 June

Guillot, Clare (2003) Nassiriya: Le soldat Reeves face à la foule en colère, *Le Monde*, 17 April

Hammond, Philip (2000) Reporting 'humanitarian' warfare: Propaganda, moralism and NATO's Kosovo war, *Journalism Studies*, Vol. 1, No. 3 pp 365–386

Hammond, Philip and Herman, Edward S. (eds) (2000) *Degraded Capability: The Media and the Kosovo Crisis*, London: Pluto

Harvey, Robert (2003) *Global Disorder*, London: Constable

Kampfner, John (2003) The truth about Jessica, *Guardian*, 15 May

Keeble, Richard (1997) *Secret State, Silent Press: New Militarism, the Gulf and the Modern Image of Warfare*, Luton: John Libbey

Keeble, Richard (1998) The myth of Saddam Hussein, Kieran, Matthew (ed.) *Media Ethics*, London: Routledge pp 66–81

Keeble, Richard (2001) The media's battle cry, *Press Gazette*, 5 October

Keegan, John (2003) Saddam's utter collapse shows this has not been a real war, *Daily Telegraph*, 8 April

Kellner, Douglas (1992) *The Persian Gulf TV War*, Boulder/San Francisco/Oxford: Westview Press

Knightley, Phillip (2003) Turning the tanks on the reporters, *Observer*, 15 June

Leigh, David (2003) Greasy palms in pinstripe pockets, *Guardian*, 16 September

Luckham, Robin (1983) Of arms and culture, *Current Research on Peace and Violence*, Vol. 4, Tampere, Finland pp 1–63

Lule, Jack (2002) Myth and terror on the editorial page: The *New York Times* responds to September 11, *Journalism and Mass Communication*, Vol. 79, No. 2 pp 275–293

MacArthur, Brian (2003) Changing pace of war, *Times*, 27 June

McChesney, Robert (2002) September 11 and the structured limitation of US journalism, Allan, Stuart and Zelizer, Barbie (eds) *Journalism after September 11*, London: Routledge pp 91–100

McLaughlin, Greg (2002) *The War Correspondent*, London: Pluto Press

Mailer, Norman (2003) We went to war just to boost the white male ego, *Times*, 29 April. Available online at www.timesonline.co.uk/article/0.482–662789.00.html, accessed on 12 August 2003

Marx, Karl (1871) Letter to Ludwig Kugelmann, 27 July. Available online at https://www.marxists.org/archive/marx/works/1871/letters/71_07_27.htm, accessed on 15 November 2019

Mayrhofer, Debra (2003) What's in a name?, *www.mwaw.org*, 15 April, accessed on 12 May 2003

Miller, David (2003) Embedding propaganda, *Free Press*, special issue, June

Milmo, Cahal (2003) Reporting for duty, *Independent*, 18 March

Morgan, David (2003) Climate of fear, *Morning Star*, 12 June

Norton-Taylor, Richard (2003) The BBC row has been got up to obscure the ugly truth, *Guardian*, 28 June

Peak, Steve (1982) Britain's military adventures, *Pacifist*, Vol. 20 p 10

Pilger, John (1998) *Hidden Agendas*, Verso: London

Pilger, John (2003) The big lie, *Daily Mirror*, 22 September

Plavsic, Dragan (2000) NATO's war: The truth comes out, *Socialist Review*, September

Powell, Colin (1995) *Soldier's Way*, London: Hutchinson (with Joseph Persico)

Ramsay, Robin (2003) Lying about Iraq, *Lobster*, No. 45, summer

Reich, Stephanie (2002) Slow motion holocaust, *Covert Action Quarterly*, Vol. 72 pp 22–28

Rogers, Ann (1997) *Secrecy and Power in the British State: A History of the Official Secrets Act*, London: Pluto Press

Said, Edward (2003) A window on the world, *Guardian Review*, 2 August

Stephen, Andrew (2003) America, *New Statesman*, 4 August

Thompson, Edward P. (1982) *Notes on Exterminism: The Last Stage of Civilisation, Exterminism and the Cold War*, London: Verso pp 151–163

Webster, Frank (2003) Information warfare in an age of globalization, Thussu, Daya Kishan and Freeman, Des (eds) *Information Warfare in an Age of Globalization: War and the Media*, London: Sage pp 57–86

Wolff, Michael (2003) 'I was only asking', *Guardian*, 14 April

8

OPERATION MOSHTARAK AND THE MANUFACTURE OF CREDIBLE, 'HEROIC' WARFARE

This chapter examines Fleet Street's coverage of the US-led Operation Moshtarak in Afghanistan in 2010. It outlines the major strands of US/UK military strategy since the 1980s (defined here as New Militarist) and argues that the conflict in Afghanistan, as represented in the mainstream media, is no war at all: rather it's a series of manufactured, media-hyped 'operations' led by a nation with the largest and most heavily resourced fighting force in history, against a pitifully under-resourced and yet skilful and merciless guerrilla movement in one of the most impoverished countries in the world.

So the role of the media embedded with the military is to manufacture the image of legitimate, heroic 'warfare' against a credible threat. In the process the reality of the conflict, the appalling suffering of the Afghan people, is kept secret from the British public. The chapter also considers Fleet Street's editorial stances on the Afghanistan war – which was costing the UK £5 billion a year (see Norton-Taylor 2010a)[1] – and the ways in which the views of the public (most of whom consistently call for the withdrawal of troops from Afghanistan) have been marginalised. The study draws on a range of alternative media to critique mainstream coverage.

Secret warfare

There are three major strands to New Militarist strategy – each accompanied by a particular form of media coverage. Firstly, the most important strategy is conducted in complete secrecy away from the glare of the media. This involves in the case of Afghanistan during 2010:

- the targeted assassinations in both Afghanistan and over the border in Pakistan of alleged Taliban leaders (Walsh 2010);

- the night raids by the CIA and some of its 56,000 Special Forces, such as the Green Berets and Navy SEALS, Special Boat teams, Air Force Special Tactics Teams, Task Force 121, the Joint Special Operations Command and Marine Corps Special Operations Battalions (see Gopal 2010; Turse and Engelhardt 2010; Porter 2010a; Grey 2009a; Scahill 2013; Southwell 2005: 15);[2]
- the secret detention and torture centres;
- the secret and massively expensive installation of almost 400 US and coalition military bases in Afghanistan and at least 300 Afghan National Army (ANA) and Afghan National Police (ANP) bases. According to investigative reporter Nick Turse (2010): 'Existing in the shadows, rarely reported on and little talked about, this base-building programme is nonetheless staggering in size and scope. ... It has added significantly to the already long secret list of Pentagon property overseas and raises questions about just how long, after the planned beginning of a drawdown of American forces in 2011, the US will still be garrisoning Afghanistan;'[3]
- the many disappearances;
- the increasing and largely secret use of pilotless drones to attack targets in Afghanistan and over the border in Pakistan;[4] In a celebratory feature on Britain's £124 million drones programme, Rob Waugh (2010) comments: 'Autonomous machines save money, save pilots' lives and point to a future where Stealth-enabled unmanned fighters and ultra-long-endurance surveillance planes can almost remove human beings from the aerial battlefield. But this technology has largely appeared without governments or the public questioning it';
- the penetration of allied and enemy governments by the CIA/MI6. In October 2009, for instance, it was revealed that the brother of Afghan President, Ahmed Wali Karzai, long alleged to be a powerful drug lord, had been on the CIA's payroll for almost eight years (Borger 2009). Leaks of this kind reflect the rivalries amongst the US's 17 intelligence agencies (see MacAskill, Nasaw and Boone 2010);
- and the Pakistan military offensives against the Taliban and al-Qaeda, instigated by Washington, which claimed thousands of lives and displaced over a million people in the north-western tribal areas (see Cockburn 2010a, 2010b). In particular, there are the little-reported attacks by the army against the rising independence movement in Baluchistan. This is Pakistan's largest province, covering 44 per cent of the country's area but where 60 per cent of the population live in abject poverty (Khan and Prasad 2010). Yet on 7 June 2010, it was reported that Pakistan planned to increase its military budget to a massive 442 billion rupees (the equivalent of £3.59bn) (*Morning Star* 2010).

On 7 June 2010, the *Independent* reported that US special forces were operating in more than 75 countries – from Colombia to the Philippines. The 'secret war' had vastly increased in scope and size under President Obama (Sengupta 2010a). No other information was forthcoming. Columnist Sam Leith (2010), in the

London *Evening Standard*, commented critically: 'It sounds ... cool. But how, in principle – that is, in terms of accountability and respect for law – does dropping bombs from drones or fielding teams of assassins in other countries differ from the secret bombing of Cambodia in Kissinger's day?'

UK battles: Beyond the glare of the media

In fact, every year since 1914, British forces have been deployed somewhere on the globe – mostly far away from the gaze of the media (Cobain, MacAskill and Stoddard 2014). As Steve Peak (1982: 10) pointed out, the Falklands 'war' of 1982 was the 88th deployment of British troops since 1945. These deployments took place in 51 countries and nearly all of them in Africa, the Middle East, South-East Asia, the Far East and around the Caribbean. Newsinger (1989) describes British intervention in Indonesia in 1945–1946 as a 'forgotten war'. Britain's longest running post-1945 campaign (leaving aside Northern Ireland) was in Malaya from 1948 to 1960. But this was never described as a war. Rose (1986) argues that British troops have been involved in more wars in more places across the globe than any other country since 1945.

In the case of the US, the investment in secret warfare is still greater than that of the UK. Cecil Currey (1991: 72–73) argues that since 1950, America has used either force or its threat about 500 times, mostly in Third World countries. Former CIA agent John Stockwell (1991: 70–73) suggests that the agency has been involved in 3,000 major operations and 10,000 minor operations which led to the deaths of 6m. people worldwide – mainly in Korea, Vietnam, Cambodia, Africa and Central and South America. It has overthrown functioning democracies in more than 20 countries and manipulated dozens of elections. During the 1980s, secret support from CIA and MI6 (the UK's foreign intelligence service) for the mujahedin in their fight against Soviet occupiers in Afghanistan ultimately helped in the creation of the 'Taliban' (not an organisation with a conventional command structure but a disparate insurgency involving many, largely Pashtun, groups) and al-Qaeda. As John Pilger (2003) records:

> For 17 years, Washington poured $4bn into the pockets of some of the most brutal men on earth – with the overall aim of exhausting and ultimately destroying the Soviet Union in a futile war. One of them, Gulbuddin Hekmatyar, a warlord particularly favoured by the CIA, received tens of millions of dollars. His speciality was trafficking opium and throwing acid in the faces of women who refused to wear the veil. In 1994, he agreed to stop attacking Kabul on condition he was made prime minister – which he was.

Special forces, such as the UK's SAS and the American Navy Seals, which are so crucial to secret warfare strategies, reportedly played important roles in the build-up to the 1991 Iraq conflict and during them. They were the subject of a series of 'inordinately flattering' features in the US and UK media (Ray and Schaap 1991:

11). Yet accounts of their daring deeds of courage and endurance, since they were shrouded in almost total secrecy, amount to a form of fiction (see Newsinger 1985; de la Billière 1995: 319–338; Hunter 1995: 169–175; Kemp 1994: 191–197).

By 2010, covert military action lay at the heart of US/Nato strategy in Afghanistan, the Middle East, the Horn of Africa and elsewhere. On 26 May 2010, both the *Guardian* and *Independent* followed up a report in the previous day's *New York Times* that General David Petraeus, head of the US's Central Command, had signed a directive (called the Joint Unconventional Warfare Task Force Execute Order) on 30 September 2009. Under its provisions, special forces such as Navy Seals and the Army's Delta Force would be able to 'penetrate, disrupt, defeat or destroy' terrorist organisations, allowing for the assassination of US citizens abroad suspected of being terrorists (Cornwell 2010a; MacAskill 2010).[5] Significantly, America's top commander in Afghanistan in 2010, Gen. Stanley McChrystal, had headed the Joint Special Operations Command between 2003 and 2008.

In an accompanying comment piece, Rupert Cornwell, in the *Independent*, expressed support for the move. By following in the footsteps of President George Bush in his expansion of special force operations, US President Barack Obama had shown he was 'above all a realist and a pragmatist' (Cornwell 2010b). He continues: 'Politically, Mr Obama must be seen as tough on national security. And if the CIA has many critics, no one doubts the quality of the US military.' An unsigned, hagiographic profile of McChrystal in *The Sunday Times* of 4 October 2009 describes him as a 'ruthless US special forces hunter killer', a 'mild, thoughtful and at times humorous soldier' and a 'gaunt ascetic who rises at 4.30 am, eats one meal a day and jogs for an hour'.[6]

Low Intensity Conflict (LIC)

The second New Militarist strategy is known in militaryspeak as Low Intensity Conflict (LIC): this involves the day-to-day grind of long-drawn-out engagement, occasional small-scale skirmishes with the enemy, sometimes involving pilotless drones and Apache helicopters; the taking out of snipers and the removal of roadside bombs. The regular reporting from Afghanistan of British soldier casualties ('Our Heroes'), more than 300 by June 2010, is part of the sporadic coverage of this LIC, counter-insurgency strategy.

Pentagon adviser John M. Collins (1991: 4), in his seminal analysis of LIC, points out: 'All LICs are contingencies and technically transpire in peacetime because none have yet been declared wars.' Focusing on just 60 examples over the last century, Collins shows that 33 per cent of his sample exceeded 10 years while 57 per cent lasted less than five years. A feature of American strategy since the beginning of the 20th century, it developed still further as an offshoot of the nuclear stand-off between East and West during the Cold War and in response to the US defeat in Vietnam.

As Halliday (1989: 72) argues: 'LIC theorists insisted that US combat forces should not be involved in the long-running, Vietnam-style operations. The "lesson" drawn here from Vietnam was that the US effort failed because it was too direct and too large.' Significantly, Collins's sample shows LICs mounting substantially in the post-Vietnam era. During the 1980s, LIC strategists 'came out' in the US and UK, numerous conferences were held and strategy documents were compiled exploring the concepts. But the LIC debate was largely ignored by the mainstream media.

Manufactured 'wars' and 'operations'

Finally, there are the occasional manufactured, media-hyped 'operations' such as the attack on Musa Qala in December 2007, dubbed 'Operation Snake Bite' (Grey 2009b),[7] and 'Operation Panther's Claw', focusing on Garmsir, Nad-e-Ali and Khanashin, in June 2009. And the one dubbed 'Moshtarak', launched in February 2010. In these 'operations', the nation with the largest and most heavily resourced fighting force in history faces a comparatively small movement – though one which is highly skilled in guerrilla tactics – in one of the most impoverished countries in the world. These 'operations' are then spectacular, essentially PR events providing the theatre in which the US and its allies can claim their so-called 'victories'.

They emerge from a long history of changing military strategies (driven by capitalism's relentless drive for minerals and foreign markets) which can be dated back to the mid-nineteenth century.[8] MacKenzie (1984) has described the 'spectacular theatre' of 19th century British militarism when press representations of heroic imperialist adventures in distant colonies had a considerable entertainment element. Featherstone (1993a, 1993b), too, has identified the way in which the Victorian 'small' wars of imperial expansion in Africa and India were glorified for a doting public by correspondents such as William Russell, G. A. Henty, Archibald Forbes and H. M. Stanley.

But Victorian newspapers and magazines did not have the social penetration of the mass media of today. And Victorian militarism was reinforced through a wide range of institutions and social activities: the Salvation Army, Church Army and uniformed youth organisations, rifle clubs, ceremonial and drill units in factories. 'In all these ways, a very large proportion of the population came to have some connection with military and paramilitary organisations' (MacKenzie op cit: 5–6). By the 1980s, this institutional and social militarism had given way to a new mediacentric, consumerist, entertainment militarism in which the mass media, ideologically aligned to a strong and increasingly secretive state, had assumed a dominant ideological role.

The traditional, industrialised militarism of the First and Second World Wars, in which the mass of the population participated in the war effort, either as soldiers or civilians, was founded on the widespread fear that the British state faced serious threats to its very existence. By the 1980s the supposed 'threats' to Western interests came from puny Third World countries: so the role of the media in these New Militarist adventures became even more critical in manufacturing the enemy as a credible 'threat'. During the 1980s, the military adventures of the UK in the Falklands (1982), the US in Grenada (1983), Libya (1986) and Panama (1989), culminating in the Iraq conflict of 1991, all bore the hallmarks of this new military/media strategy.

- The threats posed to US/Western interests in all these military interventions were either grossly exaggerated or non-existent. Significantly, the failure of the Soviet Union to intervene militarily in Poland in 1981 to crush the Solidarity movement under the leadership of Lech Walesa proved to the Western elites that the threat posed by their traditional 'enemy' was waning. And so the permanent war economies of Britain and America (with their military/industrial complexes) needed the manufacture of 'big enemies' to legitimise the continued massive expenditure on the weapons of war. Hence the massive displays of US/UK force in all these adventures bore little relation to the threats posed.
- They were all quickie attacks. The Libya bombings of 1986 lasted just 11 minutes. All the others were over within days.
- They were all largely risk-free and fought from the air. Since reporters were banned from accompanying pilots on the fighter jets, then the crucial air war was conducted largely in secret.
- All the attacks resulted in appalling civilian casualties. Yet the propaganda, in Orwellian style, claimed the raids were essentially for peaceful purposes. Casualty figures were covered up and the military hardware was constantly represented as 'precise', 'surgical', 'modern' and 'clean'.
- Central to the new strategy was the demonisation of the enemy leaders. In the absence of any serious military force, this demonisation served to represent the enemy states as credible threats.
- Media pools were deployed largely to keep journalists away from any action.
- All the invasions were celebrated in ecstatic language throughout the mainstream media. The editorial consensus remained firmly behind the military attacks. Administration lies were rarely challenged just as the global protests against the actions were largely ignored.

Defeat in Vietnam had proved to be a terrible trauma to the American military and political elites. With the waning of Soviet power in the 1980s, American imperialism could operate largely unchallenged. Victories were gained – and yet they were gained against largely puny Third World countries. The 'Vietnam syndrome' could only be kicked in a 'big' war. And Iraq's invasion of Kuwait in August 1990 was to prove the perfect opportunity for the manufacture of this perfect 'big' war (Keeble 2004).

The New Militarist strategy was to continue through the 1990s well into the new century. Media-hyped, spectacular 'wars' were waged – as in Somalia (1992–93), Serbia (1999), Afghanistan (2001) and Iraq (2003). With reporters embedded alongside the military, coverage remained tightly controlled (Keeble 2007).

Hiding the reality

The Afghanistan conflict launched in 2001 following the 9/11 outrages in the US clearly had little basis in international law. So, in these 'operations', the essential role of the media embedded with the military and constrained by the enormous risks involved in reporting from such a lawless country, is to manufacture the image of legitimate, heroic so-called 'warfare' against a credible threat. In other words, the conventional language of the military is deployed to describe completely asymmetrical conflict. As Bishop (2010: 13) points out:

> Wars with insurgents were always unbalanced. One side had modern conventional weapons. The other fought with what was cheap, portable and easily improvised. But in Afghanistan the scale of the asymmetry at times seemed blackly absurd.

In the process the reality of the conflict, the high-tech violence of the invading forces, the appalling suffering of the Afghan people, are kept secret from the British public. We know precisely how many coalition troops are killed (all of them, indeed, tragic and unnecessary), their names, their family histories – and how many have been wounded. As James Cogan (2010) noted on 23 April: 'Since 2001, the lives of 1,733 US and Nato troops have been squandered in Afghanistan. ... At least another 8,000 have been wounded in action, including more than 5,000 Americans. Thousands more have suffered non-battle injuries and illness.' In 2009 alone, there were 1,400 British casualties flown from Afghanistan to the UK, 212 in a critical condition (Willetts 2010).[9] But the Afghan casualties of US/UK and Taliban attacks remain largely nameless and unknown. According to a report in *Le Monde* (Follorou 2010), almost 5,000 (grossly under-funded) Afghan policemen, with more than 70 per cent of them estimated to be illiterate, had been killed since 2003.[10] Moreover, the Marjah offensive had created an estimated 27,000 internal refugees – but these are hardly ever reported in the media (Boone and Norton-Taylor 2010).

Indeed, the Taliban, supported by their al-Qaeda allies, are distinguished largely by their invisibility in the media. They lay booby traps and roadside bombs otherwise known as improvised explosive devices (IEDs: usually home-made from fertiliser[11]), snipe at their enemy – and flee (often on battered motorbikes). In the military jargon, this is known as 'shoot and scoot' (Bishop op cit: 73). Over the six-month period up to June 2010, British soldiers had come across more than 500 IEDs and engaged in more than 1,300 gunfights in central Helmand (Norton-Taylor 2010c). IEDs were accounting for 80 per cent of British injuries and fatalities (Rayment 2010). Many of the guns the Taliban were using date back to the 1890s (Sengupta 2010b). As Turse and Engelhardt stress (op cit):

> Al-Qaeda has no tanks, Humvees, nuclear submarines, or aircraft carriers, no fleets of attack helicopters or fighter jets. ... Al-Qaeda specialises in low-

budget operations ranging from the incredibly deadly to the incredibly inef-
fectual. ... In the present war on terror, called by whatever name (or, as at
present, by no name at all), the two 'sides' might as well be in different worlds.
After all, al-Qaeda today isn't even an organisation in the normal sense of the
term, no less a fighting bureaucracy. It is a loose collection of ideas and a
looser collection of individuals waging open source warfare.

Suicide bomb attacks and assaults on areas suspected of siding with the occupying
forces have been other Taliban guerrilla tactics. In 2003, there were only two suicide attacks in Afghanistan. In 2006, there were at least 136, six times more than
the year before. Eighty were directed at military targets but killed eight times as
many civilians as soldiers or policemen (ibid: 130–131). The Taliban also terrorise
individuals and communities suspected of siding with the occupation forces.
According to Julius Cavendish (2010a), the insurgents executed two civilians
whom they suspected of aiding government and international forces every three
days during 2009.

Journalists have also been targeted. The decapitation of Afghan reporter Ajmal
Naqshbandi, in 2007, was filmed and distributed on the internet[12] – but this did
not receive the global media attention given to the similar decapitation of the *Wall
Street Journal*'s Daniel Pearl, in February 2002.[13] The *Guardian*'s foreign correspondent Ghaith Abdul-Ahad was released along with two other journalists in
December 2009 after being held hostage for six days in a remote region of
Afghanistan (Taylor 2009). In January 2010, Rupert Hamer, embedded with US
Marines at Nawa in Helmand for the *Sunday Mirror*, became the first UK journalist
to be killed in Afghanistan. And this received massive media coverage. The front
page of the *Daily Mirror* of 11 January carried a large photograph of Hamer smiling
in front of troops with the headline: 'Fine, fearless, dedicated' (Hughes 2010).[14]

The Taliban's basic weapon is an AK-47 rifle of Second World War design,
augmented by machine guns and latterly home-made roadside bombs. In addition,
the 'legacy mines' left over since the time of the Soviet occupation (1979–1989)
pose a durable threat. Facing them, the US-led troops have state-of-the art satellites, spy planes and unmanned drones. Writing in 2009, Patrick Bishop commented in his book celebrating the heroics of 3 Para Battlegroup in Afghanistan
(op cit: 12):

> Anti-American rebels had made great use of IEDs and suicide bombs in Iraq
> but they had been late arriving in Afghanistan [since 2006]. Together they
> now kept the troops in a constant state of alertness and anxiety. The insur-
> gents' new methods carried less risk to themselves than did their previous
> confrontational tactics. Even when they suffered losses, though, there seemed
> to be no shortage of replacements.

With Osama bin Laden and Mullah Omar having mysteriously fled into the
unknown following the US invasion of 2001, the Taliban in 2010 had no

leader – such as the 'mad dog' Gaddafi, of Libya, or the 'new Hitler, Butcher of Baghdad' Saddam or the 'Butcher of Belgrade', 'Slobo' Milošević – on whom our patriotic editors safe in their Fleet Street bunkers and the military could direct their venom. The Taliban had no headquarters which US precision-guided missiles could 'take out'.

On 17 February 2010, the media reported American claims that the actual head of the Taliban's military operations had been seized in Karachi: a certain Mullah Abdul Ghani Baradar.[15] But like the rest of the Taliban, Mullah Abdul remains a shadowy, unknown figure. Significantly, no photographs of Taliban's toppled No. 2 accompanied the reports.

Moshtarak: Billed as the 'biggest US offensive since 2001'

Operation Moshtarak, launched on 12 February 2010 in Afghanistan, was billed as 'the biggest US military offensive since the US invasion of 2001' (note how PR-ish superlatives always accompany every new assault by the American military).

The 15,000 coalition forces drawn from the US, the UK, Canada, Denmark, Estonia and most significantly Afghanistan were equipped with a vast arsenal – including Apache, Chinook and Cobra, Black Hawk attack helicopters and unmanned predator aircraft – all of it backed up by ranks of military intelligence operatives and information-gathering hi-tech satellites. But whom were they 'battling'? Possibly just 400 Taliban, according to some US officers (Lamb 2010). On 7 February, *The Sunday Times* predicted just 1,000 Taliban would be facing the 4,000 crack British troops (Colvin 2010). For the follow-up Kandahar offensive planned for the summer, military intelligence was said to be expecting between just '500 and 1,000' insurgents (Kirkup 2010).

So this is an 'operation', not real warfare. Rather, it's a simulated, mediacentric event providing a symbolic show of US/UK military strength and proof that the new Afghan army is capable of taking over once the occupying forces withdraw. The operation had certainly no credible strategic legitimacy. The target of the US-led assaults was Marjah in Helmand province in the south of the country. But as reporter Anand Gopal told the progressive *Democracy Now!* radio station, Marjah was 'a very tiny town'. Gopal continued:

> It's more a show of force by the coalition forces, something they can offer their home audiences of how they've gone into a village and retaken some Taliban. But beyond that, nothing will really change on the ground, regardless of what happens in Marjah. It's just business as usual.[16]

Investigative reporter Gareth Porter (2010b: 8) claimed that the picture of Marjah presented by military officials and obediently reported by major news media was 'one of the clearest and most dramatic pieces of misinformation of the entire war, apparently aimed at hyping the offensive as a historic turning point in the conflict'. On 2 February 2010, Associated Press quoted 'Marine commanders' saying they expected 400 to 1,000 insurgents to be 'holed up in the southern Afghan town of 80,000 people'. According to Porter, 'that language evoked an image of house-to-house urban street fighting'. On 14 February, the second day of the 'offensive', Lt Josh Diddams said the Marines were 'in the majority of the city at this point'. He also used the language that conjured images of urban fighting, claiming the insurgents were hold some 'neighbourhoods'. Yet, as Porter stressed, Marjah is not a city nor even a real town but either a few clusters of farmers' homes or a large agricultural area covering much of the southern Helmand River Valley.

Maintaining the myth of warfare

Predictably the coalition forces were reported as 'storming' Marjah. More superlatives appeared in the press to manufacture the image of credible warfare: the town was suspected of being 'one of the biggest, most dangerous minefields Nato forces had ever faced' (Martin 2010). Brig Gen. Larry Nicholson, commander of the Marines in southern Afghanistan, was quoted as saying: 'This may be the largest IED threat and largest minefield that Nato has ever faced' while the US military were reported as saying that 'hundreds of beleaguered insurgents could insist to fight until death' (ibid).

On 13 February, Gulab Mangal, governor of Helmand, was reported as saying it was 'the most successful operation we have ever carried out'. Duncan Larcombe (2010), embedded with the Fire Support Company, 1st battalion, the Royal Welsh, in the *Sun* of 15 February trumpeted: 'Our boys are in high spirits after successfully pulling off the largest helicopter assaults in British military history.' Oliver Harvey (2010), embedded with 3 Platoon Queen's Company for the *Sun*, celebrated the flying of the Afghan national flag at the 'Taliban stronghold Marjah' as a 'sign of hope'.

Always the myth of warfare survives: usually as a future danger. So the *Sun* of 11 February reported: 'Fighting … in Helmand is expected to be ferocious.' In *The Sunday Times* of 14 February, Amoore and Colvin (2010) reported: 'Most Taliban appear to have scattered before the onslaught which was strongly signalled in advance. However, military commanders expect them to regroup and attack in the weeks ahead.' And Jon Boone (2010b), in the *Guardian* of 10 March, quoted Commanding Officer Major Joseph Brannon on the Taliban: 'They know we are making a difference here so we are expecting a pretty strong fight.'

But as John Pilger (2010) commented:

> The recent 'liberation' of the city of Marja from the Taliban's 'command and control structure' was pure Hollywood. Marja is not a city – there was no Taliban command and control. The heroic liberators killed the usual civilians, the poorest of the poor. Otherwise is was fake. A war of perception is meant to provide fake news for the folks back home to make a failed colonial adventure seem worthwhile and patriotic.

The celebritisation of 'heroic' warfare

One way in which the media hide the reality of the horror of warfare is to celebrate the visits of celebrities from the world of politics and entertainment to the troops on the frontlines. The events are pure PR – being usually accompanied by photographs of the smiling visitors shaking hands with similarly smiling troops or trying some of the military hardware for the cameras. The language used is always positive and uplifting. Typical, then, was the coverage given to President Barack Obama, on 29 March 2010, during his first visit to the war zone since ordering a 'surge' of 30,000 extra US troops in Afghanistan in November 2009. Stephen Foley (2010), in the *Independent*, quoted the President: 'I'm encouraged by the *progress* that's been made. ... One of the main reasons I am here is just to say thank you for the *extraordinary efforts* of our troops.'

On 24 May, the *Daily Mail* along with the rest of Fleet Street reported David Beckham, England football 'hero', dropping in on the troops in Camp Bastion, Afghanistan. He told troops of his 'huge admiration' for them.[17]

Fleet Street backs Moshtarak offensive – despite massive public opposition

Virtually all the New Militarist attacks have won the overall support of Fleet Street editors: Operation Moshtarak, involving 9,500 British troops, was no exception. In 2010, most of Fleet Street was still backing the Nato 'war' in Afghanistan. On 6 December 2009, *The Sunday Times* editorial, titled 'Prepare for the long haul in Afghanistan', welcomed President Obama's 'surge' strategy: 'He took his time, but President Barack Obama reached the right decision with his announcement last week the United States is to send 30,000 more troops and 250 helicopters to Afghanistan.' On 14 February, the same newspaper was hailing, cautiously, Operation Moshtarak: 'Maybe this is the end of the beginning.' According to the *Independent*'s editorial of 9 February 2010, the strategy of General Stanley McChrystal, to put Afghan troops alongside Western troops, had 'logic' and 'should at least be given an opportunity to prove itself'.

On 2 June, the *Daily Telegraph* editorialised: 'The heroic work undertaken by the British forces these past four years has laid the foundations for the new American-led strategy.' The *Guardian*'s editorial on the following day suggested the British government 'could make a bold decision – to withdraw troops from the front, use them to secure Kabul and set themselves the more modest aim of doing things that work'. But by 24 June 2010, the *Guardian* was describing the war as 'dysfunctional' and 'unwinnable'. According to *The Times*'s editorial of 10 June 2010, the new Prime Minister, David Cameron, 'to his credit ... has chosen to reaffirm the importance of success in Afghanistan and to offer unbridled support to the military'. A follow-up leader the next day concluded, firmly, that 'at a time of austerity, it is imperative that this nation spends more on its defence'. But as during the Nato attacks on Serbia in 1999, the *Independent on Sunday* dared to stand outside the consensus. On Remembrance Sunday, 8 November 2009, its editorial commented:

> It is time, on this solemn day on which we remember the sacrifice of those who gave their lives for our freedom and security, for a change in policy. It is time to say that this war was ill-conceived, unwinnable and counter-productive. It is time to start planning a phased withdrawal of British troops.

Fleet Street's general support for the UK government's Afghan strategy did not match the public mood with polls consistently calling for troops to be withdrawn (Milne 2009). In July 2009, the BBC/*Guardian*, ITN, *The Times* and *Independent* all published polls showing Britons wanted immediate or rapid withdrawal of troops. Yet Polina Aksamentova (2009) argued that the media largely downplayed their findings. For instance, the ICM study, reported in the *Guardian* on 11 July, found 42 per cent wanted Britain to pull out immediately and 14 per cent by the end of the year. The *Guardian*, however, titled the article 'Public support for Afghanistan is firm, despite deaths.' It stressed that support for the war had increased from 30 per cent in 2006 to 46 per cent but left the call for withdrawal to the last three sentences of the article. Few of the newspapers wrote about any of the other polls.

On 11 November 2009, the *Independent* published a vote showing four out of five did not believe the government's main justification – and did not believe that British involvement was keeping the streets of Britain safe from terrorist attacks. Some 46 per cent felt the war actually increased the threat of attacks by creating anger and resentment among the Muslim population (Sengupta and Morris 2010). Even while Operation Moshtarak was under way, another poll by ComRes for the *Independent* and ITV News showed that almost three-quarters of electors viewed the conflict as unwinnable – and more than half said they did not understand why British troops were still in Afghanistan (Morris 2010). Similar massive public opposition to the war was being recorded in the US. A *Washington Post*/ABC poll released in June 2010 showed 53 per cent of respondents saying the war was 'not worth fighting' – the highest percentage in three years.[18]

Opposition has appeared in the mainstream media from a number of prominent columnists – such as Simon Jenkins, Seamus Milne, Peter Preston (all *Guardian*), Andreas Whittam Smith, Johann Hari (*Independent*), Max Hastings and Andrew Alexander (*Daily Mail*), Jeff Randall (*Daily Telegraph*), Peter Beaumont (*Observer*) and Denis McShane MP. But, intriguingly, the loudest protests in the media came largely from those calling for still more investment in the war. The *Sun, Mail, Express* and *Telegraph*, to name but a few of Fleet Street's most hawkish members, criticised loudly the supposed failures of the Gordon Brown New Labour government to equip 'our heroes' properly. Particular attention focused on the alleged failings of the Snatch Land Rover (Sturke 2008; Bulstrode 2010). The claims of a Catholic bishop at a military funeral that soldiers in Afghanistan urgently needed more helicopters and vehicles in late April 2010 received substantial media coverage (e.g Bowcott 2010).

The row promoted an illusion of critical media holding the rulers to account. And yet the controversy was entirely manufactured. The US military spent around one trillion dollars on its post 9/11 wars up to 2009 (Stiglitz and Bilmes 2009); it has 1.4 million active duty men and women and another 1.3 million reserve personnel; it employs more than 700,000 civilians in support roles while there are estimated 100,000 members in its civilian intelligence community. Its military budget in 2009 amounted to $661 billion.[19] In June 2010, Congress was set to approve an 'emergency' supplemental financing Bill including more than $33 billion, mainly for funding the American military 'surge' in Afghanistan (Astore 2010). Britain had already spent £9.4 billion on its Afghanistan operations by 2010 (Turse and Engelhardt op cit; see also Turse 2008). Its annual military spending was the equivalent of $53.8 billion, the fourth highest in the world (after the US, France and China).[20] So much for under-resourcing.

'Operations' certainly help provide a 'theatre' in which some of these massively expensive weapons and the various branches of the military (army, navy, air force, special forces, satellites, intelligence and so on) can be tested. Significantly, Adam Ingram, a former armed forces minister, suggested that a desire within the army to try out a new range of recently purchased Apache helicopters was a factor in the deployment of British troops to Helmand in 2006 (Haynes 2010). Before the 3,000 British troops arrived, the province had been 'relatively quiet', according to Andrew Krepinevich, who served on the personal staff of three US secretaries of defence, but their arrival 'stirred up a hornet's nest' (Evans 2010).

The contradictions of New Militarism and the failure of Operation Moshtarak

Central to manufacture of New Militarist 'operations' is the celebration of 'victory' to applauding home audiences usually just days after their launch. But after 2001 and the US/UK invasions of Afghanistan and Iraq, the New Militarist strategy faced significant setbacks. The occupations of Iraq and Afghanistan attracted massive opposition from local forces and, by 2010, substantial majorities in the UK were calling for the troops to be withdrawn from Afghanistan.

Thus while the US/UK military remained committed to the launch of media-hyped 'operations', by 2010 they were often no longer achieving their desired results. In the case of Operation Moshtarak, its launch was given predictably massive media coverage yet its conclusion was hardly covered at all. Almost immediately afterwards, the focus shifted to US plans to take over Kandahar, Afghanistan's second city, in the summer. Typical was the report by Julius Cavendish (2010b), in the *Independent* of 21 April 2010. Buried in the coverage of the assassination of the deputy mayor of Kandahar in a mosque was a comment from provincial council member Haji Moqtar Ahmed on Operation Moshtarak: 'My thinking is [there was] no result. It failed. ... If they start without consulting ordinary people, thousands of families will move to Kandahar city. There will be great misery.' And Cavendish added: 'Nato's strategy for Kandahar was partly tested in its campaign to restore government control over the town of Marjah in neighbouring Helmand. The campaign, which began in February, has been held up by the Taliban.'

The *Morning Star* reported in early May 2010 that resistance forces continued to operate in Marjah and that locals had largely refused to collaborate with occupation troops or Karzai government officials (Mellen 2010). Kim Sengupta (2010e) reported on 28 May 2010 claims by Hajj Mohammad Hassan, a local tribal elder, that there remained no security in Helmand. 'By day there is government. By night it's the Taliban.' The *Guardian*'s editorial of 3 June 2010 commented: 'The Marjah campaign, which was designed as a blueprint for how the Taliban could be rolled back, has become – in Gen. McChrystal's words – a bleeding ulcer of the campaign. There could be bigger wounds yet.' On 9 June 2010, the BBC reported Nato and Afghan official claiming 'success' for the Marjah campaign, but there were reports of continuing violence and Taliban intimidation.[21] And by 17 June, the writer and historian, William Dalrymple (2010), reported: '…it appears that the Taliban have regained control of the opium-growing centre of Marjah in Helmand province, only three months after being driven out by McChrystal's forces amid much gung-ho cheerleading in the US media.'

Serious splits over strategy for the planned summer follow-up 'operation' in Kandahar, amongst military and civilian leaders in both the UK and US, also surfaced prominently in the media (e.g. Helm and Beaumont 2010; Sengupta 2010c).[22] They culminated (amazingly) in the sacking of Gen. McChrystal by President Obama on 23 June 2010 after his outspoken criticisms of the civilian leadership of the US were published in a *Rolling Stone* feature by investigative reporter Michael Hastings. As Jeremy Scahill (2013: 349) comments:

> McChrystal was finished, his run as commander of the most elite units in the US military brought down by a story published in an issue of a magazine that featured on its cover an almost naked Lady Gaga sporting a brassière with two rifles protruding from it.

Moreover, Nato officials were warning that there were no quick fixes in Afghanistan with British and foreign troops expected to be engaged in a combat role there for at least three or four more years (Norton-Taylor 2010d).

The performance of local Afghan forces in Operation Moshtarak was also disappointing, according to reports. It was thrown into further disarray with the resignations of two of the 'most internationally respected' members of Karzai's government – interior minister Hanif Atmar and spy chief Amrullah Saleh – after a gathering of 1,600 leaders in Kabul came under Taliban rocket attack (Boone 2010a). Moreover, a survey of 1,994 people in Afghanistan, commissioned by Gen. McChrystal found that 85 per cent viewed the Taliban as 'our Afghan brothers'. More than two thirds said they viewed Karzai's government as totally corrupt while the occupying forces and Afghan police were considered the greatest threat to personal security by 56 per cent (Cogan op cit).

Missing from the coverage: The massive, global opposition

Largely missing from the Moshtarak coverage is any acknowledgement of the views and protests of the massive anti-war movement in this country and globally. CND, the Anti-War Coalition, War Resisters International, the Peace Pledge Union, Pax Christi, Campaign Against the Arms Trade, Respect are but a handful of the many groups in the UK largely ignored by the mainstream. On 3 April 2010, for instance, PressTV reported that thousands of peace activists had taken to the streets in 30 towns and cities across Germany demanding an immediate end to the country's unpopular presence in Afghanistan.[23]

While the mainstream media, with a few notable exceptions (such as veteran reporter Kathy Gannon of Associated Press, Patrick Cockburn and Robert Fisk, of the *Independent*, Jonathan Steele, of the *Guardian*) are failing in their coverage of Afghanistan there are still some excellent reports in alternative media to be accessed via the internet. To name but two: *TomDispatch.com*, edited by the US historian Tom Engelhardt, has carried a series of excellent investigative pieces on the conflict contextualising it historically and highlighting the vast military/industrial complex which is promoting it. The Indian journal *Frontline* (at https://frontline.thehindu.com/) has also a history of covering US imperialistic adventures with a detailed and critical eye. For journalism students and critical media consumers there are, indeed, many models out there of good, brave reporting to admire and learn from.

Conclusion: New Militarism transformed into disaster militarism

Since 2003, Western interventions in the Middle East and Africa have all proven disasters. New militarism (from 1982 to 2003) was built on the manufacture of 'quickie' attacks against puny opposition against whom 'victories' could be rapidly won. The decline and demise of the Soviet Union following the collapse of the Berlin Wall in 1989 meant that US-led forces for a few years indulged in a series of military adventures – with little attention given to the consequences.

From 1976 to January 2004 as few as 900 US service people died overseas due to hostile action, about 38 per cent occurring in Iraq during the ten-month period 19 March to January 2004 (Conetta 2004: 13). Since then US and UK casualties have been mounting. As the years progressed Western forces were pulled into an appalling quagmire in Iraq with local opposition to the occupation mounting, while the war in Afghanistan – which began in 2001 after the US elite, with UK support, sought an immediate target for their anger over the 9/11 atrocity – dragged on. As Rajiv Chandrasekaran (2012: 331) comments: 'Afghanistan stands alone in the annals of American warfare. It is the country's longest war. It is a forgotten war – with no draft, the fighting has been left to a small cadre of professional officers and volunteer grunts.'

With US bases expanding across the globe in an effort to counter mounting opposition to US imperialism, Afghanistan rapidly deteriorated into a narco-state. As Jane Shallice (2009: 15) reports: 'Warlords paid by the coalition to curb opium production instead pocketed the money while yields increased. With the economy in ruins, poppy cultivation became the only reliable source of income for farmers.'

British troops 'handed over security responsibilities to Iraqi authorities' Iraq in 2009.[24] And in October 2014, according to official sources, the last UK combat troops left Afghanistan.[25] Yet, as Curtis and Kennard (2019) report, some British troops stayed behind to help create and train an Afghan special forces unit while, in 2018, the SAS were fighting almost every day in Afghanistan.

In Iraq, some 348 journalists were killed while an estimated 1,455,590 Iraqis died directly due to the invasion of 2003.[26] Mark Weisbrot went so far as to call this a 'holocaust' (2007). Such a sorry tale, then, of unnecessary death and devastation.[27] Massive civilian deaths also resulted from the US military operations in Yemen (backed by a Western coalition including the UK and France) that began in 2002 while millions starved following the blockade imposed on the country by Saudi Arabia.

The monstrous expansion of the media–military–industrial complexes in both the UK and US continued to appear out of control[28] as US special forces were being deployed in 149 countries – far beyond the gaze of the international corporate media (Turse 2018). US general Joseph Votel, chief of the Special Operations Command, told the senate armed services committee that 'on any given day, 10,000 special operators are deployed or forward stationed conducting overseas missions' (*Private Eye* 2016). A freedom of information request in the US also revealed that UK special forces were involved with American forces in Libya and South Sudan 'in strength' (ibid). From 2007 to 2014, the US even tripled its deployment of special operations forces to Latin America, according to documents obtained via a Freedom of Information request by the non-profit Washington Office on Latin America (WOLA) (Hardt 2016).

By mid-2019, there were reports that US troops might quit Afghanistan following a deal with the Taliban, though the CIA and CIA-backed paramilitary groups such as the Khost Protection Force were expected to remain (Fitsanakis 2019). All this after billions of dollars have been spent on the conflict – and the deaths of 2,372 Americans, 454 British soldiers, 689 Nato forces and 111,000 Afghans (Loyd 2019). In addition, 71 journalists have been killed in Afghanistan since 2006.[29]

Indeed, with Western special forces embroiled in covert conflicts in Syria and US/UK military strategists increasingly resorting to special forces interventions, secret drone attacks and targeted assassinations in Somalia, Afghanistan, Iraq, Pakistan and Yemen together with little reported attacks from the air in Libya and Mali causing countless civilian casualties[30] – New Militarism has become Disaster Militarism (Keeble 2017: 293–320; Curtis and Kennard 2019).[31, 32]

Acknowledgements

This essay is based on a chapter with the same title in *Afghanistan, War and Media: Deadlines and Frontlines*, edited by Richard Lance Keeble and John Mair, Bury St Edmunds: Arima, 2010 pp 229–260.

Notes

1 At a time of general spending cuts (imposed by the government as a response to the global credit crisis and in an attempt to reduce the massive national debt) the defence budget was due to be increased in 2010 by more than £500 million to £38 billion (Norton-Taylor 2010b). David Swanson (2010) reported that Congress was expected to vote on $33 billion extra war funding for the Afghan troop 'surge'. According to the Congressional Budget Office, Congress had already approved $345 billion for the war in Afghanistan and $708 billion for the Iraq war. Government figures released on 19 June 2010 showed that Britain had spent at least £9.24 billion in Iraq and £11.1 billion since 2001. The actual cost, which did not include soldiers' salaries or caring for the wounded, was expected to be much higher (see http://news.bbc.co.uk/1/hi/uk/10359548.stm). The Pentagon also spends an enormous amount on fuel. In 2009 alone, according to the Pentagon's Defense Energy Support Centre, the military spent $3.8 billion on 31.3 million barrels (around 1.3 billion gallons) of oil consumed at posts, camps and bases overseas. Another $974 million was spent by the ground-fuels division just on the Afghan war in 2009. Also in 2009, the military awarded $22.5 billion in energy contracts. The largest contractor was BP which received more than $2.2 billion – almost 12 per cent of all petroleum-contract dollars awarded (see http://www.lobelog.com/tom gram-nick-turse-bp-and-the-pentagons-dirty-little-secret/)

2 After the killings of civilians during a night raid provoked massive protests in eastern Afghanistan, Nato commander Gen. McChrystal ordered his troops to avoid night raids (see Afghanistan: Protest erupts over Nato killings, *Morning Star*, 15–16 May 2010). Nato spokesman Gen. Joseph Blotz claimed in June 2010 civilian casualties had fallen by 44.4 per cent over the previous three months due to more stringent rules of engagement (see http://news.bbc.co.uk/1/hi/world/asia_pacific/10356741.stm)

3 According to Turse (2010), quoting Colonel Kevin Wilson, head of the building operations in southern Afghanistan for the US Army Corps of Engineers, the Americans were spending $3 billion on base-building in Afghanistan in 2010. In Iraq in August 2009, there were still almost 300 American bases and outposts. In addition to those in Iraq and Afghanistan, the Pentagon listed 716 overseas sites across the globe – especially in the Middle East, Europe, Japan and South Korea

4 See Evans and Norton-Taylor (2010). A Freedom of Information request by the *Guardian* revealed that the RAF had fired 845 missiles from Reaper drones since they were first deployed in June 2008. They planned to double the number of drones in use over the next two years. They were launched from a base in Kandahar but remotely controlled by a squadron of 90 RAF personnel at Creech US Air Force base in Nevada. Harvey (2009) reported that Predator drones were to rack up 1 million flight hours and that there were 35 Predators in the air at any one time. Harvey described the drones as being 'so successful in the fight against the Taliban and al-Qaeda'. Focusing on the new Avenger drone, Harvey said it could fly practically undetected at 60,000ft and was being 'fine-tuned' at Gray Butte flight operations facility of General Atomics Aeronautical Systems, Inc. But citing figures compiled by Pakistan's Interior Ministry, the Karachi-based daily, *News International*, reported that 'Afghanistan-based US Predators carried out a record number of 12 deadly missile strikes in the tribal areas of Pakistan in January 2010, of which 10 went wrong and failed to hit their targets, killing 123 innocent Pakistanis' (Van Auken 2010). Significantly, the US claimed in January 2010 that a drone

attack had killed the head of the Pakistan Taliban, Hakimullah Mehsud, in North War-zirstan. But in April 2010, new intelligence suggested that he had escaped – as the Taliban had always insisted (Buncombe and Waraich 2010; Walsh 2010a). In May 2010, the Americans claimed that Mustafa Abu al-Yazid, prominent in al-Qaeda in Afghanistan (and arrested over the killing of the Egyptian President Anwar Sadat in 1981), had been assassinated by missiles fired from a drone in Pakistan (Sengupta 2010d). His wife, three daughters and a granddaughter were all said to have also died in the attack. Al-Yazid was erroneously reported dead by Pakistan officials after a drone strike in August 2008 (Walsh 2010b)

5 Kim Sengupta (2010b) reported that the law on assassinations was aimed specifically at future attempts to target Anwar al-Awlaki, suspected of being the mentor to the 2009 Christmas Day 'underpants bomber' Umar Farouk Abdulmuttallab and US Army Major Nidal Malik Hasan who killed 13 people at Fort Hood in Texas in November 2009

6 See http://www.iiss.org/whats-new/iiss-in-the-press/october-2009/profile-stanley-mcchrystal/, accessed on 1 May 2010

7 A substantial genre of books has emerged celebrating the heroics of 'Our Boys' in Afghanistan. They include Moore (2003), Scott (2008), Kemp (1994), Hughes (2010), Kemp and Hughes (2009) and Junger (2010). Geoff Dyer (2010) argues that writing in this non-fiction genre is best able to capture the essence of US-style warfare today: 'Reportage, long-form reporting – call it what you will – has left the novel looking superfluous. The fiction lobby might respond: it's too soon to tell.' He adds: 'We are moving beyond the non-fiction novel to different kinds of narrative art, different forms of cognition. Loaded with moral and political point, narrative has been recalibrated to record, honour and protest the latest, historically specific instance of futility and mess'

8 Significantly, the *Mail* Foreign Service reported on 15 June 2010 that untapped ore – including huge veins of gold, iron, copper, cobalt and industrial metals such as lithium – valued at more than £820 billion had been discovered by geologists in Afghanistan. The article commented that the find 'will also raise question marks over the motives behind the long and costly war launched in the wake of the 9/11 attacks'. Later in the same week, the Americans tripled the estimated value of the untapped mineral wealth to $3 trillion

9 Some 23 of the 55 British deaths in Afghanistan from January to June 2010 had taken place around Sangin. Of the total Nato casualties of 1,849 on 21 June 2010 (drawn from the 25 countries of the coalition and including 125 US women), 1,125 were American, 147 Canadian, 44 French and 42 German (see Higginson, John (2010) 'Highest price must be paid', *Metro*, 22 June). Soldiers were also suffering major psychological problems. In June 2010, some 20,000 ex-servicemen were in prison or on probation in Britain – one in ten of the jail population. Since of 1982, 264 veterans of the Falklands conflict of that year have committed suicide, compared with 255 who died in action (Newton Dunn 2010)

10 The Americans, in addition to funding the Afghan police, had directed $1 million on building up private security forces (see Follorou 2010). Yet these companies were operating in a 'culture of impunity' that was encouraging lawlessness and corruption, according to Britain's most senior commander in southern Afghanistan, Major General Nick Carter (Norton-Taylor 2010e). According to investigative reporter Pratap Chatterjee (2010), the US had spent $7 billion on police training since 2003 but had left 'the country of 33 million people with a strikingly ineffective and remarkably corrupt police force. Its terrible habits and reputation have led the inhabitants of many Afghan communities to turn to the Taliban for security'. Fears were also growing that the Taliban had infiltrated the Afghan police (Wintour and Norton-Taylor 2010)

11 According to the *Sun*: 'Evil Taliban improvised bombs are usually packed with filth – they hope those they fail to kill outright die later from infection' (Willetts op cit). A UN Security Council report in June 2010 said that over the previous four months roadside bomb attacks rose by 94 per cent compared with the same period in 2009 while there

were three suicide bombings every week. See http://news.bbc.co.uk/1/hi/world/a sia_pacific/10356741.stm

12 See http://www.democracynow.org/2009/8/17/fixer_the_taking_of_ajmal_naqshba ndi, accessed on 1 May 2010

13 See http://www.truthtube.tv/play.php?vid=2795, accessed on 1 May 2010

14 Colin Hughes, of the *Daily Mirror*, was later sent death threats after he posted a blog that criticised a charity motorbike ride through Wootton Bassett, through which pass the hearses carrying the bodies of repatriated soldiers (Milmo 2010). After more than 5,000 Facebook members called for a boycott of the *Mirror*, the newspaper apologised for Hughes's posting

15 Soon after the arrest of Baradar Pakistan arrested two more senior Taliban figures, Mullah Abdul Salam and Mullah Mir Mohammad. Mystery surrounded the arrests. Some commentators considered that Islamabad was shifting away from its secret support for the Taliban. But as Shah (2010) commented in the *Guardian*: 'A more cynical interpretation suggested that instead of turning its back on the Taliban, Pakistan was simply putting pressure on them to come to the negotiating table'

16 See http://www.medialens.org/forum/viewtopic.php?t=3070&sid=76d871d7f9209d50c 8b991fc950f2a5d, accessed on 3 June 2010

17 See also Patrick Mulchrone's report on Beckham's visit and his praise for the 'fallen heroes' in the *Daily Mirror*. Available online at http://www.mirror.co.uk/celebs/news/ 2010/05/24/becks-silence-for-the-fallen-115875-22280836/, accessed on I June 2010

18 See http://www.wsws.org/articles/2010/jun2010/afgh-j19.shtml, accessed on 19 June 2010

19 See http://www.globalfirepower.com/defense-spending-budget.asp, accessed on 4 June 2010. Britain's figure represented a $3.7 billion increase on the previous year. *Guardian* columnist Simon Jenkins (2010) called for all the £45 billion defence spending 'against fantasy enemies' to be cut

20 ibid

21 See http://news.bbc.co.uk/1/hi/world/south_asia/10274262.stm, accessed on 9 June 2010

22 Nato strategy in Afghanistan was thrown into further disarray with the resignation of the German President, Hörst Kohler, after he had suggested that military deployments were central to the country's economic interests (Connolly 2010)

23 See inthesetimes.com/2010/04/03/german-easter-rallies-decry-afghanistan-killings, acces- sed on 4 May 2010

24 See http://www.telegraph.co.uk/news/worldnews/middleeast/iraq/3699368/British-for ces-to-withdraw-from-Iraq-timeline-of-our-military-presence.html, accessed on 19 August 2016. The British mainstream media faithfully reported this as 'withdrawal'. 'In reality, the handover was essentially to the Shia militias who had long controlled Basra province' (Curtis 2010: 327). A BBC poll conducted in Basra found that only 2 per cent believed the British presence had had a positive impact on the province since 2003 while 86 per cent said the impact had been negative (ibid: 329)

25 http://www.bbc.co.uk/news/uk-35159951

26 http://www.justforeignpolicy.org/iraq

27 See http://watson.brown.edu/costsofwar/costs/human/civilians, accessed on 26 Octo- ber 2016

28 Under President Barack (Nobel Peace Prize-winning) Obama US defence spending rose to $663.4 billion per year, though if military-related spending by the CIA, Homeland Security, Energy, Justice or State Departments, and interest payments on past military spending are included, this figure rises to $1.3 trillion a year. See http://warisacrime.org/ content/record-us-military-budget?link_id=5&can_id= ed31bf4cbc8f991980718b21b49ca26d&source=email-the-unbearable-awesomenes s-of-the-us-military&email_referrer=the-unbearable-awesomeness-of-the-us-military& email_subject=the-unbearable-awesomeness-of-the-us-military, accessed on 19 August 2016. By the early years of the 21st century, the US defence establishment, in fact, could

be ranked as the world's 17th largest economy. It is the largest oil consumer in the US and 31st in the world. On its books, officially, are listed 725 overseas sites deploying 254,788 personnel in 153 countries (Todd, Bloch and Fitzgerald 2009: 76)

29 See https://en.unesco.org/themes/safety-journalists/observatory/country/223649, accessed on 6 September 2019. Details of casualties in all theatres of conflict are available at the website of the US-based Armed Conflict and Location Project, www.acleddata.com

30 See also https://www.thebureauinvestigates.com/category/projects/drones. A report by Drones Wars UK claimed that the government had spent more than £2 billion on buying and developing military drones over the previous five years. The UK's Reaper drones in Afghanistan flew 11,000 hours and fired over 280 laser-guided Hellfire missiles and bombs at suspected insurgents between May 2011 and May 2012. See https://www.theguardian.com/world/2012/sep/26/drone-spending-britain-tops-2bn, accessed on 22 August 2016. On 10 June 2016, James Dean (2016) reported that the RAF's new artificially intelligent drone would have the ability to attack targets of its own accord. It was being developed under the Unmanned Combat Air System project, an Anglo-French programme costing £1.5 billion – successor to the RAF's Taranis programme and its French equivalent, Neuron

31 Even as early as July 2004, a survey by Zogby International in six targeted Arab countries showed support for the US in virtual freefall – with those in favour dropping over a two-year period from pre-Iraq figure of 38 per cent to 11 per cent in Morocco, the main supporter of the group (see Todd, Bloch and Fitzgerald 2009: 45)

32 I would like to thank my son, Gabriel Keeble-Gagnère, for suggesting this phrase for describing the New New Militarism. It builds on Naomi Klein's brilliant exposure of disaster capitalism (namely 'the rapid-fire corporate reengineering of societies still reeling from shock') in her *Shock Doctrine*, of 2007 (see http://www.naomiklein.org/shock-doctrine)

References

Aksamentova, Polina (2009) Withdrawal majority censored, *Peace News*, September, No. 2513

Amoore, Miles and Colvin, Marie (2010) British spearhead allied offensive, *Sunday Times*, 14 February

Astore, William J. (2010) Doubling down in Afghanistan, *tomdispatch*, 3 June. Available online at http://www.tomdispatch.com/archive/175256/, accessed on 2 June 2010

Bishop, Patrick (2010) *Ground Truth: Back on Afghanistan's Frontline – 3 Para's Epic New Challenge*, London: Harper Press

Boone, Jon (2010a) Afghan minister resigns over jirga attack, *Guardian*, 7 June

Boone, Jon (2010b) Afghanistan: 24-hour patrols in Kandahar to win hearts and find mines, *Guardian*, 10 March

Boone, Jon and Norton-Taylor, Richard (2010) Poppy town that became deathtrap for British army, *Guardian*, 22 June

Borger, Julian (2009) Karzai's brother in pay of CIA for eight years, US officials claim, *Guardian*, 29 October

Bowcott, Owen (2010) Army shortages cost lives, bishop warns, *Guardian*, 29 April

Bulstrode, Mark (2010) Snatch Land Rovers blamed for dozens of deaths, *Independent*, 9 March

Buncombe, Andrew and Waraich, Omar (2010) Taliban leader was not killed by drone strike, says Pakistan, *Independent*, 30 April

Cavendish, Julius (2010a) Fighters switch back to Taliban after 'broken promises', *Independent*, 23 April

Cavendish, Julius (2010b) Mosque murder leaves Kandahar on edge, *Independent*, 21 April

Chandrasekaran, Rajiv (2012) *Little America: The War Within the War for Afghanistan*, London: Bloomsbury

Chatterjee, Pratap (2010) Policing Afghanistan: How Afghan police training became a train wreck, *tomdispatch.com*, 21 March. Available online at www.tomdispatch.com/blog/175220/, accessed on 3 June 2010

Cobain, Ian, MacAskill, Ewen and Stoddard, Katy (2014) Britain's hundred years of conflict, *Guardian*, 11 February. Available online at https://www.theguardian.com/uk-news/ng-interactive/2014/feb/11/britain-100-years-of-conflict, accessed on 11 June 2019

Cockburn, Patrick (2010a) The secret war – and the hidden lair of the Taliban, *Independent*, 16 April

Cockburn, Patrick (2010b) Caught in the crossfire of Pakistan's secret war, *Independent*, 22 April

Cogan, James (2010) Afghanistan: Another massacre as a bloody summer looms in Kandahar, *wsws.org*, 23 April. Available online at www.wsws.org/articles/2010/apr2010/afgh-a23.shtml, accessed on 24 April 2010

Collins, John M. (1991) *America's Small Wars*, London/Washington DC: Brasseys (US)

Colvin, Marie (2010) Special forces assassins infiltrate Taliban strongholds in Afghanistan, *Sunday Times*, 7 February

Conetta, Carl (2004) *Disappearing the Dead: Iraq, Afghanistan and the Idea of 'New Warfare'*, Project on Defense Alternatives Research Monograph 9. Available online at http://www.conw.org/pda/0402rm9.html, accessed on 30 May 2004

Connolly, Kate (2010) German President quits amid accusations of 'gunboat diplomacy' after Afghanistan gaffe, *Guardian*, 1 June

Cornwell, Rupert (2010a) US to launch covert strikes on terror targets, *Independent*, 26 May

Cornwell, Rupert (2010b) When it comes to terrorism, Obama is following Bush's lead, *Independent*, 26 May

Currey, Cecil (1991) Vietnam: Lessons learned, Helling, Phil and Roper, Jon (eds) *America, France and Vietnam: Cultural History and Ideas of Conflict*, Aldershot: Avebury pp 71–90

Curtis, Mark (2010) *Secret Affairs: British Collusion with Radical Islam*, London: Serpent's Tail

Curtis, Mark and Kennard, Matt (2019) Britain's seven covert wars: An explainer, *dailymaverick.co.za*, 17 September. Available online at https://www.dailymaverick.co.za/article/2019-09-17-britains-seven-covert-wars-an-explainer/

Dalrymple, William (2010) The British army overwhelmed by Afghan warriors. No, not today but in 1842. So can we learn lessons of history before it happens again?, *Daily Mail*, 17 June

de la Billière, Sir Peter (1995) *Looking for Trouble: SAS to Gulf Command*, London: HarperCollins

Dyer, Geoff (2010) The human heart of the matter, *Guardian*, 12 June

Evans, Michael (2010) Complacent British ignored advice that force was too small, say Pentagon officials, *Times*, 10 June

Evans, Rob and Norton-Taylor, Richard (2010) RAF strategy in Afghanistan shifts to drones, *Guardian*, 8 February

Featherstone, Donald (1993a) *Victorian Colonial Warfare: Africa*, London: Blandford

Featherstone, Donald (1993b) *Victorian Colonial Warfare: India*, London: Blandford

Fitsanakis, Joseph (2019) Despite imminent US–Taliban deal, CIA plans to keep proxy units in Afghanistan, *intelnews.org*, 9 August. Available online at https://intelnews.org/2019/08/09/01-2605/, accessed on 13 August 2019

Foley, Stephen (2010) Obama rallies the troops on surprise visit to Afghanistan, *Independent*, 29 March

Follorou, Jacques (2010) Le état d'âmes des policiers afghan, privés de moyens et minés par la corruption, *Le Monde*, 9 June

Gopal, Anand (2010) Afraid of the dark in Afghanistan, 28 January. Available online at www.tomdispatch.com/dialogs/print/?id=175197, accessed on 29 January 2010

Grey, Stephen (2009a) *Operation Snake Bite: The Explosive True Story of an Afghan Desert Siege*, London: Viking

Grey, Stephen (2009b) New elite force for Helmand, *Sunday Times*, 6 September

Halliday, Fred (1989) *Cold War, Third World: An Essay on Soviet–American Relations*, London: Radius

Hardt, Neil (2016) US triples special operations deployment in Latin America, *wsws.org*, 14 September. Available online at https://www.wsws.org/en/articles/2016/09/14/lati-s14.html, accessed on 18 November 2019

Harvey, Mike (2009) Avenger of the skies: Next wave of drones takes off, *Times*, 3 October

Harvey, Oliver (2010) The *Sun* goes into Helmand with our brave army medics, *Sun*, 26 February

Haynes, Deborah (2010) The Whitehall brass and mandarins who set up the bloodiest mission since Korea, *Times*, 10 June

Helm, Toby and Beaumont, Peter (2010) Cameron calls Chequers summit as strains grow over coalition's aims in Afghanistan, *Observer*, 30 May

Hughes, Chris (2010) Fine, fearless, dedicated, *Daily Mirror*, 11 January

Hunter, Robin (1995) *True Stories of the SAS*, London: Virgin

Jenkins, Simon (2010) My once-in-a-generation cut? The armed forces. All of them, *Guardian*, 9 June

Junger, Sebastian (2010) *War*, London: Fourth Estate

Keeble, Richard (2004) Information warfare in an age of hyper-militarism, Allan, Stuart and Zelizer, Barbie (eds) (2004) *Reporting War: Journalism in Wartime*, London and New York: Routledge pp 43–58

Keeble, Richard (2007) The necessary spectacular 'victories': New Militarism, the mainstream media and the manufacture of the two Gulf conflicts 1991 and 2003, Maltby, Sarah and Keeble, Richard (eds) *Communicating War: Memory, Media and Military*, Bury St Edmunds: Arima pp 200–212

Keeble, Richard Lance (2017) *Covering Conflict: The Making and Unmaking of New Militarism*, Bury St Edmunds: Abramis

Kemp, Anthony (1994) *The SAS: Savage Wars of Peace*, London: Signet

Kemp, Col.Richard and Hughes, Chris (2009) *Attack State: Taking the Fight to the Enemy. The Awesome Untold Story of a Landmark Tour of Duty in Afghanistan*, London and New York: Michael Joseph

Khan, Sartaj and Prasad, Yuri (2010) Crisis and conflict in Pakistan, *International Socialism*, Vol. 126, 14 April. Available online at http://www.isj.org.uk/index.php4?id=636&issue=126, accessed on 12 May 2010

Kirkup, James (2010) Kandahar offensive to target 1,000 Taliban, *Daily Telegraph*, 2 June

Lamb, Christina (2010) Battle for town is small step on the path to victory, *Sunday Times*, 14 February

Larcombe, Duncan (2010) Mud 'n guts, *Sun*, 15 February

Leith, Sam (2010) The secret war on terror sets a bad example, *Evening Standard*, 7 June

Loyd, Anthony (2019) We're back and ready to take power, declare Taliban, *Times*, 20 July pp 38–39

MacAskill, Ewen (2010) US sends more soldiers on covert mission, *Guardian*, 26 May

MacAskill, Ewen, Nasaw, Daniel and Boone, Jon (2010) CIA agents in Afghanistan are 'menace to themselves', former operatives claim, *Guardian*, 6 January

MacKenzie, John (1984) *Propaganda and Empire: The Manipulation of British Public Opinion 1880–1960*, Manchester: Manchester University Press

Martin, Patrick (2010) US military noose tightens on Afghanistan town, *wsws.org*, 12 February. Available online at http://www.wsws.org/articles/2010/feb2010/afgh-f12.shtml, accessed on 13 February 2010

Mellen, Tom (2010) Afghans 'not ready to fight yet', *Morning Star*, 8–9 May

Milmo, Cahal (2010) Forces of Facebook turn on the *Daily Mirror*, *Independent*, 19 March

Milne, Seamus (2009) In a war for democracy, why worry about public opinion, *Guardian*, 15 October

Moore, Robin (2003) *Taskforce Dagger: The Hunt for Bin Laden*, New York: Random House

Morning Star (2010) Pakistani military gets 17% boost to spending, *Morning Star*, 7 June

Morris, Nigel (2010) Afghan war is unwinnable and we should pull it now, say voters, *Independent*, 21 April

Newsinger, John (1989) A forgotten war: British intervention in Indonesia, *Race and Class*, Vol. 30, No. 4 pp 51–66

Newsinger, John (1995) The myth of the SAS, *Lobster*, Vol. 30 pp 32–36

Newton Dunn, Tom (2010) Troops to get trauma help, *Sun*, 7 June

Norton-Taylor, Richard (2010a) British troops may leave Helmand as tension grows over Afghan role, *Guardian*, 22 April

Norton-Taylor, Richard (2010b) Cost of war in Afghanistan soars to £2.5bn, *Guardian*, 13 February

Norton-Taylor, Richard (2010c) Afghan police failings fuelling Taliban, say UK army chiefs, *Guardian*, 4 June

Norton-Taylor, Richard (2010d) Four more years of Afghan war, warns Nato official, *Guardian*, 30 April

Norton-Taylor, Richard (2010e) Afghan private security firms 'fuelling corruption', *Guardian*, 14 May

Peak, Steve (1982) Britain's military adventures, *The Pacifist*, Vol. 20 p 10

Pilger, John (2003) What good friends left behind, *Guardian Weekend*, 20 September pp 43–49

Pilger, John (2010) A predatory ideology in denial, *Morning Star*, 27–28 March pp 10–11

Porter, Gareth (2010a) Night raids belie McChrystal's new image, *Asia Times*, 2 April. Available online at inthesetimes.com/2010/04/03/night-raids-belie-mcchrystals-new-image/#more-11017

Porter, Gareth (2010b) Marja, the city that never was, *Coldtype Reader* pp 8–9. Available online at http://www.coldtype.net/Assets.10/Pdfs/0410.Reader45.pdf, accessed on 22 May 2010

Private Eye (2016) Nothing special here, No. 1427, 16–29 September p 37

Ray, Ellen and Schaap, William H. (1991) Disinformation and covert action, *Covert Action Information Bulletin*, No. 37, summer pp 9–13

Rayment, Sean (2010) The hidden victims of war: 1,000 casualties of the Afghan conflict, *Sunday Telegraph*, 21 February

Rose, Stephen (1986) Spend, spend, spend – on military only, *New Statesman*, 3 January

Scahill, Jeremy (2013) *Dirty Wars: The World is a Battlefield*, London: Serpent's Tail

Scott, Jake (2008) *Blood Clot: In Combat with the Patrols Platoon, 3 Para, Afghanistan, 2006*, Solihull: Helion

Sengupta, Kim (2010a) US cruise missile parts found in Yemeni village where 52 died, *Independent*, 7 June

Sengupta, Kim (2010b) Army given new rifles to engage enemies from further away, *Independent*, 7 June

Sengupta, Kim (2010c) British military split over plan to move troops to Kandahar, *Independent*, 27 April

Sengupta, Kim (2010d) UN asks drone attacks to be taken out of CIA's hands, *Independent*, 3 June 2010

Senguta, Kim (2010e) Warning to politicians about early Afghan troop pull-out, *Independent*, 28 May

Sengupta, Kim and Morris, Nigel (2010) Afghan war is bad for security, voters say, *Independent*, 11 November

Shah, Saeed (2010) Taliban arrests in Pakistan amid talk of policy shift, *Guardian*, 19 February

Shallice, Jane (2009) Afghanistan: A brief history, *Red Pepper*, No. 166, June/July p 15

Southwell, David (2005) *Secrets and Lies: Exposing the World of Cover-Ups and Deception*, London: Sevenoaks

Stiglitz, Joseph and Bilmes, Linda (2009) *The Three Trillion Dollar War*, London: Penguin

Stockwell, John (1991) *The Praetorian Guard: The US Role in the New World Order*, Boston: South End Press

Sturcke, James (2008) SAS commander quits in Snatch Land Rover row, *Guardian*, 1 November. Available online at http://www.guardian.co.uk/uk/2008/nov/01/sas-comma nder-quits-afghanistan, accessed on 1 May 2009

Swanson, David (2010) Afghan escalation funding, *tomdispatch.com*, 11 May. Available online at http://www.tomdispatch.com/blog/175246/tomgram%3A_david_swanson,_did_you_ say_$33_billion__/, accessed on 12 May 2010

Taylor, Matthew (2009) Kidnapped *Guardian* journalist released, *Guardian*, 17 December

Todd, Paul, Bloch, Jonathan and Fitzgerald, Patrick (2009) *Spies, Lies and the War on Terror*, London and New York: Zed Books

Turse, Nick (2008) The trillion dollar tag sale, *nickturse.com*, 26 October. Available online at http://www.nickturse.com/articles/tom_trillion.html, accessed on 1 May 2009

Turse, Nick (2010) The 700 military bases of Afghanistan, *tomdispatch.com*, 9 February. Available online at http://www.tomdispatch.com/blog/175204/tomgram:_nick_turse, _america's_shadowy_base_world/, accessed on 10 February 2010

Turse, Nick (2018) Commandos Sans Frontières: The global growth of US Special Operations Forces, *tomdispatch.com*, 17 July. Available online at http://www.tomdispatch.com/ blog/176448/tomgram%3A_nick_turse%2C_special_ops%3A_133_countries_down%2C_ 17_to_go, accessed on 12 June 2019

Turse, Nick and Engelhardt, Tom (2010) Shooting gnats with a machine, *tomdispatch.com*, 14 January. Available online at www.tomdispatch.com/dialogs/print/?id=175191

Van Auken, Bill (2010) Obama's surge: Killing spree on both sides of Afpak border, *wsws.org*, 3 February. Available online at http://www.wsws.org/articles/2010/feb2010/afpk-f03.shtml, accessed on 1 May 2010

Walsh, David (2010) US military's private spy and murder ring continues to operate in Afghanistan, Pakistan, *wsws.org*, 18 May. Available online at www.wsws.org/articles/ 2010/may2010/cont-m18.shtml, accessed on 20 May 2010

Walsh, Declan (2010a) Taliban leader in Pakistan survived CIA drone strike said to have killed him, spy agency says, *Guardian*, 29 April

Walsh, Declan (2010b) US hails 'big victory' after Islamist website confirms drone strike killed al-Qaida veteran, *Guardian*, 2 June

Waugh, Rob (2010) The rise of the robo-fighters, *Daily Mail*, 5 May

Willetts, David (2010) A wing and a prayer, *Sun*, 7 June

Wintour, Patrick and Norton-Taylor, Richard (2010) Commanders fear Taliban infiltration as troops hunt assassin, *Guardian*, 11 May

9

GIVING PEACE JOURNALISM A CHANCE

Introduction

Since the 1970s, a movement has emerged amongst academics and social movement activists promoting the theory of peace journalism – and aiming to inspire further activities. This chapter will argue that the theory has inappropriately prioritised mainstream activities – and failed to acknowledge adequately the role of the alternative media – both historically and today. Such a debate raises a number of important questions. For instance, how are both the peace movement and journalism defined? Is there not a danger of exaggerating the distinctions between alternative and mainstream media? Are there not some progressive spaces within the mainstream to be exploited by peace journalists?

This chapter seeks to highlight the corporate media's historic function to promote overall the dominant political, military, economic, ideological and cultural interests in society. Research has confirmed that the mainstream, professionalised media, given its close ties to the military/industrial/entertainment complex, tends to support warfare and downplays opportunities for the peaceful resolution of conflicts (e.g. Carruthers 2000; Andersen 2006). In this context, it can be seen that, historically, the non-corporate, alternative media have played a crucial role in promoting the interests of the peace movement globally – thus providing a voice to the otherwise marginalised or silenced. The chapter will provide a brief history of peace journalism (PJ), a survey of the overall state of PJ today – and a brief focus on two major, contemporary examples of PJ.

The emergence of peace journalism theory and its focus on the mainstream

Peace journalism theory emerged during the 1970s amongst peace researchers, activists and academics, but the activities of the alternative media were hardly acknowledged (Shinar and Kempf 2007: 9). The seminal theoretical study was conducted by Johan Galtung (1998; see also Lynch 1998: 44), one of the founders of the academic subject of Peace Studies, who essentially contrasted the elements of what he described as 'peace/conflict journalism' with those of 'war/violence journalism'. The theory, then, emerged as a critique of the dominant mode of covering conflict in the mainstream media – and solutions were sought from within the mainstream.

PJ, according to Galtung, gives 'a voice to all parties', emphasises the invisible effects of violence (psychological trauma, damage of social structures), aims to 'expose untruths on all sides', is 'people-oriented', gives a 'voice to the voiceless' and is solution-oriented. In contrast, war journalism dehumanises the enemy, focuses on only the visible effects of violence, is propaganda-oriented, elite-focused and victory-obsessed – and tends to concentrate on institutions (the 'controlled society'). Another seminal text, by Jake Lynch and Annabel McGoldrick offers a 17-point plan for developing PJ (Lynch and McGoldrick 2005: 28–31), in which improving professional practice within the mainstream remains the priority. Their points include:

- avoid concentrating always on what divides parties, on the differences between what each say they want. Instead, try asking questions which may reveal areas of common ground;
- avoid focusing on the suffering, fears and grievances of only one party ... Instead, treat as equally newsworthy the suffering, fears and grievances of all parties.

In keeping with their stress on professional media, Lynch and McGoldrick suggest the London-based *Independent* as one of the best examples of peace journalism. While the newspaper carries the outstanding reports of veteran reporters Robert Fisk (see Keeble 2012) and Patrick Cockburn, critical research suggests that the newspaper tends to reproduce Fleet Street's dominant news values (Zollmann 2009; Keeble 1997, 1999, 2000, 2004). Another important text, *Peace Journalism: The State of the Art* (Shinar and Wilhelm Kempf 2007), contains the work of some of the leading theorists in the field, though most concentrate on professional issues and only rarely acknowledge any 'alternative' outlets. Susan Dente Ross ends a highly detailed overview of peace journalism literature by suggesting that no 'revolutionary' changes are needed: 'Peace journalism does not involve any radical departure from contemporary journalism practice. Rather peace journalism requires numerous subtle and cumulative shifts in seeing, thinking, sourcing, narrating and financing the news' (Ross 2007: 74).

The dominant strand of peace journalism theory views journalism as a privileged, professional activity. It fails to acknowledge the critical intellectual tradition which considers professions as essentially occupational groupings with a legal monopoly of social and economic opportunities in the marketplace, underwritten by the state (Althusser 1969; Illich 1973; Parkin 1979; Collins 1990). PJ theory, in short, is too elitist and too utopian in suggesting that improvements in professional routines and reforms in journalistic training can bring about significant changes (Keeble 2010). And it is too reluctant to acknowledge the crucial role played by the alternative media – both historically and today – in promoting peace.

Is change possible from within the mainstream?

Yet PJ theory and practice should not totally exclude the mainstream. Its closeness to dominant economic, cultural and ideological forces means that the mainstream largely functions to promote the interests of the military–industrial–political–entertainment complex (Herman and Chomsky 1988; Der Derian 2001). Yet within advanced capitalist economies, currently suffering acute downturns following the 2008 crisis (which, to a large extent, stemmed from the over-resourcing of US/UK military and imperial adventurism) the contradictions within corporate media provide certain spaces for progressive journalism.

Chris Atton (2004: 10) warns against presenting a polarised vision of the mainstream and alternative spheres, positing a 'hegemonic approach' that 'suggests a complexity of relationships between radical and mainstream that previous binary models have been unable to identify'. Robert Hackett (2007) suggests that a way ahead for PJ is to reform mainstream journalism from within. Herman and Chomsky's (1988: 2) propaganda model stresses the role of the corporate media in forming a single propaganda system where 'money and power are able to filter out the news fit to print, marginalise dissent and allow the government and dominant private interests to get their message across to the public'. But for Hackett, their model is too deterministic. It thus fails to 'identify the scope and conditions under which newsworkers could exercise the kind of choices called for by PJ' and to acknowledge that individual journalists are 'active and creative agents' able to combine an involvement in the corporate media with regular contributions to alternative, partisan, campaigning media (Hackett 2007: 93).

Hackett also draws on the 'hierarchy of influences' model of Shoemaker and Reese (1996) and Bourdieu's (1998) notion of the media as a relatively autonomous institutional sphere to theorise further the activities of progressive newsworkers within the corporate media to promote the interests of the peace movement. Arguing that both models suggest some degree of agency for newsworkers, Hackett (2007: 93) stresses: 'There is, indeed, a necessary role for dedicated journalists to take the lead.' At the same time, he acknowledges the severe constraints on progressive journalists operating within the mainstream: 'Ultimately it seems probable that in Western corporate media at least, journalists have neither sufficient incentives nor autonomy *vis-à-vis* their employers to transform the way news is done without support from powerful external allies' (ibid). Oliver Boyd-Barrett (2010) also highlights the propaganda model's failure to acknowledge journalists' individual agency, though his focus is more on the penetration of corporate media by covert intelligence and their sympathisers.

The historical role of the alternative media (in brief)

Conventional histories of the media tend to marginalise or ignore altogether the non-corporate media. This should not come as a surprise: the essential ideological function of the dominant political and cultural spheres is to silence the voices of progressive and revolutionary social movements (Keeble 1997). Yet the historic role of the alternative media (of which the peace movement media is a part) in the formation of a counter or oppositional public sphere is considerable both in the UK and internationally, and as has been highlighted by scholars (see, for example, Atton and Hamilton 2008; Couldry and Curran 2003; Downing 1984; Forde 2011; Harcup 2003, 2013; Nelson 1989; Rodriguez 2001; Sparks 1985; Waltz 2005).

To take just a few specific examples: John Hartley (1996) has highlighted the importance of journalists such as Robespierre, Marat, Danton and Hébert to the French Revolution of the 1790s (see also Chapman 2008). In the first half of the 19th century in the UK, a popular, radical, unstamped (and hence illegal) press played a crucial role in the campaign for trade union rights and social and political reforms (Black 2001; Conboy 2004; Curran and Seaton 2004). Many feminists and suffragettes (such as Sylvia Pankhurst: see Davis 1999) were radical journalists, pacifists and political agitators. Most studies of the Vietnam War (1965–1973) have failed to identify the role of the many anti-war newspapers that cropped up in the armed services during the course of the conflict in both reflecting and inspiring opposition to the conflict. On the other hand, Jonathan Neale (2001: 122–130) identified around 300 anti-war newspapers: for instance, a small group of Trotskyists were behind *Vietnam GI*, which was produced in Chicago with a print run of 15,000 and a mailing list of 3,000 in Vietnam. At Fort Bragg, a chapter of GIs United Against the War put out *Bragg Briefs*.

After the 1964 Gulf of Tonkin incident (in which a US naval destroyer was allegedly attacked by North Vietnamese torpedo boats, providing President Johnson the pretext to launch the war on the North) the corporate media were either hawkish or believers in the 'official word'. I. F. Stone, self-publisher of the *I. F. Stone Weekly*, was alone in highlighting the administration's lies and in running the views of the two lone Senators who opposed the war, Wayne Morse and Ernst Gruening (MacPherson 2006). Moreover, for many, the greatest scoop of the Vietnam conflict was Seymour Hersh's exposure of the Mai Lai massacre of up to 500 women and children by US soldiers in March 1968 – significantly this was first published by the alternative news agency, Despatch News Service (Knightley 1982: 259–260).

Defining the global contemporary peace movement

Consideration of contemporary PJ needs to begin with a definition of the global peace movement which it is aiming to inform, inspire and, indeed, entertain. One of the most useful overviews appears in *Housmans Peace Diary*, produced over the last 61 years by Housmans radical bookshop in London. In its 2014 edition there is a listing of around 1,500 peace groups from around the world. It begins with international organisations: from Abolition 2000 International Secretariat through the European Bureau for Conscientious Objection, the Global Anabaptist Peace and Justice Network and Mayors for Peace through to the South Asia Peace Alliance, War Resisters' International and the World Peace Council. It moves on to national organisations in 136 countries: from the Women, Peace and Security Research Institute of Afghanistan and Footprints for Peace of Australia, through Britain's Campaign for a Nuclear-Free Middle East and Coalition of Resistance to Zimbabwe's Institute of Peace, Leadership and Governance.

The list highlights the global breadth of the peace movement. It is hardly a distinct, unified grouping, but one closely intertwined with broader (and often competing) social, environmental, religious, feminist, gay rights, educational and human rights movements. Thus, in the Canada section, Toronto Action for Social Change/Homes not Bombs is listed; in Rwanda, there is Shalom: Educating for Peace and in the US Psychologists for Social Responsibility (among more than 180 entries). To complicate the issue even further, within these individual organisations there are often factions competing for prominence. Despite its enormity and complexity, the list might even be seen as failing to convey the full picture since trade unions and political parties are excluded – even though those (particularly of the left, such as the Socialist Workers Party, the Socialist Equality Party, the Communist Party and their international affiliates) can play important roles in peace movements.

All of the organisations listed have internet sites, newsletters or journals and email contacts. Many have a presence on YouTube and Facebook. In other words, via the web and blogosphere – far beyond Jürgen Habermas's (1974) original conception of a national public sphere – it could be argued that a global alternative public sphere (with all its internal contradictions and complexities) has emerged. Indeed, PJ activities are perhaps best understood as operating in this counter-public sphere and global network society (Castells 2009). Certainly, the activities of this extraordinarily dynamic, diverse, imaginative and global alternative peace movement (and its associated media activities) have been too often ignored by mainstream journalists and the academy.

Peace journalism: Broadening the definitions of journalism and journalist

Peace movement media, like other non-corporate outlets, have always tended to rely on the work of non-professional journalists: citizens and community/political activists. As in Chris Atton's (2002: 25) definition of alternative media: 'They typically go beyond simply providing a platform for radical or alternative points of view: they emphasise the organisation of media to enable wider social participation in their creation, production and dissemination than is possible in the mass media.' Thus, these well-established working arrangements long pre-dated recent discussions about the nature of journalism – provoked by the emergence of the internet and its many communicative forms. Stuart Allan (2006: 7), for instance, celebrates the bloggers and the 'extraordinary contribution made by ordinary citizens offering their first-hand reports, digital photographs, camcorder video footage, mobile telephone snapshots or audio clips'. John Hartley (2008: 42) even draws on Article 19 of the Universal Declaration of Human Rights to proclaim the radical, utopian-liberal ideal that everyone has the right not only to seek and receive but also to 'impart' (in other words, communicate) information and ideas.

Alternative journalists

This broadened definition of journalism certainly helps to incorporate a wide range of media and political activists into the discussion on PJ. For instance, it could include radical, progressive journalists and their associated media such as, in the United States, *Democracy Now!* an alternative broadcast station (with allied website) run by the award-winning Amy Goodman, which is overtly committed to peace journalism. As its website stresses:

> *Democracy Now!*'s War and Peace Report provides our audience with access to people and perspectives rarely heard in the US corporate-sponsored media, including independent and international journalists, ordinary people from around the world who are directly affected by US foreign policy, grassroots leaders and peace activists, artists, academics and independent analysts. In addition, *Democracy Now!* hosts real debates – debates between people who substantially disagree, such as between the White House or the Pentagon spokespeople on the one hand, and grassroots activists on the other (www. democracynow.org).

Other peace-oriented, progressive journals include *Middle East Report* (www.merip. org), *Nation* (www.thenation.com), *Mother Jones* (www.motherjones.com), *Z Magazine* (www.zcommunications.org/zmag), and *In These Times* (www.inthesetimes.com). In Chennai, India, there is *Frontline* (https://frontline.thehindu.com/) while in London there is the investigative website *Corporate Watch* (www.corporatewatch.org). Media such as these often draw inspiration from Noam Chomsky's (1988) critique of the corporate myths of 'balance' and 'objectivity' and emphasise instead their explicitly partisan character. Moreover, they seek to 'invert the hierarchy of access' to the news by explicitly foregrounding the viewpoints of 'ordinary' people (activists, protestors, local residents), citizens whose visibility in the mainstream media tends to be obscured by the presence of elite groups and individuals (Atton 2002: 20).

The role of progressive intellectuals

A broadened definition of journalist should also acknowledge the role of progressive intellectuals within peace journalism. For instance, the American historian Tom Engelhardt, with his colleague Nick Turse, runs the radical, investigative website *tomdispatch.com*. Other radical intellectuals prominent in the blogosphere have included the late Edward Said, Noam Chomsky, Norman Solomon, James Winter, Mark Curtis and the late African intellectual, campaigner and journalist Tajudeen Abdul-Raheem. The website *Coldtype.net* publishes the work of many of these writers in PDF magazine format. In the UK, Professor David Miller and William Dinan are part of a collective running *Spinwatch* (www.spinwatch.org) which critiques the PR industry from a radical, peace perspective. David Edwards and David Cromwell edit the radical media monitoring site *Media Lens* (www.medialens.org), which maintains a constant critique of the mainstream print and broadcast media from a radical Chomskyite, Buddhist perspective and in support of the global peace movement. It also seeks to encourage peace activists to be inspired by their critiques to engage in follow-up protest activities (such as letter writing and demonstrating) against the mainstream media. As its website states:

> Since 2001, we have been describing how mainstream newspapers and broadcasters operate as a propaganda system for the elite interests that dominate modern society. The costs of their disinformation in terms of human and animal suffering, and environmental breakdown, are incalculable. We show how news and commentary are 'filtered' by the media's profit-orientation, by its dependence on advertisers, parent companies, wealthy owners and official news sources. We check the media's version of events against credible facts and opinion provided by journalists, academics and specialist researchers. We then publish both versions, together with our commentary, in free Media Alerts and invite readers to deliver their verdict both to us and to mainstream journalists through the email addresses provided in our 'Suggested Action' at the end of each alert. We urge correspondents to adopt a polite, rational and respectful tone at all times – we strongly oppose all abuse and personal attack.

The website *globalresearch.ca* is run by the Center for Research and Globalisation, an independent media and research group based in Montreal, Canada. It carries articles by Michel Chossudovsky, Professor of Economics at the University of Ottawa, amongst other prominent activist academics. Special thematic sections on the site have focused on '9/11 and the "War on Terrorism"', 'Crimes against Humanity', 'Media Disinformation', 'Militarisation and WMD', 'Poverty and Social Inequality' and 'Women's Rights'. Subjects of in-depth reports include 'Syria: Nato's Next War?', the 'Arab Protest War' and 'Occupy Wall Street'.

Human rights and peace journalism

Ibrahim Seaga Shaw (2012) extends the debate over peace journalism with a special focus on human rights reporting. Drawing on Johan Galtung's (1998) theories relating to visible and invisible violence, his concerns embrace:

> ... direct physical violence – such as genocide, arbitrary arrest and detentions, extra-judicial killings, rape, torture, ethnic cleansing and the mistreatment of prisoners – or indirect forms of cultural and structural violence such as hate speech, racism, xenophobia, poverty, famine, corruption, colonialism, slavery, unfair trade, forced migration, forced labour, human trafficking, margin-alisation or the exclusion of minorities (Shaw 2012: 11).

From this perspective, international human rights organisations that produce campaigning sites and publications (reports, magazines, leaflets) can be seen as practising activist peace journalism. Reprieve (www.reprieve.org.uk) campaigns on behalf of those often unlawfully detained by the US and UK in the 'war on terror' and its director Clive Stafford Smith writes regular pieces for the 'quality' press and the leftist *New Statesman* magazine. Amnesty International (www.am nesty.org.uk) highlights human rights abuses and members are active in peace movement activities globally. While many in the peace movement denounce Israel as a 'terrorist' and apartheid state, on the Israel/Palestine conflict, Amnesty International stresses:

> The innocent imprisoned. Movement restricted. Homes demolished. Human Rights abuses are rife in Israel and the Occupied Territories. We do not take up a position on issues of statehood. We stand with those demanding that all sides respect human rights and that the perpetrators of human rights abuses are brought to justice (see www.amnesty.org.uk).

In the US, both the American Civil Liberties Union (www.aclu.org) and Human Rights Watch (www.hrw.org) have consistently campaigned to expose the human rights abuses that have accompanied the 'war on terror' and produced a number of important reports on the subject.

Peace News and *CounterPunch*: Peace journalism in action

Since its founding in early 1936, *Peace News* has been a site of citizen journalism for the promotion of peace and social justice. Take a look at the back pages of any edition of *Peace News* (http://peacenews.info). Listed there are scores of events happening all across the UK: in September 2012, for example in Liverpool there was a concert for peace; in Leeds a talk by Chris Cole, of the Drones Campaign Network; in Bromley, a Peace Day event. All this is evidence of an imaginative, vast, committed and growing progressive and alternative community whose activities (most significantly) are almost totally ignored by the corporate media. A co-editor of *Peace News*, Milan Rai, comments:

> For *Peace News*, citizen journalism has meant activist journalism, with self-reporting by large numbers of social movement activists through the years. ... Throughout the past thirty years, a staple of *PN* coverage has been the self-documentation by members of various peace camps around Britain, most famously Greenham Common Women's Peace Camp in the 1980s and now including Faslane nuclear submarine base in Scotland and the Atomic Weapons Establishment in Aldermaston, Berkshire. The number of *PN* street sellers may have shrunk over the years, but the number of journalist–activists has increased correspondingly (Rai 2011: 211).

Rai argues that *Peace News*'s primary function is 'to assist and encourage people who are seeking to make positive social changes through non-violent means' (cited in Forde 2011: 84). The November 2013 edition is typical in the way it highlights the work of peace movement activists. Its front page lead story reports on a new nonviolence campaign in the US, *Pace e Bene*, which is calling for an end to drone warfare, extreme poverty and environmental destruction. Inside, a whole page is devoted to the case of the 'Waddington Six': peace activists found guilty of criminal damage during a protest at the drone base at RAF Waddington, Lincolnshire. Other items focus on the actions of Stop the Arms Fair activists, peaceful anti-fracking protests in Balcombe, West Sussex, and peace activists facing 30-year sentences for breaking into a US nuclear bomb-making factory in Oak Ridge, California, in July 2012.

Another function of media such as *Peace News* is to promote a form of 'counter-journalism'. Rai provides an example of a report on a poll in Iraq in 2007 which suggested a total of 1,220,580 deaths since 2003, a finding which was almost totally ignored by the mainstream media (Rai 2011: 216–220). For Rai the aim of counter-journalism is:

> ... to search the output of the mass media with diligence and a sceptical eye, cutting through the mass of misrepresentation and fraud to discover nuggets that can help citizens to better understand – and to more effectively alter the world in which we are living and acting (Rai 2011: 217).

Another example of PJ as 'counter-journalism' is *CounterPunch* (www.counterpunch.org), a regularly updated, investigative website with an associated printed monthly journal sent to subscribers and a book imprint. Run since 1996 by Jeffery St Clair and, until his death in 2012, Alexander Cockburn, from its Washington DC base, it depends entirely on donations from readers and subscriptions – so entirely free from corporate pressure (though almost permanently financially insecure). It is firmly in the American 'muckraking' tradition and has consistently opposed US/Western imperialistic adventures, Israel's oppression of the

Palestinians, the military/industrial/surveillance complex, the corporate destruction of the environment and global threats to civil liberties. On its magazine format, St Clair commented:

> Personally, I prefer it. There's something more permanent about a magazine that you can walk around with, sit on the toilet and read, annotate, pass around to others and use as a fire-starter. It seems weightier and more substantial. The magazine/newsletter/pamphlet also has such a rich history on the left, going back to Tom Paine, to Marat and Hébert in the French Revolution, Hazlitt, Lamb and Blake in England to the American anti-slavery movement and Prairie populists to the Catholic Workers and then Stone. It's a tradition that Cockburn and I saw ourselves as a part of and didn't want to renounce entirely for the 'new thing'.
>
> Of course, the 'new thing' also seems to be always morphing and changing. Online journalism is captive to the latest trends in technology, in software, and tech gizmos. Once you're online you have to continually upgrade and update. It's expensive and time-consuming. Plus, you begin to feel that you're catering to the latest fetishes of your readers. For example, now about 40 per cent of *CP*'s online readers access the site through cellphones. In fact, we had to redesign the website to make it cellphone compatible. The technology also dictates reading habits. For social media purposes, each story now requires a photo to encourage 'sharing'. Because so many people are 'reading' on cellphones the trend is to keep stories short, 500 words or so. It's the revenge of *USA Today*. We haven't succumbed to this trend yet, though we are under constant pressure to do so (Keeble 2017: 306).

Many of its pieces are contributed by activist academics and specialist journalists – they not only provide alternative perspectives but information missed by the mainstream. In the July 2019 issue, for instance, Laura Carlsen, Director of the Americas Program of the Center for International Policy, Mexico City, contributes a piece on the plans of the country's President to halt the Merida Initiative, the $3 billion US counter-narcotics aid package that has fuelled the drugs war; T. J. Coles, an associate researcher at the Organisation for Propaganda Studies, highlights the rarely considered links between modern slavery and Western-backed conflicts, militarism and corporations; while Dan Glazebrook, the political writer and journalist (particularly associated with *middleeasteye.net*), reports on how Nato has spent seven years entrenching militia misrule in Libya.

Conclusion

In Britain, a predictable media panic erupted in 2011 after Fleet Street journalists were discovered hacking to the phones of celebrities, top politicians, royals and the occasional 'ordinary' person, such as missing schoolgirl Milly Dowler (see Keeble and Mair 2012). An expensive inquiry was then launched into the ethics of the corporate press. Not surprisingly then, the alternative sector was entirely ignored. Yet, as this chapter has attempted to show, the importance of the alternative media both historically and today as a site for 'good' journalism cannot be under-estimated. Tony Dowmunt draws our attention to the term 'alternative media', noting that it might be thought of as denoting activities of secondary importance to the mainstream. Yet this need not need be the case: 'In that they provide resistance, opposition and counter-examples to tired and reactionary mainstream uses of media, they are of primary social, cultural and political importance. Nevertheless they remain, by definition, significantly less powerful and privileged than the mainstream' (Dowmunt 2007: 10).

There are, though, as I hope this chapter has shown, reasons for optimism. Beyond the gaze of the elite, a global counter-public sphere (though full of tensions) is bursting with people constantly challenging the lies and mystifications of the powerful and their propaganda media, bravely protesting (through the alternative media and in so many other imaginative ways) against the warmongers – and for peace.

Acknowledgements

This essay is based on a chapter with the same title in *The Routledge Companion to Community and Alternative Media*, London: Routledge, edited by Chris Atton, 2015 pp 335–346.

Further reading

Important sites for academic discussions on peace journalism globally include: http://www. cco.regener-online.de/, http://globalmedia.emu.edu.tr/, *Peace Review* at https://www.ta ndfonline.com/loi/cper20, the *Journal of Peace Research* at https://journals.sagepub.com/ home/jpr, the *Peace Journalist* at https://issuu.com/peacejournalism and Johan Galtung's http://www.transcend.org/.

For the alternative media in the US see Kessler, Lauren (1984) *The Dissident Press: Alternative Journalism in American History*, Newbury Park, London: Sage Publications, and Ostertag, Bob (2006) *People's Movements, People's Press: The Journalism of Social Justice Movements*, Boston: Beacon Press. Rips, Geoffrey (1981) *The Campaign Against the Underground Press*, San Francisco, CA: City Lights Books, is also an invaluable source. Following a three-year study of government documents acquired through the Freedom of Information Act, Rips concludes that the alternative, peace movement press was the target of 'surveillance, harassment and unlawful search and seizure by US government agencies'. Nancy R. Roberts contributes a section on the pacifist press to the *Encyclopedia of American Journalism*, edited by Stephen L. Vaughn, New York and London: Routledge, 2008 pp 378–380.

References

Allan, Stuart (2006) *Online News: Journalism and the Internet*, Maidenhead: Open University Press
Althusser, Louis (1969) *For Marx*, London: Penguin
Andersen, Robin (2006) *A Century of Media, a Century of War*, New York: Peter Lang

Atton, Chris (2002) *Alternative Media*, London: Sage

Atton, Chris (2004) *An Alternative Internet: Radical Media, Politics and Creativity*, Edinburgh: Edinburgh University Press

Atton, Chris and Hamilton, James F. (2008) *Alternative Journalism*, London: Sage

Black, Jeremy (2001) *The English Press 1621–1861*, Stroud, Gloucestershire: Sutton Publishing

Bourdieu, Pierre (1998) *On Television*, London: Pluto Press

Boyd-Barrett, Oliver (2010) Recovering agency for the propaganda model: The implications for reporting war and peace, Keeble, Richard Lance, Tulloch, John and Zollmann, Florian (eds) *Peace Journalism, War and Conflict Resolution*, New York: Peter Lang pp 31–48

Carruthers, Susan L. (2000) *The Media at War: Communication and Conflict in the Twentieth Century*, London: Macmillan Press

Castells, Manuel (2009) *Communicative Power*, Oxford: Oxford University Press

Chapman, Jane (2008) Republican citizenship, ethics and the French revolutionary press, Keeble, Richard (ed.) *Communication Ethics Now*, Leicester: Troubador pp 131–141

Collins, Richard (1990) Market closure and the conflict theory of professions, Burrage, Michael and Torstendahl, Rolf (eds) *Professions in Theory and History: Rethinking the Study of Professions*, London, Newbury Park and New Delhi: Sage pp 24–42

Conboy, Martin (2004) *Journalism: A Critical History*, London: Sage

Couldry, Nick and Curran, James (eds) (2003) *Contesting Media Power: Alternative Media in a Networked World*, Lanham, MD: Rowman & Littlefield

Curran, James and Seaton, Jean (2004) *Power Without Responsibility: The Press, Broadcasting and New Media in Britain*, London: Routledge, seventh edition

Davies, Mary (1999) *Sylvia Pankhurst: A Life in Radical Politics*, London: Pluto

Der Derian, James (2001) *Virtuous War: Mapping the Military–Industrial–Media–Entertainment Network*, New York: Basic Books

Downing, John (1984) *Radical Media: The Political Experience of Alternative Communication*, Boston, MA: South End Press

Dowmunt, Tony (2007) Introduction, Coyer, Kate, Dowmunt, Tony and Fountain, Alan (eds) *The Alternative Media Handbook*, Oxon and New York: Routledge pp 1–12

Forde, Susan (2011) *Challenging the News: The Journalism of Alternative and Community Media*, Basingstoke: Palgrave Macmillan

Galtung, Johan (1998) High road – low road: Charting the course for peace journalism, *Track Two*, Vol. 7, No. 4, Centre for Conflict Resolution, South Africa. Available online at http://ccrweb.ccr.uct.ac.za/archive/two/7_4/p07_highroad_lowroad.html, accessed on 7 April 2009

Habermas, Jürgen (1974) The public sphere, *New German Critique*, Vol. 3 pp 49–59

Hackett, Robert A. (2007) Is Peace Journalism possible? Shinar, Dove and Kempf, Wilhelm (eds) *Peace Journalism: The State of the Art*, Berlin: Regener pp 75–94

Harcup, Tony (2003) The unspoken – said: The journalism of the alternative media, *Journalism*, Vol. 4, No. 3 pp 356–376

Harcup, Tony (2013) *Alternative Journalism: Alternative Voices*, London: Routledge

Hartley, John (1996) *Popular Reality: Journalism, Modernity and Popular Culture*, London and New York: Arnold

Hartley, John (2008) Journalism as a human right: The cultural approach to journalism, Loffelholz, Martin and Weaver, David (eds) *Global Journalism Research: Theories, Methods, Findings, Future*, Oxford: Backwell pp 39–51

Herman, Edward S. and Chomsky, Noam (1988) *Manufacturing Consent: The Political Economy of the Mass Media*, New York: Pantheon Books

Illich, Ivan (1973) The professions as a form of imperialism, *New Society*, 13 September

Keeble, Richard (1997) *Secret State, Silent Press: New Militarism, the Gulf and the Modern Image of Warfare*, Luton: John Libbey

Keeble, Richard (1999) A Balkan birthday for Nato, *British Journalism Review*, Vol. 10, No. 2 pp 16–20

Keeble, Richard (2000) New Militarism and the manufacture of warfare, Hammond, Philip and Herman, Edward S. (eds) *Degraded Capability: The Media and the Kosovo Crisis*, London: Pluto Press pp 59–69

Keeble, Richard (2004) Information warfare in an age of hyper-militarism, Allan, Stuart and Zeliger, Barbie (eds) *Reporting War*, London: Routledge pp 43–58

Keeble, Richard Lance (2010) Peace Journalism as political practice: A new, radical look at the theory, Keeble, Richard Lance, Tulloch, John and Zollmann, Florian (eds) *Peace Journalism, War and Conflict Resolution*, New York: Peter Lang pp 49–67

Keeble, Richard Lance (2012) The war reporting of Robert Fisk: Relentlessly exposing the horror, Keeble, Richard Lance and Tulloch, John (eds) *Global Literary Journalism: Exploring the Journalistic Imagination*, New York: Peter Lang pp 237–252

Keeble, Richard Lance (2017) The progressive left: Better read than dead, Mair, John, Clark, Tor, Fowler, Neil, Snoddy, Raymond and Tait, Richard (eds) *Last words? How Can Journalism Survive the Decline of Print?*, Bury St Edmunds: Abramis pp 302–307

Keeble, Richard Lance and Mair, John (eds) (2012) *The Phone Hacking Scandal: Journalism on Trial*, Bury St Edmunds: Abramis

Knightley, Phillip (1982) *The First Casualty: The War Correspondent as Hero, Propagandist and Myth Maker*, London: Quartet

Lynch, Jake (1998) *The Peace Journalism Option*, Taplow: Conflict and Peace Forums

Lynch, Jake and McGoldrick, Annabel (2005) *Peace Journalism*, Stroud: Hawthorn Press

MacPherson, Myra (2006) *All Governments Lie: The Life and Times of Rebel Journalist I. F. Stone*, New York: Simon & Schuster

Neale, Jonathan (2001) *The American War: Vietnam 1960–75*, London: Bookmarks

Nelson, Elizabeth (1989) *The British Counter-Culture, 1966–73: A Study of the Underground Press*, London: Macmillan

Parkin, Frank (1979) *Marxism and Class Theory: A Bourgeois Critique*, London: Tavistock Publications

Rai, Milan (2010) Peace journalism in practice – *Peace News*: For non-violent revolution, Keeble, Richard Lance, Tulloch, John and Zollmann, Florian (eds) *Peace Journalism, War and Conflict Resolution*, New York: Peter Lang pp 207–221

Rodriguez, Clemencia (2001) *Fissures in the Mediascape: An International Study of Citizen's Media*, New Jersey: Hampton Press

Ross, Susan Dente (2007) (De-)constructing conflict: A focused review of war and peace journalism, Shinar, Dove and Kempf, Wilhelm (eds) *Peace Journalism: The State of the Art*, Berlin: Regener pp 53–74

Shaw, Ibrahim Seaga (2012) *Human Rights Journalism: Advances in Reporting Distant Humanitarian Interventions*, Houndmills, Basingstoke: Palgrave Macmillan

Shinar, Dove and Kempf, Wilhelm (eds) (2007) *Peace Journalism: The State of the Art*, Berlin: Regener

Shoemaker, Pamela J. and Reese, Stephen D. (1996) *Mediating the Message: Theories of Influences on Mass Media Content*, New York: Longman

Sparks, Colin (1985) The working-class press: Radical and revolutionary alternatives, *Media, Culture and Society*, Vol. 7 pp 133–146

Waltz, Mitzi (2005) *Alternative and Activist Media*, Edinburgh: Edinburgh University Press

Zollmann, Florian (2009) Is it either or? Professional ideology v. corporate media constraints, *Westminster Papers in Communication and Culture*, Vol. 6, No. 2 pp 97–118

PART IV

Scoops and spooks: Journalism in an age of surveillance capitalism

10

JOURNALISTS AND THE SECRET STATE

Elements of the 'democratic' state are part of the very air people breathe in Britain: parliament, the rule of law, the 'free press', human rights, *habeas corpus* and so on. But alongside the 'democratic' state (and sometimes overlapping it) there exists a secret, massively resourced,[1] extremely powerful and highly centralised state occupied by the intelligence and security services:[2]

- MI5 for domestic security – with links to intelligence services in more than 100 countries (Hennessey and Thomas 2009: 604).[3]
- MI6 – otherwise known as the Secret Intelligence Service (SIS) – supplying the government with foreign intelligence.
- GCHQ, the Cheltenham-based signals (SIGINT) spying centre. Plus the little known but 'hugely important' Her Majesty's Government Communications Centre, in Hanslope.[4] All the spy services are increasingly using new technologies to analyse social media for intelligence and surveillance use.[5]
- Secret cabinet committees set up to deal with specific emergencies – such as Margaret Thatcher's MISC 57, chaired by Peter Gregson, which planned for the miners' strike of 1984 by making sure there was a huge stockpile of coal for the power stations (Marsden 2013).
- The Metropolitan Police's special 'domestic extremism unit' monitoring the activities of protestors (Evans 2016).
- Special Branch, responsible for security in British and Commonwealth police forces.
- The RAF Police – providing the policing, counter-intelligence and specialist security support to the RAF.[6]
- The National Crime Agency, set up in October 2013, to gather intelligence in the fight against serious and organised crime.[7]

- The National Cyber Security Centre, launched in 2015 to counter cyber attacks: in its first two years, it claimed to have dealt with 1,167 incidents (Osborne 2018). In 2017, the government quietly announced investment of £1.9 billion amidst mounting fears of 'cyber terrorism'.
- The US National Reconnaissance Office (the 'spies in the sky') which, along with the National Security Agency, runs the Menwith Hill spy base in Yorkshire (Yorkshire CND). Its ECHELON operation (created in the late 1960s and linking a network of 120 satellites) allows for the interception of more than 8 million phone calls, faxes, emails and text messages per hour (Southwell 2005: 105).
- The secret armaments research centres at Porton Down, in Wiltshire, and Fort Halstead, in Kent.
- Undercover police units.[8]
- And special military forces, such as the SAS, together with mercenary groups and individuals with links to covert intelligence.[9]

According to Clive Bloom (2015: 191), there are also very close ties between the intelligence services and the highly secretive City of London, a massive tax haven at the heart of the British establishment.[10]

The Five Eyes intelligence alliance links the security services of Australia, Canada, New Zealand, the US and UK. The former NSA contractor Edward Snowden described Five Eyes as a 'supra-national intelligence organisation that does not answer to the known laws of its own countries'.[11] And according to Bloch and Fitzgerald (1983: 142), MI6 exchanges information on Palestinians with Mossad, the Israeli secret service. The Joint Intelligence Committee of the Cabinet Office oversees the priorities for the security services – and members of the Australian, Canadian and US intelligence communities take part in JIC discussions (Plesch 2004).

As Anthony Sampson (2004: 151) highlights, MI5 and MI6 and their many competing factions are only part of a much wider intelligence community: 'This includes private companies, often employing ex-MI6 officers, which have their own interests in cultivating mystery and which rapidly expanded in the 1980s and 1990s, benefiting from the global market-place.' Such companies include Control Risks, Oxford Analytica, Sandline and the Hakluyt & Company.[12]

The secret state and the law

The secret state is variously described and theorised: as 'shadow government', 'invisible government', 'deep state', 'security state', 'clandestine state' (Wilson 2009; Scott 2017). It operates both within and outside the law. It is crucially protected by a raft of legislation:

- The Official Secrets Acts of 1889, 1911, 1920, 1939, revised in 1989 to remove the 'public interest' defence from whistleblowers.

- The Intelligence Services Act of 1994 which placed the intelligence services on a legal basis.
- The Regulation of Investigatory Powers Act (2000) allows the authorities to secure the phone records of journalists in cases of 'national security'. In 2015, the Interception of Communication Commissioner's Office revealed that police forces had used RIPA against 82 journalists over a three-year period to access confidential material.
- The Justice and Security Act of 2013 which allows for secret courts to consider, for instance, allegations of torture against MI5. Government ministers can apply for special courtroom measures known as 'closed material procedure' whenever the government or its secret services are being sued in UK courts. The fact that a hearing is being held in secret can itself be kept secret.
- The Data Retention and Investigatory Powers Act 2014 allows for the creation of a privatised database of everyone's communications activity. According to Joseph Cannataci, the first UN privacy chief, surveillance in the UK is 'worse than Orwell imagined' (Alexander 2015).
- The largely unnoticed re-writing of clause 10 of the Computer Misuse Act, which came into force in March 2015, effectively makes lawful GCHQ's hacking operations (Bowcott 2015).

Significantly, the Freedom of Information legislation (of 2000) fails in any way to cover the activities of the secret state (and, interestingly, the royal family, too). Members of the public can bring complaints against the security service by using the Investigatory Powers Tribunal (IPT) – but in its 15-year history it has only once ruled against the intelligence services (Verkaik 2016). But then, in May 2019, the Supreme Court ruled that IPT decisions were subject to review by the High Court.

The system of Defence and Security Media Advisory (DSMA) Notices (better known as D Notices) also serves to restrain the media in their coverage of sensitive security issues (Wilkinson 2009). Once a notice is issued by the secretary of the DSMA committee, editors are asked to censor reporting. The system, introduced in 1912 to prevent breaches in security by German spies, is entirely voluntary (see its website at http://www.dsma.uk/). According to John Turner, linked to the centralisation of power is the secrecy 'which pervades British politics and the patronising assumption that the government knows best. Britain's culture of secrecy is buttressed by harsh libel laws, weak rights of access to official information, the Official Secrets Act and the D Notice system' (Turner 2006: 190).

There is little democratic accountability in the secret state: the Intelligence Services Act of 1994 created the Intelligence and Security Committee of the House of Commons though this provides hardly any credible oversight. The first 'grilling' of the heads of MI5 (Andrew Parker), MI6 (Sir John Sawers) and GCHQ (Sir Iain Lobbam) in November 2013 proved an embarrassing flop. As Shami Chakrabarti, director of Liberty, commented: 'These public servants presided over blanket surveillance of the entire population without public, parliamentary or democratic mandate. Yet they faced a grilling that wouldn't have scared a puppy' (Walker 2013).

The Ministry of Defence and Foreign and Commonwealth Office also keep secret, illegally, thousands of files that should have been declassified and transferred to the National Archive under the 30-year rule. As Iain Cobain reports:

> More than 66,000 separate [MoD] files are being stored at an enormous warehouse operated by TNT Archive Service at Swadlincote in southern Derbyshire, despite the department's legal obligation to assess them for declassification once they are three decades old and either hand them to the archives at Kew, south-west London, or publicly give a reason for keeping them classified (Cobain 2013).[13]

Moreover, it was also revealed that the Foreign Office has hoarded 1.2 million files – some of them dating back to the 1840s. A number of leading academics from Oxford, Cambridge and London universities planned to take legal action to bring the archive into the public domain (Cobain 2014a).

Newspapers 'playthings of MI5'

According to Roy Greenslade, media blogger at the *Guardian* and editor of the *Mirror* at the time of the Gulf crisis in 1991: 'Most tabloid newspapers – or even newspapers in general – are playthings of MI5' (Milne 1995: 262). Journalist (with *The Times, Observer* and *Economist*), former MI6 officer and Soviet spy Kim Philby once said that MI6 had penetrated the 'English mass media on a wide scale', running agents in the *Daily Telegraph, Sunday Times, Daily Mirror, Financial Times* and the *Observer* (Davies 2008: 235). Spy novelist John le Carré, who worked for British intelligence for a number of years, has even claimed that the British secret service then controlled large parts of the press – just as they may do today (Dorril 1993: 281).[14] In 2015, Frederick (*Day of the Jackal*) Forsythe, best-selling spy novelist and former journalist, revealed in his autobiography he had worked for British intelligence for 20 years.[15]

David Leigh (2000) records a series of instances in which the secret services manipulated prominent journalists. He says reporters are routinely approached by intelligence agents:

> I think the cause of honest journalism is best served by candour. We all ought to come clean about these approaches and devise some ethics to deal with them. In our vanity, we imagine that we control these sources. But the truth is that they are very deliberately seeking to control us.

Leigh identifies three ways in which the secret intelligence services manipulate journalists:

1. They attempt to recruit journalists to spy on other people or to go themselves under journalistic 'cover'.

2.   Intelligence officers are allowed to pose as journalists 'to write tendentious articles under false names'.[16]
3.   And 'the most malicious form: when intelligence agency propaganda stories are planted on willing journalists who disguise their origin from readers' (ibid).

Splits in the intelligence community: And the impact on the media

Yet it is wrong to see the intelligence community as unified with one single ambition. As intelligence has grown so have the competing factions within it. The media, then, become the theatre in which these various factions play out their games for supremacy. Chapman Pincher, over a very long journalistic career (he died in August 2014 aged 100), fed stories to Fleet Street from various competing factions within the intelligence services (see Andrew 2009: 627–645; Pincher 2014; Keeble 2017: 38). As the obituary in the *Daily Telegraph* recorded:

> There were many casualties in these campaigns. Pincher revealed that 'my friend' the late Sir Maurice Oldfield, former 'C' of MI6, was a homosexual. He was one of the leading protagonists for the (discredited) theory that the late Sir Roger Hollis, former head of MI5, was a traitor. Like a number of other journalists, Pincher was aware of Sir Anthony Blunt's treachery. Curiously, it was one story he did not tell.[17]

Christopher Moran (2013: 108) comments on Pincher's journalistic techniques, approvingly:

> As Pincher's fame grew, he found himself inundated with people wanting to leak him things. With seemingly little concern for the risks involved, senior figures in Whitehall often took extended lunch breaks to join the scoop-gatherer in his preferred London haunts, which included the Écu de France, the Dorchester and Kettner's Restaurant and Champagne Bar. Knowing the journalist's fondness for traditional British field sports, other officials invited him to hunts, shoots and fishing trips. ... Many went to Pincher to sell their agenda to the public, others simply to cause professional angst in their opponents.

Historian and polemist E. P. Thompson was less charitable. Pincher, he said, was like an 'official urinal' at which the great and good queued up to leak. He added: 'One can only admire their resolute attention to these distasteful duties' (Thompson 1980: 116).[18] And Paul Lashmar (2013) commented: 'Pincher was a primary conduit to the public sphere for intelligence officials and whether the flow was informal or formal was often obscure not least because it was not supposed to happen at all.'

Significantly, in the late 1990s, factions emerged which managed to marginalise traditional elements within both MI6 and the CIA. In the UK, the Rockingham Cell emerged triumphant; in the United States it was the Office of Special Plans (OSP), set up by the Defense Secretary, Donald Rumsfeld, in 2002 (Borger 2003; Baker 2007: 293).

James Bond to the rescue?

Some of the most important research into the links between hacks and spooks has been conducted by Phillip Knightley, author of *The First Casualty* (Knightley 2003 [1982]), a seminal history of war correspondents, and *The Second Oldest Profession* (Knightley 1986), a history of the intelligence services. He even claimed that at least one intelligence agent is working on every Fleet Street newspaper (Keeble 2003). Moreover, he said he was convinced 'MI5 has agents in newspapers, printers and publishing houses who tip off MI5/SIS about impending publication of material that would be of interest to the services'.[19]

In particular, Knightley highlights the activities, immediately after the Second World War, of the Kemsley Imperial and Foreign Service, better known by its cable address, Mercury. It was part of the Kemsley and then the Thomson chain of newspapers, which provided foreign news and features to newspapers such as *The Sunday Times* and *Empire News*.

The head of Mercury was Ian Fleming, celebrated author of the James Bond spy novels, who had served in British naval intelligence during the war. In his official history of MI6, Keith Jeffery (2011: 406) significantly records Fleming being chosen to communicate to the press the disinformation relating to 'Paul Lewis Claire', a French naval officer taken on by SIS, who had been suspected of defecting to the fascist Vichy regime in France and who had been killed during a struggle in a car: 'The official story (as communicated by Commander Ian Fleming of Naval Intelligence to the British Red Cross in July 1942) represented Claire as "missing believed drowned", en route to Britain on the SS Empire Hurst, sunk by enemy aircraft on 11 August 1941.' It was all lies.

In 1942, Fleming created 30CU (later known as 30AU), a covert unit of soldiers expert in armed combat and intelligence gathering.[20] Charles Wheeler, who later went on to become the BBC's longest serving correspondent, and Donald McLachlan, who became editor of the *Sunday Telegraph*, were key men in the unit (Cabell 2008: 60–71). Veterans of the unit interviewed by Cabell remembered Wheeler as 'being a fierce interrogator of enemy captors' (ibid: 172).

After the war, Fleming controlled, as head of Mercury, a worldwide network of 88 journalists many of whom had wartime intelligence backgrounds (Trelford 2009). Cedric Salter, formerly of the secret military organisation, the Special Operations Executive, was sent to Barcelona; Ian Colvin (who had close SIS links) to Berlin and Henry Brandon, an 'SIS asset', to Washington. Donald McCormick, formerly in naval intelligence, became Mercury's correspondent in Tangier and later foreign manager at *The Sunday Times*. He was also to write on intelligence matters under the pseudonym, Richard Deacon. Anthony Terry, *The Sunday Times*'s man in Bonn, also worked as a Mercury correspondent and as an officer of British intelligence in Berlin and Vienna. Fleming required his correspondents to write regular 'situation reports', or 'sitreps' providing background information – not for publication – about activities in their parts of the world. Fleming's biographer Andrew Lycett (1996: 170) records McCormick saying that material from these sitreps was 'passed on to branches of Intelligence as and when this seemed justified'. Anthony Cavendish, a former SIS officer, writes:

> At the end of the war a number of MI6 agents were sent abroad under the cover of newspapermen. Indeed, the Kemsley press allowed many of their correspondents to co-operate with MI6 and even took on MI6 operatives as foreign correspondents (Knightley 2006: 8).

IRD: Propaganda arm of the Empire

The release of Public Record Office documents in 1995 about some of the operations of the MI6-financed propaganda unit, the Information Research Department of the Foreign Office, threw light on this secret body – which even George Orwell aided by sending them his list of 'crypto-communists' from his death bed in 1949 (Smith 2013: 145–151). Set up by the Labour government in 1948, it 'ran' dozens of Fleet Street journalists and a vast array of news agencies across the globe until it was closed down by foreign secretary David Owen in 1977. Such famous names as Denis Healey, Stephen Spender, Bertrand Russell and Guy Burgess helped or backed the work of IRD (Lashmar 2013). It was funded, like MI6, by the 'secret vote' and was thus beyond parliamentary scrutiny. John Rennie, its second head between 1953 and 1958, was later appointed head of MI6.

IRD distributed across the globe 'white' (true), 'grey' (partially true) and 'black' (false) propaganda, planting smears, lies, false rumours and forged official reports in the media. As Phillip Deery comments: 'IRD worked hard to ensure that its propagandists – speechwriters, broadcasters, journalists and politicians – used the most effective words and phrases in their articles and speeches.'[21] And according to John Pilger (1998: 495–496):

> In the anti-colonial struggles in Kenya, Malaya and Cyprus, IRD was so successful that the journalism served up as a record of those episodes was a cocktail of the distorted and false, in which the real aims and often atrocious behaviour of the British was suppressed. Thus the bloodshed in Malaya was and still is misrepresented as a 'model' of counter-insurgency; the anti-imperial uprising in Kenya was and still is distorted as a Mau Mau terror campaign against whites; and the struggle for basic human rights in Northern Ireland became and remains a noble defence of order and stability against IRA terror.

Lashmar and Oliver (1998) argue:

... the vast IRD enterprise had one sole aim: to spread its ceaseless propaganda output (i.e. a mixture of outright lies and distorted facts) among top-ranking journalists who worked for major agencies, papers and magazines, including Reuters and the BBC, as well as every other available channel. It worked abroad to discredit communist parties in Western Europe which might gain a share of power by entirely democratic means, and at home to discredit the British Left.[22]

By 1960, IRD was the largest and fastest-growing department of the post-war Foreign Office though the official *Diplomatic List* for the year would have given no such indication (Aldrich 1998: 2–3). From 1970–1972 IRD staff were secretly drafted to serve on the European Community Information Unit: a covert propaganda operation aiming to persuade the British public to accept the Common Market (Ramsay 2003). When PM Edward Heath's files on the Common Market were released 30 years later, the ECIU's work was kept secret but some 200 files were quietly released a few months later at the National Archives, Kew. According to Ramsay (ibid), the IRD staff were used 'to soften up the public for huge price rises in basic commodities such as butter' while a government hospitality fund 'was used to entice supposedly independent-minded personalities to speak in favour of Europe'. 'Independent' people were to deluge newspapers with pro-Europe letters and to tour the country speaking on behalf of the pressure group, the British Council of the European Movement. Moreover, 'the unit persuaded Gwyn Morgan, Labour's assistant general secretary, to reveal Harold Wilson's campaign plans and to leak a copy of a report on the issue by Labour's national executive' (ibid).

But under Harold Wilson, the Labour Party cut funding to IRD when it took office in 1964, again in 1968 and 'slashed' funding in 1970 (Dorril and Ramsay 1991: 110). Col. 'Sammy' Logan, then-secretary of the D Notice committee, was actually on MI5's payroll and spent his £500 retainer spying on reporters and feeding the intelligence service 'titbits' about them (McCrystal 1999: 32). David Leigh suggests that IRD had '60 or so' newspaper, television and BBC and radio journalists on its mailing list in 1977 (Leigh 1980: 221). And the IRD played a crucial role in the psychological warfare waged in Northern Ireland by the British state during the 1970s (Ramsay 2008: 191). As Rory Cormac (2018: 214) comments:

> Newly released documents and recent inquiries reveal black propaganda discrediting the IRA, undercover disruption operations authorized to use lethal force, and a context in which collusion with loyalist para-militaries thrived. ... They were not the work of rogue agents but can be traced back to Whitehall and Number 10.

The CIA's expansion in 1965 of the London-based propaganda unit, Forum World Features (FWF), with the knowledge and co-operation of British intelligence, was probably a response to the political and financial pressures on IRD (Dorril and Ramsay op cit: 110). Nick Davies suggests (op cit: 227) that FWF supplied reports to 140 newspapers around the world.

Then in December 2015, Shadow Home Secretary Andy Burnham revealed during a parliamentary debate about the convictions of 24 pickets in 1972 (including the actor Ricky Tomlinson) that the Information Research Department had played a significant role in the making of the Anglia Television documentary *Red Under the Bed*. A note from IRD to the Foreign Office said: 'We had a discreet but considerable hand in this programme. Mr [Woodrow] Wyatt [the leader of the investigation] was given a large dossier of our own background material. It is clear from internal evidence in the programme that he drew extensively on this' (James 2015).[23]

The press – and the extraordinary plot to oust a prime minister

One of the most famous whistleblowers of all time, Peter (*Spycatcher*) Wright (1987), revealed that MI5 had agents in newspapers and publishing companies whose main role was to warn them of any forthcoming 'embarrassing publications'. Wright also disclosed that the *Daily Mirror* tycoon, Cecil King, 'was a longstanding agent of ours' who 'made it clear he would publish anything MI5 might care to leak in his direction' (ibid: 369). King was also closely involved in an extraordinary plot in 1968 to oust Prime Minister Harold Wilson (suspected of radical left/communist leanings) and replace him with a coalition headed by Lord Mountbatten, Prince Charles's uncle (Marr 2007: 305–308; Cottrell 2008: 22–25, 28). Harold Evans, celebrated editor of *The Sunday Times* (1967–1981), intriguingly records in his memoir *Good Times, Bad Times* (Evans 1983: 226) that in the late 1960s, *The Times* 'encouraged Cecil King's lunatic notion of a coup against Harold Wilson's Labour government in favour of a government of business leaders led by Lord Robens'. According to Phillip Knightley (1986: 352), MI5 did tell the Home Secretary, James Callaghan, about the plot – 'but Callaghan apparently decided against informing either Wilson or the Cabinet.'

Wilson had taken the unprecedented step of forbidding MI5 to carry out any form of surveillance of MPs including telephone tapping, the opening of letters and the examination of bank accounts. Five days later, Wilson announced the bugging ban also applied to members of the House of Lords (Cobain 2014b). In 1997, with the development of email and other electronic communication, Prime Minister Tony Blair even assured the Commons that the ban extended 'to all forms of warranted interception of communications' (ibid). But as Dorril and Ramsay (op cit: 65) comment: 'Unfortunately, Wilson's attempts to curtail MI5's activities did not work.' MI5 secretly planted bugs in 10 Downing Street despite repeated official denials, it was revealed in April 2010. This revelation was to have been included by Christopher Andrew in his best-selling history of MI5, published in 2009 but was suppressed by Whitehall officials to protect the 'public interest' (Norton-Taylor 2010). In any case, Labour MP Ken Livingstone had revealed in an article in the *Independent* in November 1998 that MI5 continued to receive the phone-tapping information on MPs via the CIA and GCHQ – without Wilson knowing this. Moreover, MI5 also continued to use a Tory MP, Captain Henry Kerby, who had ingratiated himself with a Labour MP, George Wigg, whom Harold Wilson made responsible for MI5 and MI6 (Livingstone 1998).[24]

The official MI5 history did, however, record that the intelligence service held a secret file on Wilson (who was given the pseudonym 'Norman John Worthington') since 1947 and throughout the time he was Prime Minister (1964–1970 and 1974–1976). This was supposedly because of his contacts with Eastern European businessmen, KGB officers – and a belief amongst communist civil servants in Whitehall that he had similar political sympathies. Harold Wilson was, in fact, the only serving Prime Minister to have a permanent security service file (Evans 2009). Baroness Manningham-Buller, director general of MI5 from 2002 to 2007, told *The Times* (ibid): 'You might well have a file, supposing you were a person who was a target for a terrorist attack. There was no plot, no conspiracy.'[25]

Peter Wright later confessed that just before the 1974 general election he had planned to leak a secret MI5 file on the Prime Minister to the press. 'The plan was simple. MI5 would arrange for selective details of intelligence about leading Labour Party figures, but especially Wilson, to be leaked to sympathetic pressmen' (Hollingsworth and Fielding 1999: 23). Richard Briginshaw, general secretary of the printing union, Natsopa, later claimed that his union 'had foiled attempts by the *Daily Mail* and *Daily Express* to print smear stories against Labour during the election simply by threatening to stop the presses' (Dorril and Ramsay op cit: 271).

On one occasion, Wilson confided in cabinet minister Shirley Williams (who later became one of the 'Gang of Four' founders of the Social Democratic Party in 1981) that his office in the cabinet chamber was bugged. Andy Beckett (2010: 166) records: 'Williams thought at the time that Wilson was "off his trolley". But afterwards she changed her mind: "There was a real attempt to try to undo him of a non-constitutional kind."'

David Leigh, in *The Wilson Plot* (1989), his study of the smearing of Harold Wilson before his sudden resignation in 1976, quotes an MI5 officer: 'We have somebody in every office in Fleet Street.' Selective details about Wilson and his alleged affair with his secretary, Marcia Falkender, were leaked by the intelligence services to sympathetic Fleet Street journalists and via the satirical journal, *Private Eye* (McConnachie and Tudge 2005: 42; Ramsay 2008: 147), and the *Spectator*. John Simpson (2010: 465), in his history of the reporting of the last century, *Unreliable Sources*, records that in 1974, Patrick Marnham, of *Private Eye*, was handed a dossier on Wilson which he was told had come from MI5. Simpson adds (ibid): 'The general thrust of the documents he used in his articles was that Wilson was a Zionist-Soviet agent; not an easy double function to carry out, one would have thought.' Richard Norton-Taylor (1990: 96) also suggests that William Massie, defence correspondent of the *Sunday Express*, and Jak (Raymond Jackson), the *Evening Standard* cartoonist, had particularly close ties with intelligence.

According to Wright there were also suspicions that Hugh Gaitskell, Wilson's predecessor as Labour leader, had been murdered by the KGB. Soviet defector Anatoliy Golitsyn stoked these suspicions – reporting that the KGB had plotted to kill a major European leader 'to get their man in place' (ibid: 42). Edward Short, deputy leader of the Labour Party and leader of the House of Commons, was also smeared: it was suggested he was involved in tax evasion, channelling secret funds via a Swiss bank account to offshore locations (Hollingsworth and Fielding 1999: 22).[26] Wright comments: 'No wonder Wilson was later to claim that he was the victim of a plot' (Wright op cit: 370).

Shortly after resigning in 1976, Wilson gave his version of events to two BBC journalists, Barrie Penrose and Roger Courtiour. He even alleged that officers of BOSS, the South African intelligence service, were involved in moves to discredit his government. Penrose and Courtiour went on to publish the interviews in *The Pencourt File* (Penrose and Courtiour 1978).

MI5 was cleared of plotting by two Prime Ministers – James Callaghan in 1977 and Margaret Thatcher in 1987. But Callaghan later said he was not confident that he had not misled the Commons in his 1977 statement when he dismissed the allegations (Norton-Taylor 1990: 97). Again, in 1994, Stella Rimington, then MI5's director general, denied the existence of any anti-Wilson plot. But two years later, Lord Hunt, cabinet secretary throughout the 1974–1979 Labour government, told Channel 4's *Secret History* programme:

> There is absolutely no doubt at all that a few malcontents in MI5 who were right-wing, malicious and had serious personal grudges, were giving vent to this and spreading damaging and malicious stories about some members of the Labour government.[27]

Moreover, according to Peter Wright, MI5 always had about twenty senior journalists working for it in the national press. 'They were not employed directly by us, but we regarded them as agents because they were happy to be associated with us.'[28]

Hugh Cudlipp, editorial director of the *Mirror* from 1952 to 1974, was also closely linked to intelligence, according to Chris Horrie, in his history of the newspaper (Horrie 2004: 237). And Cudlipp was closely involved in the anti-Wilson coup plot (Newton 2008/9: 7). Wright referred to a 'senior executive' at the *Mirror* who was controlled by an MI5 Section D4 agent runner. Seamus Milne (1995: 263) reports that Cyril Morten, the *Mirror*'s managing editor, worked closely with MI6 and happily employed an MI6 agent as a *Mirror* photographer. David Walker, the *Mirror*'s foreign correspondent in the 1950s, was named as an MI6 agent following a security scandal while Stanley Bonnett, editor of the Campaign for Nuclear Disarmament's journal, *Sanity*, in the early 1980s, was exposed as an intelligence agent by whistleblower and former MI5 officer Cathy Massiter in a *20/20 Vision* programme on Channel 4 (Urban 1996: 46–47; Dorril 1993: 25–28).

Thatcher: The spooks and the media

Mark Urban (op cit) reports that during Margaret Thatcher's years at Number 10 (1979–1990) spending on the intelligence services doubled and MI5 became a key player in the government machine. Milne comments (1995: 341): 'The cosy relationship between elements of the intelligence service and the right-wing of the Tory Party proved to be a vital lubricant in smoothing Margaret Thatcher's rise to power.' Yet rivalries between the various branches of intelligence could often spill out into the pages of newspapers. For instance, soon after Thatcher became PM in 1979 she sent Sir Maurice Oldfield, head of MI6, to Belfast to co-ordinate intelligence. MI5 reacted furiously considering the appointment of an MI6 chief to oversee their officers in Northern Ireland amounted to public criticism of their work. As Hollingsworth and Fielding (1995: 123) report: 'Suddenly, journalists in Belfast were receiving calls from RUC Special Branch alleging that Oldfield was a closet homosexual who combed the towns of Ulster looking to seduce young men. These malicious stories were traced back to MI5.'

Significantly, following his appointment as MI5 director general in 1985, Sir Anthony Duff, and Bernard Sheldon, his legal advisor, made special efforts to cultivate close links with the press. Urban (1996: 54–55) reports:

> Duff and Sheldon focused their early efforts on the editors of quality newspapers, meeting them for lunch with the aim of convincing them that the service was modern, forward-looking organisation which did not conspire against the Labour Party and was not stuffed with KGB agents.

Maxwell and Mossad – and further revelations

According to Stephen Dorril (1993), intelligence gathering during the miners' strike of 1984–1985 was helped by the fact that during the 1970s MI5's F Branch had made a special effort to recruit industrial correspondents – with great success. *Guardian* journalist Seumas Milne (1995) claimed that three quarters of Fleet Street's industrial correspondents were at that time agents for MI5 or for Scotland Yard's Special Branch. MI5 was also suspected of leaking smears to the Robert Maxwell-owned *Daily Mirror* as part of an elaborate disinformation campaign against miners' leaders Arthur Scargill and Peter Heathfield in 1990. Both were accused of using Libyan funds to pay the mortgages on their homes during the earlier strike (Ramsay 2009: 78). There was one major problem with the story: neither Scargill nor Heathfield had mortgages.[29]

In 1991, just before his mysterious death, *Mirror* proprietor Robert Maxwell was accused by the US investigative journalist Seymour Hersh in his book, *The Sampson Option* (Hersh 1991), of acting for Mossad, the Israeli secret service, though Dorril (1993: 276) suggests his links with MI6 were equally as strong. In particular, Maxwell was suspected of orchestrating the discrediting and exposure of Mordechai Vanunu after he revealed the existence of Israel's nuclear programme, in *The*

Sunday Times of 5 October 1986. Hersh claimed Vanunu's London address had been betrayed to Mossad on Maxwell's orders by the *Daily Mirror*'s foreign editor Nick Davies. Tom Bower (1996: 263–264), however, discounts the theory that Maxwell was a Mossad agent. Hersh's source was Ari Ben-Menasche, an Israeli who had been introduced to Maxwell in 1989. 'Since Ben-Menasche had, earlier, falsely claimed to be a former Mossad officer, Hersh's allegations were sharply devalued,' according to Bower (ibid: 264).

The intimate links between journalists and the secret services were highlighted in the autobiography of the eminent newscaster Sandy Gall (1994). He reports without any qualms how, after returning from one of his reporting assignments to Afghanistan, he was asked to lunch by the head of MI6. 'It was very informal, the cook was off so we had cold meat and salad with plenty of wine. He wanted to hear what I had to say about the war in Afghanistan. I was flattered, of course, and anxious to pass on what I could in terms of first-hand knowledge' (ibid: 158).[30]Aldrich and Cormac (2016: 362) record how MI6 turned to Gall in 1984 to report on the 'secret' guerrilla war being fought against the Soviets in Afghanistan.

Growing power of the secret state

Thus from this evidence alone it is clear there has been a long history of links between hacks and spooks in both the UK and US. After the 11 September 2001 attacks in the US, all of Fleet Street immediately became awash in warnings by anonymous intelligence sources of terrorist threats. According to Hewitt and Lucas (2009: 109), the Iraqi National Congress, the opposition group with close ties to the Bush administration and US intelligence agencies, was the source for 108 English language news reports published between October 2001 and May 2002.

The former UN arms inspector, Scott Ritter, revealed in his book, *Iraq Confidential* (2005), the existence of an MI6-run psychological warfare effort, known as Operation Mass Appeal. According to Ritter: 'Mass Appeal served as a focal point for passing MI6 intelligence on Iraq to the media, both in the UK and around the world. The goal was to help shape public opinion about Iraq and the threat posed by WMD' (Davies op cit: 231; see also Meacher 2003; Thursby 2004; Woodcock 2003).[31] Ritter, for instance, described how he would be asked by MI6 agents for information on Iraq that could be planted in newspapers in India, Poland and South Africa from where it would feed back to Britain and America (Rufford 2003). He also noted that many reports had appeared in the international media about 'secret underground facilities' in Iraq and nerve-gas programmes. 'All of them were garbage,' he added (cited in Aldrich and Cormac 2016: 431). MI6 propaganda specialists, at the time, claimed they could spread the misinformation through 'editors and writers who work with us from time to time'. Thus there were constant attempts to scare people – and justify still greater powers for the national security apparatus.

Early in 2004, as the battle for control of Iraq continued with mounting casualties on both sides, it was revealed that many of the lies about Saddam Hussein's supposed WMD had been fed to sympathetic journalists in the US, Britain and Australia by the exile group, the Iraqi National Congress. Moreover, later in 2004 it emerged that the Iraqi defector codenamed 'Red River', who made false claims about Iraq's germ warfare programme and failed a lie-detector test, had maintained his links with British intelligence (Borger and Norton-Taylor 2004). 'Red River' was listed in a US Senate report as one of four sources for claims made at the UN in February 2003 by US Secretary of State Colin Powell that Iraq had developed mobile germ warfare laboratories.

In his evidence to a special immigration appeal commission in July 2002, the *Observer* reporter and intelligence expert, Martin Bright (2002) highlighted the way in which journalists were constantly fed unverifiable information by the intelligence services about alleged al-Qaeda threats to the UK.

In 2008, it was reported that the government had resurrected the Information Research Department with a new title, the Research, Information and Communication Unit, to target the BBC and other media organisations with anti-al-Qaeda propaganda (Travis 2008; Cormac op cit: 256). A report leaked to the *Guardian, Challenging Violent Extremist Ideology Through Communications*, said: 'We are pushing this material to UK media channels, e.g. as a BBC radio programme exposing tensions between AQ leadership and supporters. And a restricted working group will communicate niche messages through media and non-media.'

Sexed up – and missed out

During the controversy that erupted following the end of the 2003 'war' and the death of the arms inspector Dr David Kelly (and the ensuing Hutton Inquiry) the spotlight fell on BBC reporter Andrew Gilligan and the claim by one of his sources that the government (in collusion with the intelligence services) had 'sexed up' a dossier justifying an attack on Iraq. Intriguingly Dr Kelly also had close ties with intelligence. Part of his work involved liaising with the shadowy Rockingham Cell, which Scott Ritter, the maverick US arms inspector, described as a 'secretive intelligence activity buried inside the defence intelligence staff which dealt with Iraqi WMD and the activities of the UN Special Commission' (see Baker 2007: 9; Aldrich and Cormac 2016: 430). Kelly also had a close and somewhat mysterious relationship with the American Mai Pederson who introduced him to the Baha'i faith. She was also alleged to be a spy (Baker op cit: 257–274).

The Hutton Inquiry, its every twist and turn massively covered in the mainstream media, was the archetypal media spectacle that drew attention away from the broader and more significant issues – including mainstream journalists' links with the intelligence services. Moreover, Sir Kevin Tebbit, permanent secretary at the Ministry of Defence, did tell the inquiry that Prime Minister Tony Blair had chaired the key meeting at which a question-and-answer strategy leading to the naming Dr Kelly had been agreed (Evans 2003; see also Bower 2016: 382–383). But as Georgina Born (2005: 456) comments:

…Hutton's narrow remit, defined by Downing Street and backed by unprecedented and dramatic evidence of formerly hidden governmental and editorial processes, drew the public mind away from bigger questions about the legitimacy of the government's case for war. By expiating the wrongdoings of the Kelly affair, the effect of Hutton was to ward off awareness of larger possible misdemeanours.

Admitting (and not admitting) mistakes

Significantly, on 26 May 2004, the *New York Times* carried a 1,200-word editorial admitting it had been duped in its coverage of WMD in the lead-up to the invasion by dubious Iraqi defectors, informants and exiles. Chief among the dodgy informants to reporter Judith Miller of the *Times*, was Ahmed Chalabi, leader of the Iraqi National Congress (INC) who enjoyed a strangely mixed fate in Iraq: firstly a Pentagon favourite before his Baghdad house was raided by US forces on 20 May 2004; then becoming one of the country's three deputy prime ministers while being accused of giving US intelligence secrets to Iran (Fisk 2008: 287).[32]

Then, in the *Observer* of 30 May 2004, David Rose admitted he had been the victim of 'calculated set-up' devised to foster the propaganda case for war. 'In the 18 months before the invasion of March 2003, I dealt regularly with Chalabi and the INC and published stories based on interviews with men they said were defectors from Saddam's regime.' For instance, a report by Rose in the London *Evening Standard* of 9 December 2002 was headlined: 'Saddam and al-Qaeda – the link we've all missed.' Rose concluded:

> The information fog is thicker than in any previous war, as I know now from bitter personal experience. To any journalist being offered apparently sensational disclosures, especially from an anonymous intelligence source, I offer two words of advice: *caveat emptor* (Rose 2004).

No British mainstream newspaper apologised for being duped over the WMD rationale for war in 2003. As the *Press Gazette* editorial of 23 November 2007 ('Manipulation: Have we learned from Iraq war?') commented: 'There has been no *mea culpa* in the UK press for its failure to see through the non-existent WMDs and the bogus threats whipped up by dubious groups such as the Iraqi National Congress.'

Snowden and WikiLeaks: Questions

In 2013, the NSA employee Edward Snowden revealed through the *Guardian* (with reports co-ordinated by Glenn Greenwald) and other leading Western newspapers highly classified information about the (illegal) global surveillance activities of the NSA and Five Eyes countries. His actions provoke a series of important questions.

- How legitimate was it for Greenwald and his close circle of journalists (later grouped around the *Intercept*)[33] subsequently to hold a monopoly on the distribution of the Snowden revelations?
- Are there not serious conflict of interest issues to consider when the *Intercept* is funded by the billionaire eBay founder, Pierre Omidyar, who also has a stake in PayPal?
- Is it not interesting that Sibel Edmonds, whistleblower and founder of the *boilingfrogspost* website (later *newsbud.com*), reported an NSA leaker revealing close ties between the NSA and PayPal corporation? [34]
- Why has only one media outfit (the website *Cryptome*) kept a tally on the publication of the Snowden files.[35]
- How many files are there, in fact? We, the public, have still no idea. We know that only a tiny proportion has been revealed – just 2 per cent possibly. Why? What is being held back? And was not the *Intercept*'s decision in March 2019 to close down the archive a 'disservice to the source … and to the public for whom Snowden had blown the whistle', as claimed by Laura Poitras?[36]
- Was not the dissemination of the Snowden files an extremely 'managed operation'? *Guardian* editor Alan Rusbridger said he had over a hundred meetings with government representatives discussing publication.[37] Intriguingly Chris Blackhurst, of the *Independent*, said he would never have published the revelations. 'If MI5 warns that it is not in the public interest who am I to disbelieve them?'[38] Edward Lucas, a senior correspondent for the *Economist*, said that, had Snowden brought the documents to him, he would have marched him straight down to a police station.[39]
- Should we share the concerns of Mark Curtis and Matt Kennard that the British intelligence services appear to have 'neutralised' the *Guardian*'s critical coverage of the secret state since Katherine Viner took over the editorship in 2015 (Curtis and Kennard 2019)?
- How original were Snowden's revelations? Had not much of the same data been previously revealed on *Cryptome* website and by James Bamford (in, say, his *The Shadow Factory: The Ultra Secret NSA from 9/11 to the Eavesdropping on America*, New York: Doubleday, of 2008)?
- Journalism is dependent on the ability of reporters to maintain sources' confidentiality. Yet do not Snowden's revelations about state surveillance of electronic communications (emails, Google, social media) mean that such confidentiality is no longer possible?[40]
- Do not the revelations about intelligence and police snooping[41] on reporters' communications and the attacks on whistleblowers in the UK and US (John Kiriakou,[42] Russell Tice,[43] Thomas Drake,[44] Jeffery Sterling,[45] William Binney[46], Mark Klein[47] etc[48]) provide evidence of further threats to journalistic activities?[49]
- Do not the jailings of Julian Assange, whose WikiLeaks website revealed criminal activities by Western states – in the *Collateral Murder* video in April 2010, the Afghanistan war logs in July 2010, the Iraq war logs in October 2010 and Cablegate in November 2010 – together with the jailing of

WikiLeaks' source, Chelsea Manning (see Madar 2012), amount to serious attacks on press freedom?

In 2015, the Interception of Communication Commissioner's Office reported that police forces in the UK had used the Regulation of Investigatory Powers Act 2000 against 82 journalists over a three-year period to access confidential material.[50] In April 2016, Privacy International revealed that the security services had been using Section 94 of the Telecommunications Act 1984 to requisition personal data from potentially thousands of public and private organisations. This includes data held by financial institutions and could include anything from confidential NHS health records to databases of people who have signed online petitions. According to Privacy International, the term 'Bulk Personal Datasets' was first used in March 2015 in an Intelligence and Security committee report. Even the ISC was unaware of the use of BPDs until recently.[51]

GCHQ staff, intelligence officers and police have been given immunity from prosecution for hacking into computers, laptops and mobile phones under legislative changes that were never fully debated by parliament.[52] Moreover, the Investigatory Powers Act 2016 enables the tracking of everyone's web and social media use, but also moves to strengthen the security services' warranted powers for the bulk interception of the content of communications.[53]

How to react?

How should journalists and citizens react to the ever-increasing powers of the secret state? Do not schools of journalism now have to problematise notions of professional neutrality and teach that only radical journalism is relevant? Is not all the rest mere 'churnalism' for the powerful interests in society? With radical politics there have to be radical journalistic techniques: for instance, since electronic communication is now compromised, face-to-face interviewing of sources on sensitive topics and the teaching of encryption techniques have to be the priority. Do not journalists need to speak out more and join citizen campaigns in defence of Assange and Manning – and other reporters who are attacked, intimidated, tortured and killed throughout the world? (Keeble 2018). Should more publicity be given campaigns calling for an opening up of the police and intelligence agencies to democratic scrutiny? As *discoversociety.org* argues:

> The collaboration of the security establishment with official enemies and the total lack of transparency around the use of spies and informers by the intelligence agencies is a key but unsung element of the 'blowback' effect. If we want to see a reduction in 'terrorist' attacks in the UK, we need to stop invading and bombing foreign countries, stop providing support to proxy groups in regime change operations (as in Libya and Syria) and arms to allied repressive regimes such as Israel, the UAE, Bahrain and Saudi Arabia, and instead uphold international law.[54]

And are not now the most important media on the secret state and its secret wars non-corporate alternatives (always to be read critically, of course) such as *anti-war. com, coldtype.net, counterpunch.org, cryptome.org, globalresearch.ca, intelnews.org, lobster-magazine.co.uk, statewatch.org, tomdispatch.com, whowhatwhy.com, wsws.org*, the writing of Pepe Escobar at *Asian Times* (http://www.atimes.com/atimes/Others/Escobar. html), the freelance work of Dahl Jamail (*dahrjamail.net*) and of the maverick American intellectual/political activist Noam Chomsky (*chomsky.info*) etc?[55]

Acknowledgements

This essay is based on a chapter with the same title in *Covering Conflict: The Making and Unmaking of New Militarism*, Bury St Edmunds, Abramis, 2017 pp 31–76.

Notes

1 Precise figures on funding of the intelligence services are difficult to identify. Richard Norton-Taylor, of the *Guardian*, reported that the three intelligence services (MI5, MI6 and GCHQ) spent £2.4 billion each year (see Inside the doughnut, *Guardian*, 19 June 2010)

2 The secret state is also theorised as the 'clandestine, parallel state' (that operates both inside and outside the law), 'shadow government', 'invisible government', 'deep state' and 'national security state'. See Tunander 2009

3 As Hennessey and Thomas (2009: 605, 615) report, MI5 has established regional stations around Britain to work closely with police forces – with a presence in the Midlands, North East, North West, South, East and Scotland

4 See Beaumont, Paul (2016) Whitehatters: Seeking a new generation, *Eye Spy*, No. 105, October pp 44–47

5 See http://motherboard.vice.com/read/your-government-wants-to-militarize-social-media-to-influence-your-beliefs, accessed on 15 November 2016

6 As former MI5 undercover agent Gary Murray (1993: 7) comments: 'RAF "spooks" have played an integral part in numerous undercover operations, and have contributed to the detection and apprehension of a number of foreign agents, both in the United Kingdom and abroad'

7 See http://www.nationalcrimeagency.gov.uk/

8 See http://undercoverresearch.net/undercover-profiles/, accessed on 2 April 2016. They include the Counter Terrorism Specialist Firearms unit set up in 2016 following a wave of terrorist attacks in Europe

9 For instance, British mercenaries, the SAS and Saladin Security have fought alongside Sri Lankan forces in their war against the Tamil people (see Miller 2014)

10 Bloom (2015: 191) also quotes Peter Wright claiming MI5 was 'controlled by Masonic connections'. On the City of London as an offshore tax haven, see http://www.newsta tesman.com/economy/2011/02/london-corporation-city, accessed on 9 May 2016

11 See http://www.ndr.de/nachrichten/netzwelt/snowden277_page-2.html, accessed on 13 June 2016

12 In the US, the NSA has around 30,000 employees but it relies on a larger workforce of some 60,000 private contractors (Foster and McChesney 2014: 26). The privatisation of US military intelligence is highlighted by Pratap Chatterjee (2006)

13 *Private Eye* reported (19 August–1 September 2016: 11) that the body that is meant to scrutinise and represent the public interest on disclosure of items in the National Archive, the obscure advisory council on national records and archives, is dominated by former diplomats, police officers, spooks and civil servants

14 Le Carré had previously worked for intelligence as an informant while at Oxford University. When le Carré decided to retire from MI6 following the enormous global success of his novel *The Man Who Came in From the Cold* (1963) it was suggested he continue spying under the cover of being either a journalist or an academic (Sisman 2015: 254–255)

15 See http://www.independent.co.uk/arts-entertainment/books/news/frederick-forsyth-reveals-he-once-worked-for-mi6-10478684.html, accessed on 7 November 2015

16 For instance, SIS agent Richard Tomlinson travelled around Serbia in the early 1990s carrying a press card saying he was a member of the National Union of Journalists and a British passport describing him as Ben Presley. 'Both documents were forged by MI6's Technical Services Department' (Thomas 2009: 286)

17 See http://www.telegraph.co.uk/news/obituaries/11016167/Chapman-Pincher-obituary. html, accessed on 18 June 2016

18 See http://www.bbc.co.uk/news/uk-26781900, accessed on 18 June 2016

19 This quotation from an email sent by Phillip Knightley to the author on 12 May 2000

20 See www.30au.co.uk – a website packed with details about the assault unit

21 The terminology of terrorism: Malaya 1948–1952, *Journal of South East Asian Studies*, June 2003 Available online at http://www.accessmylibrary.com/coms2/summary_0286-4205179_ITM, accessed on 11 June 2008

22 See http://www.spinprofiles.org/index.php/Information_Research_Department, accessed on 14 February 2010

23 The bugs in No. 10 Downing Street were only removed by PM Jim Callaghan in 1977, the year he cleared MI5 of a plot to oust Wilson's government

24 In 2000, Northern Ireland secretary Mo Mowlam even admitted that Gerry Adams of Sinn Fein had been bugged. Four years later Sinn Fein's Martin McGuinness was also shown to have been bugged after a new biography carried transcripts of telephone conversations. And in 2008 it was reported in *The Sunday Times* that MP Sadiq Khan was bugged while meeting a constituent Babar Ahmad, being held at a north London prison while fighting extradition to the United States on terrorism charges (Cobain 2014b)

25 The MI5 history also revealed that the telephone of Jack Jones, general secretary of the Transport and General Workers' Union from 1969 to 1978, was also bugged by MI5. See Michael Evans: MI5 bugged Jack Jones's phone over fears he was agent of KGB, *Times*, 6 October 2009

26 Richard Norton-Taylor (1990: 98) records how, in 1974, Chapman Pincher was given a copy of a forged Swiss account claiming Ted Short, later Lord Glenamara, was illegally investing in a foreign bank. Lord Glenamara believed it was all part of a 'dirty campaign by people in MI5'

27 See Newton, Scott (2000/1) MI5 and the Wilson plot, *Lobster*, No. 40 winter p 28. Significantly, the intelligence plots against Wilson occurred at roughly the same time when social democratic governments in Australia, New Zealand and West Germany were also being subjected to destabilisation campaigns. See Willy Brandt: The 'Good German', by Stephen Dorril, *Lobster*, No. 22 pp 12–15. On the 1975 coup to remove Gough Whitlam in Australia see The British-American coup that ended Australian independence, by John Pilger, *Guardian*, 23 October 2014

28 See British intelligence and the covert propaganda front. Available online at http://nelsonmandela2.blogspot.com/, accessed on 14 June 2008

29 Roy Greenslade, the then-editor of the *Daily Mirror*, later apologised for his role in the Scargill smears affair. See http://www.guardian.co.uk/media/2002/may/27/mondaymediasection.politicsandthemedia, accessed on 6 April 2009. During the miners' strike of 1972, the leader of the National Union of Mineworkers was Joe Gormley. While Richard Vinen (2009: 39) reports that Gormley was 'conspicuously non-communist and may even have been an MI5 informant'. Rory Cormac, working with official documents, stresses (op cit: 302): 'Gormley was a Special Branch informant during the 1970s and passed on details of Arthur Scargill's and other miners' plans for industrial action'

30 Anthony Frewin, in *Lobster*, No. 30 p. 42 argues that 'the proximate cause of the attack on Gott … was his review of the memoirs of the ITN journalist, Sandy Gall, in the *Guardian* of 12 February 1994, in which he pointed out that Gall had been working with SIS in his reporting of the war in Afghanistan'

31 The government later admitted the existence of Mass Appeal. See Revealed: How MI6 sold the Iraq war, Nicholas Rufford, *Sunday Times*, 28 December 2003

32 The agent known as Curveball, who became one of the CIA's most valuable sources on Iraq's fictitious WMD, was later revealed to be Rafid Ahmed Alwan al-Janabi, who worked in Division Four of Iraq's intelligence services (see Meanwhile Curveball – the man whose lies made the case for war – looks on from afar, Martin Chulov, *Guardian*, 29 June 2009)

33 See https://firstlook.org/theintercept/

34 http://www.boilingfrogspost.com/2013/12/11/bfp-breaking-news-omidyars-paypal-corporation-said-to-be-implicated-in-withheld-nsa-documents/

35 http://motherboard.vice.com/read/cryptome-is-pushing-for-all-of-the-snowden-docs-to-be-made-public

36 See https://www.thedailybeast.com/the-intercept-shuts-down-access-to-snowden-trove

37 http://www.nytimes.com/2013/12/04/business/media/after-snowden-revelations-a-changed-world-for-journalists.html?_r=0 and http://zelo-street.blogspot.co.uk/2013/12/snowden-guardian-editor-speaks.html

38 http://www.independent.co.uk/voices/comment/edward-snowdens-secrets-may-be-dangerous-i-would-not-have-published-them-8877404.html

39 See http://www.cjr.org/opinion/edward_snowden_impact.php

40 http://www.theguardian.com/world/2013/sep/05/nsa-gchq-encryption-codes-security

41 See http://www.mirror.co.uk/news/uk-news/phone-hacking-legal-loophole-allows-4472109

42 http://www.newyorker.com/magazine/2013/04/01/the-spy-who-said-too-much

43 http://www.huffingtonpost.com/2013/06/20/russ-tice-nsa-obama_n_3473538.html and http://www.nytimes.com/2005/12/16/politics/16program.html?pagewanted=all&_r=1&

44 See https://couragefound.org/2015/03/government-rejects-thomas-drakes-retaliation-claims/ and http://www.wsws.org/en/articles/2011/06/leak-j13.html and http://www.theguardian.com/us-news/2016/may/22/how-pentagon-punished-nsa-whistleblowers

45 http://rt.com/news/226455-sterling-cia-iran-guilty/ and http://www.wsws.org/en/articles/2014/06/03/rise-j03.html; http://www.wsws.org/en/articles/2015/05/12/ster-m12.html – Jeffrey Sterling was sentenced to 42 months on 11 May 2015 for leaking secrets to *New York Times*'s James Risen about 'Operation Merlin', launched by the CIA in 2000 to sabotage Iran's nuclear programme using dirty tricks, including the provision of flawed nuclear bomb blueprints

46 http://timshorrock.com/?p=1950

47 https://sites.google.com/site/markklein2009/Home

48 http://www.politifact.com/punditfact/statements/2014/jan/10/jake-tapper/cnns-tapper-obama-has-used-espionage-act-more-all-/

49 http://www.theguardian.com/uk-news/2015/jan/19/gchq-intercepted-emails-journalists-ny-times-bbc-guardian-le-monde-reuters-nbc-washington-post

50 http://www.pressgazette.co.uk/use-anti-terror-legislation-against-journalists-sees-uk-slip-down-world-press-freedom-rankings

51 https://privacyinternational.org/node/853

52 See http://www.theguardian.com/uk-news/2015/may/15/intelligence-officers-have-immunity-from-hacking-laws-tribunal-told

53 See http://www.theguardian.com/uk-news/2015/may/27/security-services-investigatory-powers-bill

54 https://discoversociety.org/category/on-the-frontline/

55 See Keeble, Richard Lance (2015) Journalists and the secret state, in *News from Somewhere: A Reader in Communication and Challenges to Globalization*, edited by Daniel Broudy, Jeffery Klaehn and James Winter, Wayzgoose Press, Eugene, Oregon, USA pp 203–212

References

Aldrich, Richard (1998) *Espionage, Security and Intelligence in Britain 1945–1970*, Manchester and New York: Manchester University Press

Aldrich, Richard J. and Cormac, Rory (2016) *The Black Door: Spies, Secret Intelligence and British Prime Ministers*, London: William Collins

Alexander, Adam (2015) UK surveillance oversight weakest in west, says first UN privacy chief, *Guardian*, 24 August. Available online at https://www.theguardian.com/world/2015/aug/24/we-need-geneva-convention-for-the-internet-says-new-un-privacy-chief, accessed on 13 June 2016

Andrew, C. M. (2009) American Presidents and their intelligence communities, Andrew, Christopher, Aldrich, Richard J. and Wark, Wesley K. (eds) *Secret Intelligence: A Reader*, London: Routledge pp 116–128

Baker, Norman (2007) *The Strange Death of David Kelly*, London: Methuen

Beckett, Andy (2010) *When the Lights Went Out: What Really Happened to Britain in the Seventies*, London: Faber & Faber

Bloch, Jonathan and Fitzgerald, Patrick (1983) *British Intelligence and Covert Action*, London: Junction Books

Bloom, Clive (2015) *Thatcher's Secret war: Subversion, Coercion, Secrecy and Government 1974–1990*, Stroud, Gloucestershire: The History Press

Borger, Julian (2003) The spies who pushed for war, *Guardian*, 17 July. Available online at http://www.theguardian.com/world/2003/jul/17/iraq.usa, accessed on 6 June 2014

Borger, Julian and Norton-Taylor, Richard (2004) British intelligence still talking to Iraqi source who made false claims, *Guardian*, 14 July

Born, Georgina (2005) *Uncertain Vision: Birt, Dyke and the Reinvention of the BBC*, London: Vintage

Bowcott, Owen (2015) Campaigners say barely debated change in law legalised GCHQ hacking, *Guardian*, 16 May. Available online at https://www.theguardian.com/uk-news/2015/may/15/intelligence-officers-have-immunity-from-hacking-laws-tribunal-told, accessed on 13 June 2016

Bower, Tom (1996) *Maxwell: The Final Verdict*, London: HarperCollins

Bower, Tom (2016) *Broken Vows: Tony Blair – The Tragedy of Power*, London: Faber & Faber

Bright, Martin (2002) Terror, security and the media, *Observer*, 21 July. Available online at http://observer.guardian.co.uk/libertywatch/story/0,1373,758265,00.html, accessed on 22 July 2002

Cabell, Craig (2008) *Ian Fleming's Secret War*, Barnsley, South Yorkshire: Pen and Sword Books

Chatterjee, Pratap (2006) Intelligence in Iraq: L-3 supplies spy support, *Corpwatch*, 9 August. Available online at http://www.corpwatch.org/article.php?id=13993, accessed on 16 September 2016

Cobain, Ian (2013) MoD unlawfully conceals files about the Troubles, *Guardian*, 7 October. Available online at http://www.theguardian.com/uk-news/2013/oct/06/ministry-of-defence-files-archive, accessed on 19 January 2016

Cobain, Ian (2014a) Academics consider legal action to force Foreign Office to release public records, *Guardian*, 13 January. Available online at http://www.theguardian.com/politics/2014/jan/13/foreign-office-secret-files-national-archive-historians-legal-action, accessed on 20 January 2016

Cobain, Ian (2014b) Are spooks bugging politicians?, *Guardian*, 15 July. Available online at http://www.theguardian.com/world/2014/jul/14/spies-flouting-wilson-doctrine-bugging-mps, accessed on 15 July 2014

Cormac, Rory (2018) *Disrupt and Deny: Spies, Special Forces, and the Secret Pursuit of British Foreign Policy*, Oxford:Oxford University Press

Cottrell, Roger (2008) The Cecil King coup plot as a precursor to Gordon Brown's 'government of all talents', *Lobster*, No. 55, Summer pp 22–28

Curtis, Mark and Kennard, Matt (2019) How the UK Security Services neutralised the country's leading liberal newspaper, *Daily Maverick*, 11 September. Available online at https://www.dailymaverick.co.za/article/2019-09-11-how-the-uk-security-services-neut ralised-the-countrys-leading-liberal-newspaper/amp/

Davies, Nick (2008) *Flat Earth News*, London: Chatto & Windus

Dorril, Stephen (1993) *The Silent Conspiracy: Inside the Intelligence Services in the 1990s*, London: Heinemann

Dorril, Stephen and Ramsay, Robin (1991) *Smear*, London: Fourth Estate

Evans, Harold (1983) *Good Times, Bad Times*, London: Weidenfeld and Nicolson

Evans, Michael (2003) Blair 'chaired talks on Kelly naming strategy', *Times*, 14 October

Evans, Michael (2009) MI5 compiled dosser on Harold Wilson's KGB links, *Times*, 3 October

Evans, Rob (2016) UK's top policeman challenged over intelligence unit, *Guardian*, 9 January. Available online at http://www.pressreader.com/uk/the-guardian/20160109/ 281522225076166/TextView, accessed on 11 January 2016

Fisk, Robert (2008) *The Age of the Warrior: Selected Writings*, London: Fourth Estate

Foster, John Bellamy and McChesney, Robert W. (2014) Surveillance capitalism: Monopoly finance capital, the military–industrial complex and the digital age, *Monthly Review*, Vol. 66, No. 3 pp 1–31

Gall, Sandy (1994) *News from the Frontline: A Television Reporter's Life*, London: Heinemann

Hennessey, Thomas and Thomas, Claire (2009) *Spooks: The Unofficial History of MI5*, Stroud, Gloucestershire: Amberley

Hersh, Seymour (1991) *The Sampson Option*, London: Faber & Faber

Hewitt, Steve and Lucas, Scott (2009) *All the Secrets that are Fit to Print? The Media and US Intelligence Services Before and After 9/11*, Dover: Robert and Goodman

Hollingsworth, Mark and Fielding, Nick (1999) *Defending the Realm: MI5 and the Shayler Affair*, London: André Deutsch

Horrie, Chris (2004) *Tabloid Nation: From the Birth of the Daily Mirror to the Death of the Tabloid*, London: Deutsch

James, Luke (2015) Spies rigged Shrewsbury pickets trial, 10 December, Campaign for Press and Broadcasting Freedom

Jeffery, Keith (2011) *MI6: The History of the Secret Intelligence Service 1909–1949*, London: Bloomsbury

Keeble, Richard (2003) Spooks are represented on every newspaper, *Press Gazette*, 9 October

Keeble, Richard Lance (2010) Hacks and spooks – close encounters of a strange kind: A critical history of the links between mainstream journalists and the intelligence services in the UK, Klaehn, Jeffery (ed.) *The Political Economy of Media and Power*, New York: Peter Lang pp 87–111

Keeble, Richard Lance (2018) Secret, repressive states worldwide and the threat to journalism, *Journalism*, Vol. 20, No. 1 pp 114–117

Knightley, Phillip (1986) *The Second Oldest Profession: The Spy as Bureaucrat, Patriot, Fantasist and Whore*, London: André Deutsch

Knightley, Phillip (2003 [1982]) *The First Casualty: The War Correspondent as Hero, Propagandist and Myth-Maker from the Crimea to Iraq*, London: André Deutsch

Knightley, Phillip (2006) Journalists and spies: An unhealthy relationship, *Ethical Space: The International Journal of Communication Ethics*, Vol. 3, Nos 2/3 pp 7–11

Lashmar, Paul (2013) Urinal or open channel? Institutional flow between the UK intelligence services and news media, *Journalism*, Vol. 14, No. 8 pp 1024–1040

Lashmar, Paul and Oliver, James (1998) *Britain's Secret Propaganda War 1948–1977*, Stroud: Sutton

Leigh, David (1980) *The Frontiers of Secrecy*, London: Junction Books

Leigh, David (2000) Britain's security services and journalists: The secret story, *British Journalism Review*, Vol. 11, No. 2 pp 21–26

Livingstone, Ken (1998) A cock-up that reawakens suspicions about our spies, *Independent*, 25 November. Available online at http://www.independent.co.uk/arts-entertainment/a-cockup -that-reawakens-suspicions-about-our-spies-1187129.html, accessed on 1 January 2010

Lycett, Andrew (1996) *Ian Fleming*, London: Weidenfeld and Nicolson

McConnachie, James and Tudge, Robin (2005) *The Rough Guide to Conspiracy Theories*, London: Rough Guides

McCrystal, Cal (1999) The sub-secret underworld of the D-Notice business, *British Journalism Review*, Vol. 10, No. 2 pp 26–33

Madar, Chase (2012) *The Passion of Bradley Manning*, New York: Or Books

Marr, Andrew (2007) *A History of Modern Britain*, London: Pan Macmillan

Marsden, Sam (2013) Thatcher made secret plans to bring in the military during the miners' strike, *Daily Telegraph*, 1 August. Available online at http://www.telegraph.co.uk/news/poli tics/margaret-thatcher/10213447/Thatcher-made-secret-plans-to-bring-in-the-military-dur ing-the-miners-strike.html, accessed on 28 January 2016

Meacher, Michael (2003) The very secret service, *Guardian*, 11 November

Miller, Phil (2014) *Britain's Dirty War against the Tamil People 1979–2009*, Bremen: International Human Rights Association

Milne, Seamus (1995) *The Enemy Within: The Secret War Against the Miners*, London: Pan

Moran, Christopher (2013) *Classified: Secrecy and the State in Modern Britain*, Cambridge: Cambridge University Press

Murray, Gary (1993) *Enemies of the State: A Sensational Exposé of the Security Services by a Former MI5 Undercover Agent*, New York and London: Pocket Books

Newton, Scott (2008/9) Harold Wilson, the Bank of England and the Cecil King 'coup' of May 1968, *Lobster*, Winter pp 3–8

Norton-Taylor, Richard (1990) *In Defence of the Realm? The Case for Accountable Security Services*, London: Civil Liberties Trust

Norton-Taylor, Richard (2010) MI5 bugged cabinet room at No. 10, says historian, *Guardian*, 19 April

Osborne, Samuel (2018) UK to be hit by 'Category 1' cyber emergency, intelligence chief warns, *Independent*, 16 October

Penrose, Barry and Courtiour, Roger (1978) *The Pencourt File*, London: Secker & Warburg

Pilger, John (1998) *Hidden Agendas*, London: Verso

Pincher, Chapman (2014) *Dangerous to Know: A Life*, London: Biteback

Plesch, Dan (2004) Missing link: The role played by US intelligence has been predictably omitted from the Butler report, *Guardian*, 16 July

Ramsay, Robin (2003) A guided democracy, *Lobster*, No. 46 p 15

Ramsay, Robin (2008) *Politics and Paranoia*, Hove: Picnic Publishing

Ramsay, Robin (2009) The miners and the secret state, Williams, Granville (ed.) *Shafted: The Media, the Miners' Strike and the Aftermath*, London, Campaign for Press and Broadcasting Freedom pp 73–80

Rose, David (2004) Iraqi defectors tricked us with WMD lies, but we must not be fooled again, *Observer*, 30 May. Available online at http://www.guardian.co.uk/media/2004/may/30/Iraqandthemedia.iraq, accessed on 14 October 2006

Rufford, Nicholas (2003) Revealed: How MI6 sold the Iraq war, *Times*, 28 December. Available online at http://www.timesonline.co.uk/tol/news/uk/article839897.ece, accessed on 28 December 2003

Sampson, Anthony (2004) *Who Runs This Place? The Anatomy of Britain in the 21st Century*, London: John Murray

Scott, Peter Dale (2017) *The American Deep State*, London: Rowman & Littlefield

Simpson, John (2010) *Unreliable Sources*, London: Macmillan

Sisman, Adam (2015) *John le Carré: The Biography*, London: Bloomsbury

Smith, James (2013) *British Writers and MI5 Surveillance 1930–1960*, Cambridge: Cambridge University Press

Southwell, David (2005) *Secrets and Lies: Exposing the World of Cover-Ups and Deception*, London: Sevenoaks

Thomas, Gordon (2009) *Inside British Intelligence: 100 Years of MI5 and MI6*, London: JR Books

Thompson, Edward P. (1980) *Writing by Candlelight*, London: Merlin Press

Thursby, Rowena (2004) Operation Rockingham, *globalresearch.ca*, 31 July. Available online at http://www.globalresearch.ca/articles/THU407A.html, accessed on 22 August 2016

Travis, Alan (2008) Revealed: Britain's secret propaganda war against al-Qaida, *Guardian*, 26 August

Trelford, Donald (2009) The spying game, *Independent*, 14 September

Tunander, Ola (2009) Democratic state vs. deep state: Approaching the dual state of the West, Wilson, Eric (ed.) *Government of the Shadows: Parapolitics and Criminal Sovereignty*, London: Pluto pp 56–72

Turner, John (2006) Powerful information, Keeble, Richard (ed.) *The Newspapers Handbook*, Londo: Routledge, fourth edition pp 164–191

Urban, Mark (1996) *UK Eyes Alpha: The Inside Story of British Intelligence*, London: Faber & Faber

Verkaik, Robert (2016) Why we need an ombudsman for extremism, *Guardian*, 27 January

Vinen, Richard (2009) *Thatcher's Britain: The Politics and Social Upheaval of the 1980s*, London: Simon & Schuster

Walker, Peter (2013) Questioning of spy agency chiefs 'wouldn't have scared a puppy', *Guardian*, 7 November. Available online at http://www.theguardian.com/world/2013/nov/07/questioning-spy-chiefs-wouldnt-scared-puppy, accessed on 14 January 2016

Wilson, Eric (ed.) (2009) *Government of the Shadows: Parapolitics and Criminal Sovereignty*, London: Pluto Press

Wilkinson, Nicholas (2009) *Secrecy and the Media: The Official History of the United Kingdom's D-Notice System*, London: Routledge

Woodcock, Andrew (2003) Parliament urged to probe 'disinformation operation', *PA*, 21 November

Wright, Peter (1987) *Spycatcher*, New York, Dell Publishing Group. Available online at https://wikispooks.com/w/images/a/a5/Spycatcher.pdf, accessed on 15 June 2016

Yorkshire CND (2012) Lifting the lid on Menwith Hill. Available online at https://www.statewatch.org/news/2012/mar/uk-menwith-hill-lifting-the-lid.pdf

11

TARGETING GADDAFI

Secret warfare and the media

On 30 April 2011, Nato bombs killed Saif el-Arab, the 29-year-old son of Libyan President Col. Muammar Gaddafi, and three of his grandchildren who were sheltering in his Tripoli compound. One of the grandchildren, Mastoura, was just four-months-old.[1]

This was not an isolated attempt on Gaddafi's life. Behind a wall of silence, the US and UK conducted over four decades a massive, largely secret war against Libya – often using Chad, the country lying on its southern border, as its base – and attempting to assassinate the Libyan leader. Indeed, Nato continued its relentless bombing of Gaddafi's Tripoli HQ in the Bab al-Aziziya compound over the months leading up to its seizure by the rebels in August 2011 – and his eventual assassination on 20 October 2011.

Gaddafi seizes power – and MI6 plot to restore monarchy flops

Seizing power in Libya by ousting King Idris in a 1969 coup,[2] Gaddafi (who intriguingly had undertaken a military training course in England in 1966) quickly established close links with the Soviet Union – and so became the target of massive covert operations by the French, US, Israeli and British.[3] Stephen Dorril (2000: 736), in his history of MI6, records how in 1971 a British plan to invade the country, release political prisoners and restore the monarchy ended in a complete flop (see also Cormac 2018: 184–185).

Dorril reports: 'What became known as the "Hilton assignment" was one of MI6's last attempts at a major special operation designed to overthrow a regime opposed to British interests.' The plan to bring down Gaddafi had originally been a joint MI6/CIA operation but the CIA suddenly withdrew after they concluded that 'although Gaddafi was anti-West, he was also anti-Soviet, which meant there could be someone a lot worse running Libya. The British disagreed' (2000: 736).

In 1980, according to Richard Deacon, the head of the French secret service, Col. Alain de Gaigneronde de Marolles, resigned after a French-led plan ended in disaster when a rebellion by Libyan troops in Tobruk was rapidly suppressed (Deacon 1990: 260–262). But former French intelligence chief Pierre Lethier disputes this claim:

> Mr Deacon, I am afraid, has seen fit to spread rumours fabricated by the opposition press in France. Former head of the Action Service and then Deputy Director for Intelligence in 1978, de Marolles fell from grace in 1980 after a sinister conflict within the SDECE (under Count Alexandre de Marenches from 1971 to 1981) following a highly debatable counter-intelligence operation. Unfortunately I cannot say any more about this.[4]

Throughout the early 1980s Gaddafi was demonised in the mainstream US and UK media as a 'terrorist warlord' and prime agent of a Soviet-inspired 'terror network'. According to Noam Chomsky, Reagan's campaign against 'international terrorism' was a natural choice for the propaganda system in furtherance of its basic agenda: 'expansion of the state sector of the economy; transfer of resources from the poor to the rich and a more "activist" (i.e. terrorist and aggressive) foreign policy'. Such policies needed the public to be frightened into obedience by some 'terrible enemy'. And Libya fitted the need perfectly (Chomsky 1991: 120).

Easy to hate

As Chomsky adds: 'Gaddafi is easy to hate, particularly against the backdrop of rampant anti-Arab racism in the United States and the deep commitment of the educated classes, with only the rarest of exceptions, to US–Israeli rejectionism and violence. He has created an ugly and repressive society and is, indeed, guilty of retail terrorism, primarily against Libyans' (ibid).

In July 1981, a CIA plan to overthrow and possibly kill Gaddafi was leaked to the press. At roughly the same time, Libyan hit squads were reported to have entered the United States, though this has since been revealed to have been a piece of Israeli secret service disinformation (Rusbridger 1989: 80). Joe Flynn, the infamous con man, was also able to exploit Fleet Street's fascination with the Gaddafi myth. In September 1981, posing as an Athens-based arms dealer, he tricked almost £3,000 out of the *News of the World* with his story that the Libyan leader was 'masterminding a secret plot to arm black revolutionary murder squads in Britain' (Lycett 1995).

Then in 1982, away from the glare of the media, Hissène Habré, with the backing of the CIA, Egyptian and Israeli troops, overthrew the Chadian government of Goukouni Wedeye (Cockburn and Cockburn 1992: 123; Meredith 2006: 352–356). Human Rights Watch records: 'Under President Reagan, the United States gave covert CIA paramilitary support to help install Habré in order, according to secretary of state Alexander Haig, to "bloody Gaddafi's nose".'[5] Bob

Woodward, in his semi-official history of the CIA, reveals that the Chad covert operation was the first undertaken by the new CIA chief William Casey and that throughout the decade Libya ranked almost as high as the Soviet Union as the *bête noir* of the administration (Woodward 1987: 348, 363, 410–411).

A report from Amnesty, *Chad: The Habré Legacy* (Amnesty International 2001), records massive military and financial support for Habré by the US Congress. It adds: 'None of the documents presented to Congress and consulted by Amnesty International covering the period 1984 to 1989 make any reference to human rights violations.'

US official records indicate that funding for the Chad-based secret war against Libya also came from Saudi Arabia, Egypt, Morocco, Israel and Iraq (Hunter 1991). According to John Prades (1986: 383), the Saudis, for instance, donated $7m. to an opposition group, the National Front for the Salvation of Libya (also backed by French intelligence and the CIA). But a plan to assassinate Gaddafi and take over the government on 8 May 1984 was crushed (Perry 1992: 165). One month earlier, an unarmed policewoman, Yvonne Fletcher, was shot while on duty outside the Libyan People's Bureau in St. James's Square, London. And the British accused the Libyan government of being directly responsible.[6] In the following year, the US asked Egypt to invade Libya and overthrow Gaddafi but President Mubarak refused (Martin and Walcott 1988: 255–256).

Thrilled to blitz

Frustrated in its covert attempts to topple Gaddafi, the US government's strategy suddenly shifted. In March 1986, US planes patrolling the Gulf of Sidra were reported to have been attacked by Libyan missiles. But Noam Chomsky suggests this incident was a provocation 'enabling US forces to sink several Libyan boats, killing more than 50 Libyans and, it was hoped, to incite Gaddafi to acts of terror against Americans, as was subsequently claimed' (Chomsky op cit: 124). In the following month, Gaddafi was blamed for organising the bombing of a TWA passenger jet over Greece while President Reagan next claimed to have proof that the Libyan embassy had arranged the bombing of a Berlin discothèque on 5 April 1986 – killing an American serviceman and a Turkish woman and seriously injuring 229 people.[7]

The US responded with a military strike on key Libyan targets. But the attack was widely condemned. James Adams (1987: 372) quotes a British intelligence source: 'Although we allowed the raid there was a general feeling that America had become uncontrollable and unless we did something Reagan would be even more violent the next time.'

Prime Minister Margaret Thatcher was perhaps hoping for an action-replay of the Falklands factor when she gave the US permission to fly 24 F-111 attack jets from the US 48th Tactical Fighter Wing, based at RAF Lakenheath, in East Anglia, to bomb Libyan targets. Also, according to Annie Machon (2005: 104), Mrs Thatcher was 'anxious for revenge' after the shooting of Pc Fletcher. In contrast,

Mark Curtis (1998: 29) argues that the UK was the only major ally to offer support to President Reagan 'partly in return for US intelligence support during the Falklands War [of 1982] which Britain could probably not have undertaken unilaterally'.

Dorril reports that the Arab Commando Cell, a front for terrorist Abu Nidal, killed two British hostages, Philip Padfield and Leigh Douglas: 'Mrs Thatcher had given the go-ahead for the US bombers to use British bases despite a report which originated with MI6 that the hostages would be killed in retaliation for the raid' (Dorril 1993: 289).

The Libyan attack was an archetypal move of the secret state: only a select few in Thatcher's cabinet were involved in the decision. Yet the bombings appeared to win little support from the public. Harris, Gallup and MORI all showed substantial majorities opposed.

Much of the UK mainstream press, however, responded with jingoistic jubilation. The *Sun*'s front page screamed: 'Thrilled to blitz: Bombing Gaddafi was my greatest day, says US airman.' The *Mirror* concluded: 'What was the alternative? In what other way was Colonel Gaddafi to be forced to understand that he had a price to pay for his terrorism?' *The Times* commented:

> The greatest threat to Western freedoms may be the Soviet Union but that does not make the USSR the only threat. The growth of terrorist states must be curbed while it can be curbed. The risks of extension of the conflict must be minimised. And in this case it would appear that it has been.

The *Star*'s front page proclaimed: 'Reagan was right.' In the *Sunday Telegraph*, of 1 June, columnist Paul Johnson denounced the 'distasteful whiff of pure cowardice in the air' as 'the wimps' raised doubts about the US bombing of 'terrorist bases' in Libya (Keeble 2017: 114).

But there was an intriguing mediacentric dimension to the Libyan bombings as the BBC, transformed into the 'enemy within' of the vulnerable state, was to come under some considerable attack from the Conservative government over its coverage of the attacks (ibid). Though most of the press responded ecstatically to Britain's role in the bombing, all their contrived jingoism could not hide the fact that the raid failed to capture the imagination of important elements of the elite. Opposition even came from cabinet members. Both Spain and France refused to allow the F-116s to fly over their air space (Moore 2015: 511).

How BBC became the perfect scapegoat

The BBC became the perfect scapegoat. Kate Adie's on-the-spot reports could not fail to mention the casualties (Sebba 1994: 266–267; Higgins and Smith 2011). Many of the main targets were missed. Four 2,000lb bombs fell on the suburb of Bin Ghashir, causing far more devastation than any 'terrorist' bomb could ever achieve.[8] Even so, Norman Tebbit, chairman of the Conservative Party, engaged in a highly personalised attack on Adie. Yet there was an air of theatre about the whole event. Adie was one of the most trusted BBC correspondents. And both government and BBC could benefit from the spat. The Tory right, on the ascendancy at the time, and ever hasty to criticise the BBC it so desperately wanted privatised as the 'enemy within', was satisfied and the BBC, who stuck by their star reporter throughout the attacks, could appear to be courageously defending media freedom. Amidst the many contradictions and complexities of modern-day politics, mediacentric elements are put to many diverse uses by (usually competing) factions in the ruling elites.

According to US academic Douglas Kellner (1990: 138), the bombing was a manufactured crisis, staged as a media event and co-ordinated to coincide with the beginning of the 7 pm news in the US. Two hours later President Reagan went on network television to justify the raid. Chomsky also argues that the attack was 'the first bombing in history staged for prime-time television' (Chomsky op cit: 127). Administration press conferences soon after the raid ensured 'total domination of the propaganda system during the crucial early hours'. Chomsky continues:

> One might argue that the administration took a gamble in this transparent public relations operation, since journalists could have asked some difficult questions. But the White House was justly confident that nothing untoward would occur and its faith in the servility of the media proved to be entirely warranted (ibid).

Yet the main purpose of the raid was to kill the Libyan President – dubbed a 'mad dog' by Reagan. David Yallop (1994: 713) quotes 'a member of the United States Air Force intelligence unit who took part in the pre-raid briefing': 'Nine of F-111s that left from the UK were specifically briefed to bomb Gaddafi's residence inside the barracks where he was living with his family.'[9]

In the event, the first bomb to drop on Tripoli hit Gaddafi's home killing Hana, his adopted daughter aged 15 months – while his eight other children and wife Safiya were all hospitalised, some with serious injuries. The president escaped. According to Richard J. Aldrich (2010: 457), Gaddafi escaped death by minutes because the Prime Minister of Malta warned him by telephone of the approaching military jets. David Blundy and Andrew Lycett report:

> The attack on Gaddafi's Aziziya compound was a military failure. Gaddafi himself was deep underground. The administration building, where he lives, was missed by two bombs which fell thirty yards away, knocking out the windows but doing no structural damage. The tennis courts received two direct hits and a bomb fell outside the front door of the building where Gaddafi's family lives. Blasts tore through the small bedrooms to the right of the living room, injuring two of Gaddafi's sons and killing his fifteen-month old adopted daughter, Hana. Hana was publicly acknowledged only in death. During interviews only a month before Gaddafi had said, sadly, that he had only one daughter, eight-

year-old Aisha, and wished that he had more. He did not say that his wife had adopted a baby girl ten months before (op cit: 22).

Consider the outrage in the Western media if a relative of Reagan had been killed by a Libyan bomb. There was no such outrage over the Libyan deaths. In November, the UN General Assembly passed a motion condemning the raid. Israel was one of the few countries to back the US over the raid. Yet when the Israeli representative came to justify his country's stance, he used evidence of Gaddafi's alleged commitment to terrorism taken from the German mass-selling newspaper *Bild am Sonntag* and the London-based *Daily Telegraph* (Yallop 1994: 695).

Intriguingly, in February 2011, the German newspaper *Welt am Sonntag*, the Sunday edition of *Die Welt*, reported that Hana had actually survived, lived in London for a while, trained as a doctor and was currently holding an important position in the Libyan Ministry of Health. The information was apparently gathered from Gaddafi family documents seized in Switzerland. As the rebels advanced on Tripoli in August 2011, this news was covered prominently in most leading Western media. In the *Irish Times*, Mary Fitzgerald located what appeared to be Hana's study in the overrun Bab al-Aziziya compound. But was it all disinformation?[10]

Away from the media glare, CIA aims to spark anti-Gaddafi coup

Following the April 1986 attack, reports of US military action against Libya disappeared from the media. But away from the media glare, the CIA launched by far its most extensive effort yet to spark an anti-Gaddafi coup. A secret army was recruited from among the many Libyans captured in border battles with Chad during the 1980s (Perry op cit: 166). In March 1987, the Libyans were defeated at Ouaddiddoum in northern Chad, in a major battle involving French and American secret services in league with a number of Arab powers – Egypt and Tunisia, Saudi Arabia, Iraq – and Israel.[11] And, as concern grew in MI6 over Gaddafi's alleged plans to develop chemical weapons, Britain funded various opposition groups in Libya including the London-based Libyan National Movement.

For his part, Gaddafi continued to arm various revolutionary movements including the IRA. In October 1987, French customs seized an Irish-crewed freighter, the Eksund, carrying almost 200 tonnes of arms including Kalashnikov rifles, ground-to-air SAM-7 missiles, a million rounds of ammunition and more than 2 tonnes of Semtex. This was the fifth shipment to Ireland since 1985.[12]

The Libyan leader was also blamed for the bombing of the Pan Am jumbo jet on 21 December 1988 over the Scottish town of Lockerbie in which 270 people died.[13]

Then in 1990, with the crisis in the Gulf developing, French troops helped oust Habré and install Idriss Déby as the new President of Chad in a secret operation. The French government had tired of Habré's genocidal policies while the Bush administration decided not to frustrate France's objectives in exchange for their co-operation in the war against Iraq. Yet even under Déby the abuses of civil rights by government forces have continued.[14]

Attempts to oust Gaddafi also continued. David Shayler, a former MI5 agent, even alleged that MI6 were involved in a plot in March 1996 to assassinate the Libyan leader as he attended the Libyan General People's Congress (Hunter op cit). His motorcade was attacked by dissidents with Kalashnikovs and rocket grenades but while Gaddafi escaped there were casualties on both sides. Stephen Dorril reports: 'Three fighters were killed but the leader of the hit team, Abd al-Muhaymeen, a veteran of the Afghan resistance who was possibly trained by MI6 or the CIA, "escaped unhurt"' (Dorril op cit: 793). Shayler even claims MI6 paid the al-Islamiya al-Muqatila, the Islamic Fighting Group, £100,000 to carry out the attack (ibid: 793–794; Machon op cit: 172; Jaber 2010; Thomas 2009: 235; Must 2019).

Libya welcomed back to the 'international community'

Following Libya's decision after the 9/11 US terrorist attacks to build closer ties with the West and renounce all efforts to develop nuclear weapons, UN sanctions against the country were lifted in 2003. To improve the image of Libya in the West, Gaddafi employed the Monitor Group, an American public relations company between 2000 and 2008.[15] The demonisation of Col. Gaddafi predictably declined and members of the political, financial and academic British elite lined up to welcome the Libyan leader back into the 'international community'.[16]

For instance, on 26 March 2004, an editorial in the *Guardian* commented: 'We should congratulate the Foreign Office for its quiet and effective diplomacy. ... Col. Gaddafi should be encouraged, but not at such a forced pace.' An editorial in the *Independent* on the same day described Gaddafi as merely 'the Arab world's most eccentric and unpredictable leader', adding:

> Mr Blair is right to argue that there is real cause for rejoicing in a sinner that repenteth. However distasteful to the families of those murdered, an engagement and reconciliation with Libya that leads to the admission of guilt and compensation is better than continued isolation of the North African country.[17]

Also during this period, Gaddafi was represented more as an 'eccentric and unpredictable leader' rather than an 'evil dictator'. This picture was reinforced in the coverage of the WikiLeaks revelations on Libya in December 2010. For instance, the cables disclosed that Col. Gaddafi, 68, 'suffered from severe phobias, enjoyed flamenco dancing and horse-racing, acted on his whims and irritated friends and enemies alike'.[18]

Significantly, the demonisation did not intensify even after Abdurahman Alamoudi was jailed after admitting to participating in a Libyan plot to assassinate Prince Abdullah (now King) of Saudi Arabia. According to court records, Gaddafi wanted Abdullah killed after a 2003 Arab League summit where Gaddafi felt he had been insulted. At one point, Abdullah wagged a finger at Gaddafi and said: 'Your lies precede you, while the grave is ahead of you.'[19] But Robert Fisk (deploying a fair amount of irony, too) was keen to emphasise the Blair government's double standards:

> We adore Gaddafi, the crazed dictator of Libya whose werewolves have murdered his opponents abroad, whose plot to murder King Abdullah of Saudi Arabia preceded Tony Blair's recent trip to Tripoli – Colonel Gaddafi, it should be remembered, was called a 'statesman' by Jack Straw for abandoning his non-existent nuclear ambitions – and whose 'democracy' is perfectly acceptable to us because he is on our side in the 'war on terror'.[20]

Return of the 'mad dog' demonisation discourse and the toppling of Gaddafi

The 2003–2011 period can, then, be seen as a significant interregnum in the moves by Western governments to eliminate Col. Gaddafi. Both sides in the conflict cynically decided that some kind of 'entente' best served their interests. Gaddafi certainly took the opportunity to secure the lifting of UN sanctions and build up diplomatic and commercial relations with the United States, the European Union and Asian states. The high point of Libya's rapprochement with the West came when Col. Gaddafi addressed the United Nations on 23 September 2009.[21] Yet the WikiLeaks cables revealed that Gaddafi flew into a rage after the US refused to let him pitch his Bedouin-style tent in New York. In return, the Libyan leader refused to allow a 'hot' shipment of highly enriched uranium to be loaded on to a transport plane and shipped to Russia as part of his nuclear-dismantling procedure (Leigh and Harding 2011: 143).

After the uprising against the regime was launched in Tripoli in February 2011 – enthusiastically backed by large segments of the Western corporate media (Edwards and Cromwell 2018: 78–96) and Nato began its bombing campaign on 19 March (the anniversary of the attack on Iraq in 2003), the 'mad dog', demonisation discourse returned to the media. For instance, on 4 September, *The Sunday Times* headlined a report about the Libyan leader's alleged attempts to escape via the pipes of the $33 billion Great Man-made River Project: 'Gaddafi and his sons flee like rats up a waterpipe.'[22]

And the Western elites (assisted by a compliant mainstream media) quickly reverted to their previous policy of confrontation with Libya, seizing the new opportunities in their increasingly desperate attempts to eliminate Gaddafi. Immediately after the 25 April attack on Gaddafi, Vladimir Putin, the Russian prime minister, significantly accused Nato of aiming to kill the Libyan leader – and going far beyond the remit allowed by the UN resolution 1973 authorising all necessary means 'to protect civilians'. US defence secretary Robert Gates rejected the claim.

The efforts of MI6 and the SAS in assisting the rebels and capturing Gaddafi once his Tripoli compound was raided on 24 August 2011 were reported prominently throughout the conflict.[23] For instance, *The Times* reported on 25 August 2011 that a 30-strong SAS unit had been working with Qatari special forces along the front line with rebel forces. 'The SAS has performed a more discreet role compiling information and co-ordinating with Nato pilots farther back' (Hider 2011). The SAS was said to be 'keen to restore its somewhat battered reputation after an abortive early secret mission to Benghazi when six SAS troopers and two MI6 officers were arrested by Libyan farmers'. Reports also emerged of France, Italy and Egypt (in the form of members of Unit 777) sending special forces to support the insurgents.[24]

Indeed, one of the paradoxes of contemporary warfare propaganda is that, at strategic moments such as during the Libyan crisis of 2011, the secret and the invisible are revealed.

Libya: Post-Gaddafi

The Western elite achieved their ultimate ambition – with the brutal murder of Col Gaddafi on 20 October 2011. After he was captured in a culvert close to Sirte he was lynched by a mob and sodomised with a bayonet by a soldier as revealed, appallingly, to the world in graphic video. According to Paye and Umay (2013), the gruesome images proved

> ...the objective of the war on Libya was not only conquest, leading to the plundering of oil or of Libyan assets, but also, just as was the case in the Crusades, the destruction of a symbolic order, leaving room for the sheer enjoyment of an act of killing, as displayed by the media, in a capitalist World Order run amok.

'Bullet in the head: That's for Lockerbie' headlined the *Sun*; the *Star* plunged to even further journalistic depths with: 'Mad dog put down' (see Arbuthnot 2011).

Following the toppling of Gaddafi, Libya descended into chaos – and largely disappeared from the Western media. According to historian, human rights activist and blogger Mark Curtis, the 2011 Libyan invasion spurred terrorism in 14 countries in Europe, Syria, North Africa and sub-Saharan Africa (Curtis 2019). And in September 2016, the foreign affairs committee of the House of Commons condemned the British invasion – saying it had been carried out with no proper intelligence analysis, drifted into an unannounced goal of regime change and shirked its moral responsibility to help reconstruct the country following the fall of Col. Gaddafi (Wintour and Elgot 2016).

By mid-2019, the country had splintered into three competing sections – one led by the Benghazi-based Khalifa Haftar, whose troops of the National Libyan Army were besieging Tripoli; another section headed by the US- and UN-recognised Government of National Accord in Tripoli, chaired by wealthy businessman Fayez al-Sarraj while the third rival for state power was the Islamist-dominated General National Congress, which had proclaimed itself a Salvation Government and rejected Sarraj's authority (Van Auken 2019). And tens of thousands of refugees were arriving in the country with impunity from the rest of Africa and the Middle East and sailing to Europe on perilous journeys. Between 2016 and mid-2019, some 5,993 refugees died in the Mediterranean – desperately seeking a new life.[25]

Conclusion

This study raises a number of significant questions. To what extent do the mainstream media fail to cover the activities of the secret state and their secret warfare activities – thus giving a completely distorted picture of contemporary conflicts? (see Keeble 2011). In an age of information and news overflow, how useful is it, rather, to consider the silencing function of media? And how important are the close links between the intelligence/security services and Fleet Street in influencing coverage – of both war and peace.[26] Given that this study has used a range of sources largely marginalised in the mainstream media, to what extent do journalists' routines need to change radically if they are to cover covert warfare adequately.

And in view of the absence of any media outrage over the many attempts to assassinate a head of state (as identified in this study), how important is it for academic analyses of media representations of conflict to consider the selective application of outrage – and the complex factors behind it.

Acknowledgements

This essay is based on a chapter with the same title in *Mirage in the Desert? Reporting the 'Arab Spring'*, edited by Richard Lance Keeble and John Mair, Bury St Edmunds: Arima Publishing, 2011 pp 281–296.

Notes

1 Milan Rai records dozens of night-time Nato bomb attacks on Tripoli, many of them on or near to the Bab al-Aziziya compound on 24, 25 and 28 May. See Milan Rai: The coup against Gaddafi, *Peace News*, No. 2537, September 2011 p 6. How many Nato bomb attacks were made on the compound before the rebels took it over at the end of August 2011 we will probably never know

2 The role of the CIA in the coup is disputed. Blundy and Lycett (1987: 69) report the former Libyan Prime Minister, Abdul Hamid Bakoush, saying: 'The Americans had contacts with Gaddafi through the embassy in Tripoli. They encouraged him to take over. There were dozens of CIA operatives in Libya at that time and they knew what was going on. The Americans were frightened of the senior officers and the intelligentsia in Libya because they thought that these people were independent and could not be run as puppets.' But Blundy and Lycett add (ibid): 'Bakoush's refusal to give names that might corroborate his theory does not help his credibility.' The comments of David D. Newson, US Ambassador to Libya from 1965 to 1969, suggest that the CIA was taken by surprise. He told the Foreign Affairs Oral History Project: 'The agency had reports of a group that was forming, called the Black Boots, probably a group that was centred

around an officer by the name of Abdul Azir Shalhi. But that group, if they had any intention of trying to seize power, was pre-empted by the Gaddafi group on which we had no information.' See also Ronald Bruce St John (2008: 140)

3 St John (ibid: 144) reports that the first consignment of Soviet weaponry arrived in Libya in July 1970 being displayed at a parade commemorating the One September revolution. Gaddafi continued to purchase Soviet arms throughout the decade, including a $1 billion package in 1974–1975 'that constituted its largest arms agreement'

4 In a personal email to the author, 6 May 2011

5 See https://www.hrw.org/news/2015/04/27/chronology-habre-case

6 But according to investigative journalist Joe Vialls, Yvonne Fletcher 'was assassinated on the direct orders of the American CIA in a coldly calculated "Psyop" (Psychological Operation) designed to generate intense British hatred against Libya. The operation was a complete success'. See http://www.us-uk-interventions.org/, accessed on 18 August 2011. Hope (2011) reported that the man seen firing at Pc Fletcher was Abdulmagid Salah Ameri, a junior diplomat working at the Libyan embassy. Hope reports: 'Mr Ameri was identified by a witness in a 140-page secret review of evidence conducted at the request of the Metropolitan Police. The report, seen by the *Daily Telegraph*, was written by a senior Canadian prosecutor and addressed to Sue Hemming, the head of counter-terrorism at the Crown Prosecution Service'

7 Files of the former East German secret service, the Stasi, led German prosecutors to the Libyan Musbah Eter, who had worked at the embassy in communist East Berlin. Eter and four other suspects were arrested in 1996 in Lebanon, Italy, Greece and Berlin and put on trial a year later. After a four-year trial, Musbah Eter was finally sentenced to 12 years in prison for aiding and abetting attempted murder. Two other Libyan embassy workers also received convictions for attempted murder: Palestinian Yasser Shraydi, accused of being the ringleader, and the Lebanese-born German, Ali Chanaa, who doubled as a Stasi agent. Chanaa's German wife, Verena, was the only defendant found guilty of murder after the prosecution showed she had planted the bomb. She was sentenced to 14 years' imprisonment. Prosecutors said the three men had assembled the bomb in the Chanaas' flat. The explosive was said to have been brought into West Berlin in a Libyan diplomatic bag. Verena Chanaa and her sister, Andrea Haeusler, carried it into the La Belle in a travel bag and left five minutes before it exploded. Ms Haeusler was acquitted because it could not be proved that she knew a bomb was in the bag. See http://news.bbc.co.uk/1/hi/world/europe/1653848.stm, accessed on 18 August 2011. Intriguingly a documentary broadcast on 25 August 1998 by German public television presented evidence that some of the main suspects in the 1986 Berlin disco bombing worked for American and Israeli intelligence. The report, aired by Zweites Deutsches Fernsehen (ZDF television), claimed Musbah Eter had been working for the CIA over many years. See http://www.wsws.org/news/1998/aug1998/bomb1-a 27.shtml, accessed on 18 August 2011. Charles Moore (2015: 506–507) records in his authorised biography of Thatcher: 'On 4 April, a message was picked up from the East Berlin People's Bureau in Tripoli saying: "We have something planned that will make you happy. … It will happen soon, the bomb will blow, American soldiers must be hit."' But is that not merely reproducing the official line at the time?

8 Robert Fisk (2006: 1093) says one of the F-111s was shot down during the raid and caused civilian deaths when it crashed (as well as the deaths of the two pilots, Captain Ribas-Dominicci and Captain Paul Lorence)

9 Robert Fisk (2006: 1093) also quotes a US official admitting that Gaddafi was one of the targets of Operation El Dorado Canyon. A Pentagon official told the *Washington Post* that the F-111s had been included in the raid because their pilots 'wanted a piece of the action'

10 See, for instance, http://www.time.com/time/world/article/0,8599,2088074,00.html, http://www.guardian.co.uk/world/2011/aug/26/hana-gaddafi-daughter-mystery and http://www.guardian.co.uk/world/middle-east-live/2011/aug/26/libya-rebels-hunt-gadda fi-live-updates, http://www.telegraph.co.uk/journalists/martin-evans/8725024/Libya-Hana -Gaddafi-alive-and-well.html, all accessed on 27 August 2011

11 In an email from Pierre Lethier, former colonel in the French secret services, to the author, 6 May 2011

12 See Stephen Dorril (1993: 241–242). In June 1992, Libya agreed to provide information on shipments and IRA contacts to Edward Chapman, the British chargé d'affaires at the British mission to the UN in Geneva. This followed international pressure on Libya to 'contribute to the elimination of international terrorism' following its alleged involvement in the Lockerbie bombing (ibid)

13 On 31 January 2001, Abdelbaset al-Megrahi, former head of security for Libyan Arab Airlines, had been controversially convicted by a panel of three Scottish judges sitting in a special court at Camp Zeist in the Netherlands, of 270 counts of murder for the bombing of Pan Am Flight 103 over Lockerbie in 1988. Yet evidence emerged following the trial that raised serious questions about the conviction. For instance, Tony Gauci, in whose shop in Malta al-Megrahi allegedly purchased clothes that ended up in the suitcase with the bomb, had expressed interest in receiving an award and following the conviction, Scottish police secretly sought a $2 million payment from the US Department of Justice. As part of the Libyan moves to rejoin the 'international community', in 2004 the government formally accepted responsibility for Lockerbie – though it stressed it was only doing so to end the UN sanctions. It also agreed to pay $2.7 billion in compensation to the 270 families of the victims. By 2008, those opposing the conviction included Dr Jim Swire and the Rev. John Mosey, each of whom lost a daughter in the bombing, Archbishop Desmond Tutu and the head of the Catholic Church in Scotland, Cardinal Keith O'Brien. Al-Megrahi was released on compassionate grounds by the Scottish government in August 2009 following doctors' reports that he had terminal prostate cancer and had only a few months to live. Immediately following the fall of Gaddafi's Tripoli compound to the rebels in August 2011, calls to re-arrest al-Megrahi were given prominent coverage in the mainstream media in the UK and US. Stephen Dorril, in *The Silent Conspiracy: Inside the Intelligence Services in the 1990s*, London: Heinemann 1993 pp 288–289 reports Brian Keenan, one of the released Beirut hostages, revealing in 1992 a 'strange story connected to Lockerbie'. Following his release in the summer of 1990, he was interviewed by Syrian intelligence: 'They said the British knew all about Lockerbie. They said the British had all sorts of information prior to the event.' al-Megrahi died on 20 May 2012. Following a major campaign, the Scottish Criminal Cases Review Commission announced that it would review the case on 3 May 2018

14 See http://www.amnesty.org/en/region/chad/report-2010, accessed on 1 January 2011

15 Mark Allen, the former MI6 officer, who in September 2011 was at the centre of a row over British intelligence links with Libya, later worked as an advisor to BP and with the Monitor Group. He was also involved in the 2009 release of Abdelbaset al-Megrahi and escorted Gaddafi's son, Saif al-Islam, to meetings in Oxford. See Ian Black, Man in the middle whose WMD triumph may now be overshadowed, *Guardian*, 7 September. Available online at http://www.guardian.co.uk/world/2011/sep/06/libya-masterm ind-wmd-triumph-minefield, accessed on 8 September 2011

16 John Simpson (2010: 77), the BBC's World Affairs Editor, mentions Gaddafi just once in his overview of the reporting of war over the last century, demonising him in the process by linking him with Presidents Ahmadinejad of Iran, Saddam Hussein of Iraq, Robert Mugabe of Zimbabwe and Idi Amin of Uganda. They all, he said, spoke with 'the half-mocking, half-complaining, self-obsessed tone of a man who has felt himself belittled and now believes he can hit back without any sense of restraint'

17 Both editorials cited in Noble war in Libya, *Media Lens*, 28 March 2011. Available online at http://www.medialens.org/index.php?option=com_content&view=article& id=611:noble-war-in-libya-part-2&catid=24:alerts-2011&Itemid=68, accessed on 26 August 2011

18 See http://www.telegraph.co.uk/news/worldnews/wikileaks/8188463/What-WikiLea ks-told-us-about-Colonel-Gaddafi-a-profile-of-an-unpredictable-leader.html, accessed on 26 August 2011

19 In July 2011, US Federal prosecutors asked a judge to reduce the 23-year prison sentence for Alamoudi. Libya TV commented: 'The documents explaining why prosecutors want to cut Alamoudi's sentence are under seal, and the US Attorney's Office in Alexandria declined to say how many years they are seeking to cut from Alamoudi's term. But such reductions are allowed only when a defendant provides substantial assistance to the government. It is rare for the government to seek a reduction so many years after the initial sentence was imposed.' See http://english.libya.tv/2011/07/09/prosecutors-a sk-to-cut-sentence-of-muslim-activist-in-gaddafis-plot-to-assassinate-saudi-king/, accessed on 18 August 2011
20 See chapter entitled 'Gold-plated taps' in Fisk (2008: 234). Also available online at http://www.independent.co.uk/opinion/commentators/fisk/robert-fisk-welcome-to-pa lestine-453319.html, accessed on 18 August 2011
21 See http://www.guardian.co.uk/world/2009/sep/23/gaddafi-un-speech, accessed on 8 September 2011. Significantly the report on the 100-minute speech says Gaddafi 'fully lived up to his reputation for eccentricity, bloody-mindedness and extreme verbiage'. Nowhere is he described as a dictator
22 Similar metaphors relating to 'rat in the hole' were used when the former President of Iraq, Saddam Hussein, was captured in December 2003. See, for instance, http://news. bbc.co.uk/1/hi/programmes/breakfast/3319491.stm, accessed on 8 September 2011. Gaddafi invested $25 billion in the Great Man-Made River Project, a complex 4,000-km long water pipeline buried beneath the desert that could transport two million cubic metres of water per day. As highlighted by Garikai Chengu (2019), France's global mega-water corporations, like Suez, Ondeo and Saur, control more than 45 per cent of the planet's water market, which is already a $400 billion global industry. 'For France, the 2011 revolution in Libya was about gaining control of and privatizing Libya's astounding water resources'
23 See, for instance, http://www.telegraph.co.uk/news/worldnews/africaandindianocean/ libya/8716758/Libya-secret-role-played-by-Britain-creating-path-to-the-fall-of-Tripoli. html and http://www.dailymail.co.uk/news/article-2029831/Libya–1m-bounty-Gadda fi-MI6-agents-join-hunt.html, both accessed on 27 August 2011
24 See *Libya: An Uncertain Future: Report of a Fact-Finding Mission to Assess both Sides of Libyan Conflict*, Paris, May 2011, published by International Centre for the Study and Research into Terrorism and Assistance to the Victims of Terrorism, French Centre for Intelligence Studies and the Mediterranean Peace Forum. Available online at http://www.cf2r.org/ima ges/stories/news/201106/libya-report.pdf, accessed on 8 September 2011
25 See https://missingmigrants.iom.int/region/mediterranean, accessed on 7 June 2019
26 See Keeble (2011)

References

Adams, James (1987) *Secret Armies: The Full Story of SAS, Delta Force and Spetsnaz*, London: Hutchinson
Aldrich, Richard J. (2010) *GCHQ: The Uncensored Story of Britain's Most Secret Intelligence Agency*, London: Harper Press
Amnesty International (2001) *Chad: The Habré Legacy*, AI, 16 October
Arbuthnot, Felicity (2011) Killing Gaddafi: The death of legal justice, *New Internationalist*, 25 October. Available online at https://newint.org/features/web-exclusive/2011/10/25/ga ddafi-death-us-libya, accessed on 7 June 2019
Blundy, David and Lycett, Andrew (1987) *Qaddafi and the Libyan Revolution*, London: Weidenfeld and Nicolson
Chengu, Garikai (2019) Gaddafi vs the West: Two revolutions on the wrong side of history, *counterpunch.org*, 10 September

Chomsky, Noam (1991) *Pirates and Emperors*, Montreal and New York: Black Rose Books

Cockburn, Alexander and Cockburn, Leslie (1992) *Dangerous Liaison: The Inside Story of US–Israeli Covert Relationship*, London: Bodley Head

Cormac, Rory (2018) *Disrupt and Deny: Spies, Special Forces, and the Secret Pursuit of British Foreign Policy*, Oxford: Oxford University Press

Curtis, Mark (1998) *The Great Deception: Anglo-American Power and World Order*, London: Pluto Press

Curtis, Mark (2019) How the West's war in Libya has spurred terrorism in 14 countries, *middleeasteye.net*, 3 May. Available online at https://www.middleeasteye.net/opinion/how-wests-war-libya-has-spurred-terrorism-14-countries, accessed on 4 May 2019

Deacon, Richard (1990) *The French Secret Service*, London: Grafton Books

Dorril, Stephen (1993) *The Silent Conspiracy: Inside the Intelligence Services in the 1990s*, London: Heinemann

Dorril, Stephen (2000) *MI6: Fifty Years of Special Operations*, London: Fourth Estate

Edwards, David and Cromwell, David (2018) *Propaganda Blitz: How Corporate Media Distort Reality*, London: Pluto Press

Fisk, Robert (2006) *The Great War for Civilisation: The Conquest of the Middle East*, London and New York: Harper Perennial

Fisk, Robert (2008) *The Age of the Warrior*, London: Fourth Estate

Hider, James (2011) Eyes peeled for deluded dictator in woman's garb, says ex-aide, *Times*, 25 August

Higgins, Michael and Smith, Angela (2011) Not one of US: Kate Adie's report of the 1986 US bombing of Tripoli and its critical aftermath, *Journalism Studies*, Vol. 12, No. 3 pp 344–358

Hope, Christopher (2011) Libya man suspected of killing Pc Yvonne Fletcher identified, *Daily Telegraph*, 26 August. Available online at http://www.telegraph.co.uk/news/world news/africaandindianocean/libya/8726322/Libya-Man-suspected-of-killing-Pc-Yvonne-Fletcher-identified.html, accessed on 27 August 2011

Hunter, Jane (1991) Dismantling the war on Libya, *Covert Action Information Bulletin*, summer pp 47–51

Jaber, Hala (2010) Libyans thwart Fletcher inquiry, *Sunday Times*, 19 September

Keeble, Richard Lance (2011) Hacks and spooks – close encounters of a strange kind: A critical history of the links between mainstream journalists and the intelligence services in the UK, Klaehn, Jeffery (ed.) *The Political Economy of Media and Power*, New York: Peter Lang pp 87–111

Keeble, Richard Lance (2017) *Covering Conflict: The Making and Unmaking of New Militarism*, Bury St Edmunds: Abramis

Kellner, Douglas (1990) *Television and the Crisis of Democracy*, Boulder, CO: Westview Press

Leigh, David and Harding, Luke (2011) *WikiLeaks: Inside Julian Assange's War on Secrecy*, London: Guardian Books

Lycett, Andrew (1995) I study my targets. I find out what makes them tick, *Independent*, 22 June

Machon, Annie (2005) *Spies, Lies and Whistleblowers*, Lewes, East Sussex: The Book Guild

Martin, David and Walcott, John (1988) *Best Laid Plans: The Inside Story of America's War against Terrorism*, New York: Harper & Row

Moore, Charles (2015) *Margaret Thatcher: The Authorized Biography*, London: Allen Lane

Must, Nick (2019) David Shayler, 'Tunworth' and the LIFG, *Lobster*, Winter. Available online at https://www.lobster-magazine.co.uk/free/lobster78/lob78-shayler-tunworth-lifg.pdf, accessed on 4 August 2019

Paye, Jean-Claude and Umay, Tülay (2013) The cult of killing and the symbolic order of Western barbarism, *voltairenet.org*, 16 April. Available online at http://www.voltairenet.org/article178162.html

Perry, Mark (1992) *Eclipse: The Last Days of the CIA*, New York: William Morrow

Prades, John (1986) *President's Secret Wars: CIA and Pentagon Covert Operations from World War II through Iranscan*, New York: William Morrow

Rusbridger, James (1989) *The Intelligence Game: Illusions and Delusions of International Espionage*, London: Bodley Head

Sebba, Anna (1994) *Battling for News: The Rise of the Woman Reporter*, London: Hodder and Stoughton

Simpson, John (2010) *Unreliable Sources*, London: Macmillan

St John, Ronald Bruce (2008) *Libya: From Colony to Independence*, Oxford: Oneworld Publications

Thomas, Gordon (2009) *Inside British Intelligence: 100 Years of MI5 and MI6*, London: JR Books

Van Auken, Bill (2019) Libya on the brink of all-out civil war, *wsws.org*, 9 April. Available online at https://www.wsws.org/en/articles/2019/04/09/liby-a09.html, accessed on 7 June 2019

Wintour, Patrick and Elgot, Jessica (2016) MPs deliver damning verdict on David Cameron's Libya intervention, *Guardian*, 14 September. Available online at https://www.theguardian.com/world/2016/sep/14/mps-deliver-damning-verdict-on-camerons-libya-intervention

Woodward, Bob (1987) *Veil: The Secret Wars of the CIA*, London: Simon & Schuster

Yallop, David (1994) *To the Ends of the Earth: The Hunt for the Jackal*, London: Corgi

12

SECRETS AND LIES

On the ethics of conflict coverage

This chapter will explore a wide range of ethical issues involved in the reporting of conflict. It will argue that too much of the debate over the ethics of conflict coverage is based (either implicitly or explicitly) on conventional notions of professionalism which leads to a prioritising of issues relating to the corporate media. Drawing from radical critiques of professionalism, it will aim to relocate the debate within the activist, alternative sphere. It will also explore the studies of and theories relating to the national security/deep state to examine the crucial roles of both the alternative/peace media in bringing to light the warfare activities of the secret state and that of 'the necessary mavericks' within the corporate media.

Professionalism – and its problematics

It is not without significance that William Howard Russell became one of the founders of modern, professional war correspondence ('the miserable parent of a luckless tribe', as he described himself) in his reporting for *The Times* of the Crimean War of 1854–1856 at a critical moment in the history of the British press (Knightley 2000: 2). In 1855, the last of the Stamp Acts (which had effectively served to limit the readership of newspapers to a wealthy elite) was repealed allowing for the emergence of mass-selling newspaper industry based largely on advertising. In the process, the unstamped (and hence illegal) trade union-based, republican, revolutionary and highly partisan press – which had previously been far more popular than the elite press – was marginalised. The market effectively 'censored' the radical, activist media (Curran and Seaton 1994: 32–48).

Russell's reporting on the failures of the British military in the Crimean maelstrom was said to have led to the fall of the government of the Earl of Aberdeen in January 1855 – thus adding 'ammunition' at this critical moment to the emerging myth of the corporate press as the 'fourth estate' separate from and critical of the state. Yet *The Times* played only a minor role: a significant section of the British elite was determined on Aberdeen's fall, irrespective of any views expressed in the newspaper (Keeble 1997: 193). Moreover, Phillip Knightley (2000: 16) argues that while Russell exposed the incompetence of the army in the Crimea he failed to expose and understand the cause. Though he criticised the lot of the ordinary soldier he never attacked the officers 'to whose social class he belonged himself'. And Knightley adds (ibid): 'Above all, Russell made the mistake, common to many a war correspondent, of considering himself part of the military establishment.'

The latter half of the nineteenth century also saw the emergence of professionalism – with apolitical corporate journalism (along with other professions such as teaching, law, medicine) and its associated ideologies of objectivity and press freedom being closely integrated into the operations of the bourgeois state. Yet Frank Parkin (1979) and Richard Collins (1990) stress the notion of social closure according to which occupations seek to regulate market conditions in their favour restricting access to a limited group of eligible, mainly middle-class professionals. The notion of closure is useful in helping to explain how the ideologies of professionalism serve to exclude alternative, activist, social media from even the definition of 'journalism'. Louis Althusser (1969) sees professions as part of the ideological state apparatus – crucial to the formation of bourgeois hegemony while Ivan Illich (1973) describes professions as a 'form of imperialism' operating in modern societies as repressive mechanisms undermining democracy. This ideology is certainly still so pervasive that it provides the frame around which most of the debate over media ethics in times of conflict operates today (for instance, see Owen and Purdey 2009; Moorcraft 2016).

The cynical approach

Some corporate journalists adopt a cynical, amoral approach to the reporting of conflict (Keeble 2009: 5). This was summed up by a national newspaper editor, invited to a London journalism school to give a talk on ethics. 'Efficks – wot's that?' he asked, bemused. And so he simply proceeded to tell the gathered throng of students about his life and (highly successful) times in the industry. It is an attitude based on the conviction that ethical issues have little relevance for corporate journalists. There is not enough time for them and journalists have little power to influence them anyway. Profits are at the root of all journalism, so why bother with idealistic fancies as ethics?

Such cynicism may be linked to a philosophical, existential position propounded by the nineteenth century German Max Stirner (1806–1856) which regards all human experience as essentially amoral. Ethical egotism takes a cynical view of the altruism behind moral conduct, suggesting that all actions (however much they are clothed in the rhetoric of morality) are essentially motivated by self-interest (see Paterson 1971). A variant on this appears in the thinking of Friedrich Nietzsche (1844–1900) who described himself as an 'immoralist', arguing in *Beyond Good and Evil* (1886) that there are no moral facts and that evil made no sense (see Sanders

2003: 23). Also linked to this cynicism are theories relating to the 'realist' approach to global affairs according to which elites operate either in accordance with international law or not – depending on the perceived 'interests of the state'. Drawing on the work of Niccolo Machiavelli (1469–1527) and Thomas Hobbes (1588–1679), realists argue that states are best seen as self-interested and primarily concerned with survival. Journalists' role, then, is to understand these dynamics and avoid the empty rhetoric of morality in their reporting.

The patriotic imperative

A completely opposite approach is promoted by journalists who argue that at times of conflict their essential responsibility as professionals is to support the actions of the state – perceived not as 'immoral' but 'good'. Indeed, this patriotic imperative lies at the heart of British journalists' culture (Norton-Taylor 1991). As Max Hastings, former editor of the London *Evening Standard* but most famous for being the first journalist to march into Port Stanley at the end of the Falklands War in 1982, comments:

> I felt my function was simply to identify totally with the interests and feelings of that force [the task force] … when one was writing one's copy one thought: beyond telling everybody what the men around me were doing, what can one say that is likely to be most helpful in winning the war? (Williams 1992: 156–157).

Indeed, the system of pooling (or embedding) reporters with frontline troops (widely adopted by Western militaries since the Vietnam War) has served to reinforce the corporate media's essential role as propagandists for the state at times of conflict. As *The Times* media commentator Brian MacArthur (2003) reported: 'Embeds essentially became adjuncts to the forces.' And predictably, during recent, major overt conflicts (Iraq 1991 and 2003, Kosovo 1999, Afghanistan 2001, Libya 2011) the vast bulk of editors, safe in their Fleet Street bunkers, have fervently banged the patriotic drum (Keeble 1997; Chomsky 1999; Hammond 2007a, 2007b; Forte 2012).

The war correspondent as 'eye witness' hero

A popular rhetorical strategy of mainstream war correspondents is to highlight their professional responsibilities to record accurately what they see. They do not take political stances – they are merely eye-witnesses to historic events. This approach neatly ties into dominant notions about 'objectivity', 'media freedom' 'the public interest' – and the 'fourth estate' which stresses the watchdog role of the professional media providing checks and balances on abuses of power by both government and other professions. McLaughlin (2016) rightly highlights the dangers war correspondents constantly face. Indeed, celebrations of the journalist as intrepid battler for truth appear prominently when they are either killed, injured or taken hostage while engaged in the often highly dangerous business of reporting from the frontlines. In this spirit, Peter Beaumont and John Sweeney (2000) wrote in their *Observer* tribute to two colleagues killed covering the fighting in Sierra Leone: 'The best stories are those that afflict the comfortable and comfort the afflicted, the ones that the people of power do not want told.'

Following the death of *The Sunday Times*'s award-winning reporter Marie Colvin while covering the Syrian war in 2012, Roy Greenslade began his tribute in the *Guardian* by praising her as 'a fearless but never foolhardy war correspondent who believed passionately in the need to report on conflicts from the frontline' (Greenslade 2012). And after *Times* correspondent Anthony Loyd and photographer Jack Hill were attacked while reporting the Syrian civil war in May 2014, the newspaper captured many elements of the dominant ideology when it editorialised:

> War reporters are not omniscient. Their information is inevitably partial. Yet they are honour bound to describe the world as they see it and not according to a set of ideological presuppositions. ... *The Times* is not neutral in its editorial views. Informed by the testimony of our reporters, we have no doubt that Assad bears prime responsibility for Syria's torment. Our reporting takes no side, however, but accuracy. ... The ability to distinguish fact from propaganda is what our readers expect. It is through the bravery and professionalism of Loyd, Hill and others that we seek to fulfil that obligation (*Times* 2014).

The journalism of attachment

During the Balkans crisis of the 1990s, Martin Bell, the white-suited BBC war correspondent (and later Independent MP), advocated the 'journalism of attachment'. This, he defined, as 'a journalism that cares as well as knows ... that will not stand neutrally between good and evil, right and wrong, the victim and the oppressor' (Bell 1998: 16). In the case of the Balkans this meant representing Serbian leader, Slobodan Milošević, as essentially 'evil' and Serbia's enemies (for instance, the Kosovo Albanians) as 'good' and 'worthy victims'.

Thus, in many respects, Bell's stance mirrored that of the elite. Moreover, the apparent challenge to the stress on 'objectivity' could be accommodated since the political economy of the dominant media (which underpins the ideology of professionalism) rests untouched by the critique. Greg McLaughlin (2016) suggests that the journalism of attachment leads to unacceptable moralising and self-righteousness. While veteran investigative journalist and war reporter John Pilger, in responding to Bell, warns against framing the argument in the traditional assumptions about 'objectivity' and 'subjectivity'. But he agrees that Bell was right about the 'illusion of objectivity', rejecting it as 'often a mask for established consensus and bias' (see Wilson 2007: 126–127).

The role of the 'necessary mavericks'

The closeness of the corporate media to dominant economic, cultural and ideological forces means that the mainstream largely functions to promote the interests of the military–industrial–political–entertainment complex (Herman and Chomsky 1994 [1988]; Der Derian 2001). Yet within advanced capitalist economies, many of them currently suffering acute downturns following the 2008 crisis (which, to a large extent, stemmed from the over-resourcing of US/UK military and imperial adventurism) the contradictions within corporate media have provided certain spaces for progressive journalism.

Chris Atton (2004: 10) warns against presenting a polarised vision of the mainstream and alternative spheres, positing a 'hegemonic approach' that 'suggests a complexity of relationships between radical and mainstream that previous binary models have been unable to identify'. Robert Hackett (2007) suggests that it is the ethical responsibility of journalists to reform the mainstream from within. Herman and Chomsky's (1994 [1988]: 2) propaganda model stresses the role of the corporate media in forming a single propaganda system where 'money and power are able to filter out the news fit to print, marginalise dissent and allow the government and dominant private interests to get their message across to the public'. But for Hackett, this model is too deterministic. It thus fails to 'identify the scope and conditions under which newsworkers could exercise the kind of choices called for' by a more peace-oriented journalism and to acknowledge that individual journalists are 'active and creative agents' able to combine an involvement in the corporate media with regular contributions to alternative, partisan, campaigning media (Hackett 2007: 93).[1]

Progressive journalists of this important hybrid group (of which George Orwell may be considered an earlier member) today might include Ian Cobain, Mark Curtis, Barbara Ehrenreich, Susan George, Stephen Grey, Robert Fisk, Seymour Hersh, Dahr Jamail, Paul Lashmar, Richard Norton-Taylor, John Pilger, Arundhati Roy, Ian Sinclair and Jonathan Steele.

Oliver Boyd-Barrett (2010) also highlights the propaganda model's failure to acknowledge journalists' individual agency, though his focus is more on the penetration of corporate media by covert intelligence and their sympathisers (see Keeble 2014a).

Mockery, critique and the limits of acceptable debate

How to further explain and theorise this progressive, ethical 'space' within the corporate media? Is it useful to understand it as operating within a sort of modern-day court? During the Middle Ages, one of the most important roles at courts throughout Europe (and in India, Persia and China) was occupied by the jester. Often known as 'licensed fools' their crucial function was to mock and critique their employer. After all, rulers know they will always be attacked – but clever are those who control the attacks. The court system did just that. Today, intriguingly, a modern version of the court system operates, and while there is no formal licensing, a subtler – and hence more powerful – unwritten system helps define the limits of acceptable debate and provides a crucial legitimising function for the 'democratic' state.

Daniel Hallin (1986), in his seminal analysis of US media coverage of the Vietnam War, identifies the various ideological spheres: there is the sphere of consensus around topics on which there is, in general, elite agreement; then there's the sphere of legitimate controversy, around topics on which there are significant elite disagreements; and finally there's the sphere of deviance inhabited by issues either marginalised or eliminated from the dominant debate (ibid: 116–118). In this context, it's useful to see the work of progressive journalists (such as George Orwell) within the mainstream as falling within the sphere of 'legitimate controversy'.

Significantly, Hallin argues that ideology determines the structuring of the spheres – thus the notion that the US was conducting a criminal invasion of South Vietnam constituted the 'deviant view' excluded from the dominant media. Yet Hallin may exaggerate the importance of ideology in the formation of the various spheres. The consensual formation process may be even more complex and intriguing than Hallin envisaged – one built more about the individual's position in relation to the 'court' rather than their ideology. For 'court' members – such as the *Washington Post*'s Rajiv Chandrasekaran (2006), author of an award-winning book that highlights the incompetence the Coalition Provisional Authority in Iraq following the 2003 invasion (see Keeble 2014b), can mock and criticise the elite, even leak embarrassing information which might expose lying and corruption; but if someone outside the 'court' makes the same attack they can be harassed by the state and even jailed for treason.

Let's take the example of Peter van Buren. Basing his account on his time leading a Provincial Reconstruction Team, he exposed abysmal US failures in post-2003 Iraq in his *We Meant Well: How I Helped Lose the Battle for the Hearts and Minds of the Iraqi People* (van Buren 2011) – but because he was considered by the US elite outside the 'court' he was removed from his job in the US State Department Foreign Services following his 'dangerous whistleblowing act'.

Secret state: Secret warfare – and the ethical challenges for journalists

Alongside the 'democratic' state in Britain, there exists a secret state occupied by the massively over-resourced intelligence and security services (MI5, MI6, GCHQ, the Cheltenham-based signals spying centre and the armed forces special intelligence sections), secret armies, undercover police units and a vast array of private intelligence operations. Indeed, according to Roy Greenslade, media blogger at the *Guardian*, and editor of the *Mirror* at the time of the Gulf crisis in 1991: 'Most tabloid newspapers – or even newspapers in general – are playthings of MI5' (Milne 1994: 262). Moreover, the deployment of secret armies, targeted assassinations and covertly planned coups in 'enemy' states have been crucial features of Western military strategies since 1945 (Keeble 1997: 15). Is it not remarkable, then, that the debate over the ethics of conflict coverage has hardly ever acknowledged the existence of the secret state?

Significantly, Phillip Knightley argues that journalists have a responsibility to be more aware about the activities of the secret services:

> What's the difference between a spy and a journalist? Not much. Both are in the information business. Both go out into the world and try to find out what's really going on. They look, listen and ask people questions. They assess the reliability of what they are told. They try to decide what is likely to happen next. Then they write a report for their bosses. Only now do their paths diverge. The journalist sends his or her report off expecting it will be published for the world to read. The spy sends his report off knowing it will not be published but instead will be used for political advantage. My point is that intelligence services are well aware of the similarities between journalism and spying and take full advantage them. But journalists are not so aware (Knightley 2006).

Splits in the intelligence community: The ethical implications for journalists

Yet it is wrong to see the intelligence community as unified. As the intelligence community has grown so vast so have the competing factions within it. The corporate media, then, become the theatre in which these various factions play out their games for supremacy. Some journalists side with the dominant factions; others take a principled stand reproducing the views of those critical of policies such as over torture, 'extraordinary rendition', secret/black prisons, targeted killings and the secret deployment of drones in Afghanistan, Iraq, Pakistan, Somalia, Yemen, Syria and elsewhere (Scahill 2013).

Let us take a few examples: in the late 1990s factions emerged which managed to marginalise traditional elements within both MI6 and the CIA. In the UK, the Rockingham Cell, determined to promote the Iraq invasion, emerged triumphant (Meacher 2003); in the United States it was the Office of Special Plans (OSP), set up by Defense Secretary Donald Rumsfeld in 2002. As Julian Borger (2003) explains, the OSP was created to 'second-guess CIA information' while it operated under the patronage of hardline conservatives in the top rungs of the administration, the Pentagon and at the White House, including Vice-President Dick Cheney.

> The ideologically driven network functioned like a shadow government, much of it off the official payroll and beyond Congressional oversight. But it proved powerful enough to prevail in a struggle with the State Department and the CIA by establishing a justification for war.

Accompanying the formation of the OSP was the new regime of harsh torture techniques, backed by Cheney and Rumsfeld, directed at prisoners at Guantanamo Bay with the intention to extract confessions about links between the Iraqi regime and al-Qaeda. Indeed, statements about the existence of Iraqi WMD were extracted through torture (Chomsky 2009). Norman Baker (2007: 293) explains the crucial intelligence splits in the UK this way:

> In London, it was the Foreign Office, MI6 and the Defence Intelligence Service that were cold-shouldered. In America, it was the State Department, the CIA and the DIA. In both countries, the great reservoirs of knowledge were disregarded because they provided an analysis that was unwanted.

Baker adds, somewhat murkily (ibid 294):

> Naturally this bred resentment, and some I have spoken to have suggested that one consequence was actually a deliberate collusion between the CIA and MI6 not to find any weapons of mass destruction in Iraq so as to embarrass or even destabilise the White House and Downing Street respectively.

A lot of the media coverage of the secret state emerges, then, as a consequence of splits such as these amongst the intelligence community, with each faction fighting through their trusted journos for media prominence (Dorril 1993).

Beyond the court: Whistleblowers

Many defence correspondents loyally promote the Official Line (as on Weapons of Mass Destruction before the Iraq invasion of 2003); after 30 years have passed, top level, highly classified documents are regularly released (though suitably redacted) from the National Archives. But the Official Line is deliberately broken when whistleblowers (who are distinctly non-courtiers) speak out. Bradley/Chelsea Manning (see Madar 2012), Julian Assange (Greenberg 2012; Fowler 2018) and Edward Snowden (Greenwald 2014) are only the latest in a long line of men and women who have risked so much in speaking out against the secret state. Manning, an intelligence analyst with the US Army, was originally jailed in 2010 for 35 years for exposing, via WikiLeaks, American war crimes in Iraq and Afghanistan. After seven years behind bars, she was suddenly released by President Barack Obama in an act of clemency during the final days of his presidency. Then, in 2019, she was again jailed after refusing to testify before a grand jury investigating WikiLeaks.

Assange, founder of the WikiLeaks whistleblowing site in 2006, fearing extradition to the US (and likely torture and jailing) took refuge in the Ecuadorian Embassy in London in August 2012. He was there for almost seven years until April 2019 when he was seized by police and quickly sentenced to 50 weeks in Belmarsh high security prison for breaching the Bail Act. In June 2019, Nils

Melzer, the UN Special Rapporteur on Torture, demanded an immediate end to the 'collective persecution' of Julian Assange, condemning the US and its allies for inflicting 'psychological torture' on the WikiLeaks publisher (Grenfell 2019).

And NSA contractor Edward Snowden (Fowler 2018) took refuge in Russia after revealing the global surveillance activities of the Britain and the US. They follow a long line of brave whistleblowers which continues today:

- 1971: Daniel Ellsberg who, in the *Pentagon Papers*, as reported in the *New York Times*, reveals the secret bombing of Cambodia and Laos.
- 1975: Philip Agee exposes the activities of the CIA in his book *The Company* (see Campbell 2011).
- 1976: The secret signals spy base, GCHQ, revealed for the first time in *Time Out*: leading to the trial and acquittal of Crispin Aubrey, Dave Berry and Duncan Campbell (ABC).
- 1983: Sarah Tisdall jailed after releasing information on cruise missile deployment to the *Guardian*.
- 1985: Senior civil servant at the Ministry of Defence Clive Ponting claims 'public interest' and so the jury acquits him after he reveals secrets about the sinking of an Argentinian warship (with the loss of 323 lives) during the Falklands War of 1982 (Norton-Taylor 1985).
- 1988: former M15 officer Peter (*Spycatcher*) Wright reveals plot to oust Prime Minister Harold Wilson in 1968.
- 1997: David Shayler exposes British attempt to assassinate Col. Gaddafi, President of Libya, in 1996; later jailed for six months in 2002.
- 2003: Katherine Gun, translator for GCHQ, discloses US intimidation of states before UN discussions over attack on Iraq (Sinclair 2008).
- 2005: Russell Tice, former US intelligence analyst, dismissed from job after claiming the National Security Agency and Defense Intelligence Agency were engaged in unlawful and unconstitutional wiretaps on American citizens (Wing 2013).
- 2006: Mark Klein, a former AT&T technician who reveals details of the company's cooperation with the United States National Security Agency (Kravets 2013).
- 2007: William Binney, NSA official, forced from office following his claims over illegal data collection policies (Shorrock 2013).
- 2011: Thomas Drake, former NSA executive, who is charged under the Espionage Act 1917 for revealing information about warrantless wiretapping (Martin 2011).
- 2013: John Kiriakou, a CIA analyst, jailed for 30 months for passing classified information to a reporter (Coll 2013).
- 2015: Jeffrey Sterling, former CIA agent, sentenced to 42 months for leaking secrets to *New York Times*'s James Risen about 'Operation Merlin', launched by the CIA in 2000 to sabotage Iran's nuclear programme using dirty tricks, including the provision of flawed nuclear bomb blueprints (Maass 2018).

- 2019: Daniel Hale, former NSA analyst, charged with violating the Espionage Act after handing over information to Jeremy Scahill, of the *Intercept*, on drone wars. For an overview of the Trump administration attacks on whistleblowers see Lee (2019).
- 2019: In France, the government threatens to jail journalists on the *Disclose* investigative site for revealing information about the secret sale of arms to Saudi Arabia for use in its illegal war in Yemen.
- 2019: In Australia, police raid the offices of ABC and News Corp and home of Cameron Gill, senior official in the country's electronic spying agency, following reports of unlawful killings by Australian troops in Afghanistan and plans to extend the powers of intelligence agencies to spy on citizens.

Watergate and the need for constant scepticism

Yet the case of the most famous whistleblower of all, Mark Felt – 'Deep Throat' of Watergate fame – proves how important it is for both reporters and media consumers to remain sceptical about all matters relating to secret warfare and the secret state. The source for one of the most celebrated investigative stories of all time by the *Washington Post* duo Carl Bernstein and Bob Woodward that helped topple the US President in 1974 – and the subject of the book (Woodward and Bernstein 1974) and Hollywood blockbuster, *All the President's Men*, featuring Robert Redford and Dustin Hoffman as the intrepid sleuths – was not a high-minded public servant appalled at White House corruption and the lies over the secret bombing of Cambodia; rather, it was the deputy director of the FBI, angry that he had been overlooked for promotion by President Richard Nixon with the top job going to L. Patrick Gray (see Matthew Ricketson 2014: 46–47 and Holland 2012).

Yet mystery surrounds Felt's revelations. Why was *Vanity Fair*, of all outlets, chosen? Why were the 'Woodstein' duo not informed before publication? Was it not strange that the revelation had to be written by Felt's lawyer (Felt was seriously ill and died soon afterwards). And could there not, in fact, have been a number of 'Deep Throats', as Russ Baker (2008) argues: the Felt revelation, in effect, serving to close down any further investigations?

Conclusion: The crucial role of alternative media

Conventional studies of the ethics of conflict reporting have tended to marginalise or ignore altogether the non-corporate media. This should not come as a surprise: the essential ideological function of the dominant political and cultural spheres is to silence the voices of progressive and revolutionary social movements (Keeble 1997). Yet the role of the alternative media both historically and today in the formation of a counter or oppositional public sphere is considerable both in the UK and internationally (see, for example, Atton and Hamilton 2008; Couldry and

Curran 2003; Downing, 1984; Forde 2011; Harcup 2003, 2013; Keeble 2010, Nelson, 1989; Rodriguez, 2001; Sparks, 1985; Waltz 2005).

Moreover, non-corporate outlets have tended to rely on the work of non-professional journalists: citizens and community/political activists. As in Chris Atton's (2002: 25) definition of alternative media: 'They typically go beyond simply providing a platform for radical or alternative points of view: they emphasise the organisation of media to enable wider social participation in their creation, production and dissemination than is possible in the mass media.'

Thus, these well-established working arrangements long pre-date recent discussions about the nature of journalism – provoked by the emergence of the internet and its many communicative forms. Stuart Allan, for instance, celebrates the bloggers and the 'extraordinary contribution made by ordinary citizens offering their first-hand reports, digital photographs, camcorder video footage, mobile telephone snapshots or audio clips' (Alan 2006: 7). John Hartley (2008: 42) even draws on Article 19 of the Universal Declaration of Human Rights to proclaim the radical, utopian-liberal ideal that everyone has the right not only to seek and receive but also to 'impart' (in other words, communicate) information and ideas.

This broadened definition of journalism certainly helps to incorporate a wide range of media and political activists into the discussion on the ethics of conflict coverage. For instance, it could include radical, progressive journalists and their associated media such as *Middle East Report* (www.merip.org), *Nation* (www. thenation.com), *Mother Jones* (www.motherjones.com), *Z Magazine* (www. zcommunications.org/zmag), *In These Times* (www.inthesetimes.com), *tomdispatch.com*. In France, there's *Mediapart* (mediapart.fr/en/English) and *Disclose* (disclose.ngo/en). In Chennai, India, there's *Frontline* (www.frontline.in) while in the UK there's the investigative website *Corporate Watch* (www.corporatewa tch.org), *New Internationalist* (newint.org) and the media monitoring site *Media Lens* (medialens.org).

Media such as these often draw inspiration from the critique by Edward Herman and Noam Chomsky (1994 [1988]) of the corporate myths of 'balance' and 'objectivity' and emphasise instead their explicitly partisan character. Moreover, they seek to 'invert the hierarchy of access' to the news by explicitly foregrounding the viewpoints of 'ordinary' people (activists, protestors, local residents), citizens whose visibility in the mainstream media tends to be obscured by the presence of elite groups and individuals (Atton 2002: 20).

Indeed, given the centrality of the secret state to the operations of Western militarism, one of the most important functions of journalism is to highlight where possible its operations – and this is most consistently done in a range of alternative media (normally completely ignored in the debate over the ethics of conflict coverage) (Keeble 2017). These include: *www.bigbrotherwatch.org.uk*, *Chomsky.info*, *www.coldtype.net*, *Consortium News*, *www.counterpunch.org*, *www.cryptome.org*, *Daily Maverick*, Mark Curtis's *Declassified*, *https://www.greenleft.org.au*, *intelnews.org*, *johnpilger. com*, *www.lobster-magazine.co.uk*, *middleeasteye.net*, *New Matilda*, *www.newsbud.com*, *unredacted.com*, *offguardian*, *Peace News*, *peoplesworld.org*, the Wisconsin-based *Progressive* (to which even Orwell contributed an article on the left press in Britain in 1948), *spyculture.com, tomdispatch.com, http://whowhatwhy.com/, wsws.org, zcomm.org/zmag/*.

Acknowledgements

This chapter is based on Secrets and lies: On the ethics of conflict coverage, Robinson, Piers, Seib, Philip and Frohlich, Romy (eds) *Routledge Handbook, Media, Conflict and Security*, London: Routledge, 2017 pp 9–21.

References

Allan, Stuart (2006) *Online News: Journalism and the Internet*, Maidenhead: Open University Press

Althusser, Louis (1969) *For Marx*, London: Penguin

Atton, Chris (2002) *Alternative Media*, London: Sage

Atton, Chris (2004) *An Alternative Internet: Radical Media, Politics and Creativity*, Edinburgh: Edinburgh University Press

Atton, Chris and Hamilton, James F. (2008) *Alternative Journalism*, London: Sage

Baker, Norman (2007) *The Strange Death of David Kelly*, London: Methuen

Baker, Russ (2008) *Family of Secrets*, London: Bloomsbury

Bell, Martin (1998) The journalism of attachment, Kieran, Matthew (ed.) *Media Ethics*, London: Routledge pp 15–22

Borger, Julian (2003) The spies who pushed for war, *Guardian*, 17 July. Available online at http://www.theguardian.com/world/2003/jul/17/iraq.usa, accessed on 6 June 2014

Boyd-Barrett, Oliver (2010) Recovering agency for the propaganda model: The implications for reporting war and peace, Keeble, Richard Lance, Tulloch, John and Zollmann, Florian (eds) *Peace Journalism, War and Conflict Resolution*, New York: Peter Lang pp 31–48

Campbell, Duncan (2011) Whistleblowing: From Xerox machine to WikiLeaks via Ellsberg, Agee and Vanunu, Mair, John and Keeble, Richard Lance (eds) *Investigative Journalism: Dead or Alive?* Bury St Edmunds: Abramis pp 223–229

Chandrasekaran, Rajiv (2006) *Imperial Life in the Emerald City: Inside Baghdad's Green Zone*, London: Bloomsbury

Chomsky, Noam (1999) *The New Military Humanism: Lessons from Kosovo*, London: Pluto Press

Chomsky, Noam (2009) The torture memos, *Z Magazine*, 9 June. Available online at http://www.zmag.org/zmag/viewArticle/21609, accessed on 4 June 2009

Coll, Steve (2013) The spy who said too much: Why the Administration targeted a CIA officer, *New Yorker*, 25 March. Available online at https://www.newyorker.com/maga zine/2013/04/01/the-spy-who-said-too-much, accessed on 11 June 2019

Collins, Richard (1990) Market closure and the conflict theory of professions, Burrage, Michael and Torstendahl, Rolf (eds) *Professions in Theory and History: Rethinking the Study of Professions*, London, Newbury Park and New Delhi: Sage pp 24–42

Couldry, Nick and Curran, James (eds) (2003) *Contesting Media Power: Alternative Media in a Networked World*, Lanham, MD: Rowman & Littlefield

Curran, James and Seaton, Jean (1994) *Power without Responsibility: The Press, Broadcasting and New Media in Britain*, London: Routledge, seventh edition

Der Derian, James (2001) *Virtuous War: Mapping the Military–Industrial–Media–Entertainment Network*, New York: Basic Books

Dorril, Stephen (1993) *The Silent Conspiracy: Inside the Intelligence Services in the 1990s*, London: Heinemann

Downing, John (1984) *Radical Media: The Political Experience of Alternative Communication*, Boston, MA: South End Press

Forde, Susan (2011) *Challenging the News: The Journalism of Alternative and Community Media*, Basingstoke: Palgrave Macmillan

Forte, Maximilian (2012) *Slouching Towards Sirte: Nato's War on Libya and Africa*, Montreal: Baraka Books

Fowler, Andrew (2018) *Shooting the Messenger: Criminalising Journalism*, London: Routledge

Greenberg, Andy (2012) *This Machine Kills Secrets: How WikiLeakers, Hactivists and Cypherpunks Aim to Free the Wold's Information*, London: Virgin Books

Greenslade, Roy (2012) Marie Colvin obituary, *Guardian*, 22 February. Available online at https://www.theguardian.com/media/2012/feb/22/marie-colvin, accessed on 4 September 2019

Greenwald, Glenn (2014) *No Place to Hide: Edward Snowden, the NSA and the Surveillance State*, London: Hamish Hamilton

Grenfell, Oscar (2019) United Nations Special Rapporteur: Julian Assange is being tortured, *wsws.org*, 1 June. Available online at https://www.wsws.org/en/articles/2019/06/01/pers-j01.html, accessed on 11 June 2019

Hackett, Robert A. (2007) Is Peace Journalism possible? Shinar, Dove and Kempf, Wilhelm (eds) *Peace Journalism: The State of the Art*, Berlin: Regener pp 75–94

Hallin, Daniel (1986) *The 'Uncensored' War*, Berkeley, CA: University of California Press

Hammond, Philip (2007a) *Media, War and Postmodernity*, London: Routledge

Hammond, Philip (2007b) *Framing Post-Cold War Conflicts: The Media and International Intervention*, Manchester: Manchester University Press

Harcup, Tony (2003) The unspoken – said: The journalism of the alternative media, *Journalism*, Vol. 4, No. 3 pp 356–376

Harcup, Tony (2013) *Alternative Journalism: Alternative Voices*, London: Routledge

Hartley, John (2008) Journalism as a human right: The cultural approach to journalism, Loffelholz, Martin and Weaver, David (eds) *Global Journalism research: Theories, Methods, Findings, Future*, Oxford: Backwell pp 39–51

Herman, Edward S. and Chomsky, Noam (1994 [1988]) *Manufacturing Consent: The Political Economy of the Mass Media*, London: Vintage

Holland, Max (2012) *Leak: Why Mark Felt Became Deep Throat*, Lawrence: University of Kansas Press

Illich, Ivan (1973) The professions as a form of imperialism, *New Society*, 13 September

Keeble, Richard (1997) *Secret State, Silent Press: New Militarism, the Gulf and the Modern Image of Warfare*, Luton: John Libbey

Keeble, Richard (2009) *Ethics for Journalists*, London: Routledge, second edition

Keeble, Richard Lance (2010) Peace journalism as political practice: A new radical look at the theory, Keeble, Richard Lance, Tulloch, John and Zollmann, Florian (eds) *Peace Journalism, War and Conflict Resolution*, New York: Peter Lang pp 49–67

Keeble, Richard Lance (2014a) Giving peace journalism a chance, Atton, Chris (ed.) *The Routledge Companion to Alternative and Community Media*, London: Routledge pp 335–346

Keeble, Richard Lance (2014b) Rajiv Chandrasekaran's *Imperial Life in the Emerald City*: Beyond the court jester? Keeble, Richard Lance and Tulloch, John (eds) *Global Literary Journalism: Exploring the Journalistic Imagination*, Vol 2, New York: Peter Lang pp 139–154

Keeble, Richard Lance (2017) Yemen coverage: The crucial role of the alternatives, *Peace News*, April–May 2017 p 3. Available online at www.peacenews.info/node/8634/yemen-coverage-crucial-role-alternatives

Knightley, Phillip (2000) *The First Casualty: The War Correspondent as Hero and Myth Maker*, London: Prion Books

Knightley, Phillip (2006) Why spies and scribes have a lot in common, *Khaleej Times*, 11 August. Available online at http://www.khaleejtimes.ae/DisplayArticleNew.asp?section=op inion&xfile=data/opinion/2006/august/opinion_august31.xml, accessed on 6 June 2014

Kravets, David (2013) NSA leak vindicated AT&T whistleblower, *wired.com*, 27 June. Available online at https://www.wired.com/2013/06/nsa-whistleblower-klein/, accessed on 11 June 2019

Lee, Micah (2019) The metadata trap, *Intercept*, 4 August. Available online at https://thein tercept.com/2019/08/04/whistleblowers-surveillance-fbi-trump/, accessed on 19 September 2019

Maass, Peter (2018) Jeffrey Sterling, convicted of leaking about botched CIA program, has been released from prison, *Intercept*, 19 January. Available online at https://theintercept.com/2018/01/19/jeffrey-sterling-cia-leaking-prison/, accessed on 11 June 2019

MacArthur, Brian (2003) Changing pace of war, *Times*, 27 June

McLaughlin, Greg (2016) *The War Correspondent*, London: Pluto Press, second edition

Madar, Chase (2012) *The Passion of Bradley Manning*, New York: Or Books

Martin, Patrick (2011) Espionage case against US government whistleblower collapses, *wsws. org*, 13 June. Available online at https://www.wsws.org/en/articles/2011/06/leak-j13.html, accessed on 11 June 2019

Meacher, Michael (2003) A very secret service, *Guardian*, 21 November. Available online at http://www.theguardian.com/politics/2003/nov/21/davidkelly.media, accessed on 6 June 2014

Milne, Seamus (1994) *The Enemy Within: The Secret War Against the Miners*, London: Pan Books

Moorcraft, Paul (2016) *Dying for the Truth: The Concise History of Frontline War Reporting*, Barnsley, South Yorkshire: Pen and Sword Books

Nelson, Elizabeth (1989) *The British Counter-Culture, 1966–73: A Study of the Underground Press*, London: Macmillan

Norton-Taylor, Richard (1991) Pressure behind the scenes, *Index on Censorship*, Nos 4/5 p 14

Norton-Taylor, Richard (1985) *The Ponting Affair*, London: Cecil Woolf

Owen, John and Purdey, Heather (2009) *International News Reporting: Frontlines and Deadlines*, Chichester, West Sussex: Wiley & Sons

Parkin, Frank (1979) *Marxism and Class Theory: A Bourgeois Critique*, London: Tavistock Publications

Paterson, Ronald (1971) *The Nihilistic Egoist: Max Stirner*, Oxford: Oxford University Press

Ricketson, Matthew (2014) *Telling True Stories: Navigating the Challenges of Writing Narrative Non-Fiction*, Sydney, Melbourne and London: Allen & Unwin

Rodriguez, Clemencia (2001) *Fissures in the Mediascape: An International Study of Citizen's Media*, New Jersey: Hampton Press

Sanders, Karen (2003) *Ethics & Journalism*, London: Sage

Scahill, Jeremy (2013) *Dirty Wars: The World is a Battlefield*, London: Serpent's Tail

Shorrock, Tim (2013) Bill Binney on the WSJ's NSA-telecom revelations, *timshorrock.com*, 21August. Available online at http://timshorrock.com/2013/08/21/bill-binney-on-the-wa ll-street-journals-nsa-telecom-revelations/, accessed on 11 June 2019

Sinclair, Ian (2008) Lifting the lid on US 'dirty tricks' at the UN: Interview with Katherine Gun, *Morning Star*, December. Available online at https://ianjsinclair.wordpress.com/2017/01/05/lifting-the-lid-on-us-dirty-tricks-at-the-un-interview-with-katharine-gun/, accessed on 5 September 2019

Sparks, Colin (1985) The working-class press: Radical and revolutionary alternatives, *Media, Culture and Society*, Vol. 7 pp 133–146

Times (2014) Editorial: The first casualty, 16 May, p 20

van Buren, Peter (2011) *We Meant Well: How I Helped Lose the Battle for the Hearts and Minds of the Iraqi People*, New York: Metropolitan Books

Waltz, Mitzi (2005) *Alternative and Activist Media*, Edinburgh: Edinburgh University Press

Williams, Kevin (1992) Something more important than truth: Ethical issues in war reporting, Belsey, Andrew and Chadwick, Ruth (eds) *Ethical Issues in Journalism and the Media*, London: Routledge pp 154–170

Wilson, Deborah (2007) An unscathed tourist of wars: The journalism of Martha Gellhorn, Keeble, Richard and Wheeler, Sharon (eds) *The Journalistic Imagination: Literary Journalists from Defoe to Capote and Carter*, London: Routledge pp 116–129

Wing, Nick (2013) Russ Tice, Bush-era whistleblower, claims NSA ordered wiretap of Obama in 2004, *Huffington Post*, 20 June. Available online at http://www.huffingtonpost.com/2013/06/20/russ-tice-nsa-obama_n_3473538.html, accessed on 11 June 2019

Woodward, Bob and Bernstein, Carl (1974) *All the President's Men*, London: Quartet Books

INDEX